T0152841

The Revolution of
Everyday Life

The Revolution of Everyday Life

Raoul Vaneigem

A new translation by Donald Nicholson-Smith
with a preface by the author

The Revolution of Everyday Life
Raoul Vaneigem

Originally published as *Traité de savoir-vivre à l'usage des jeunes générations* by Éditions Gallimard (Paris). Copyright © 1967 by Éditions Gallimard.

Author's preface to the first French mass-market (Folio) edition copyright © 1992 by Éditions Gallimard.

An earlier version of this translation first published in 1983 by Rebel Press (London) and Left Bank Books (Seattle); second edition, 1994.

First PM Press edition, 2012.
All rights reserved

English translation copyright © 2012 by Donald Nicholson-Smith.

The publication of this work has been facilitated by financial support from the French Community of Belgium.

Cet ouvrage publié dans le cadre du programme d'aide à la publication bénéficie du soutien du Ministère des Affaires Etrangères et du Service Culturel de l'Ambassade de France représenté aux Etats-Unis. This work received support from the French Ministry of Foreign Affairs and the Cultural Services of the French Embassy in the United States through their publishing assistance program.

Published by:
PM Press
PO Box 23912
Oakland, CA 94623
www.pmpress.org

Cover illustration by Jean-Marie Pierret
Cover design by François Rabet
Interior design by briandesign

ISBN: 978-1-60486-678-0
Library of Congress Control Number: 2009912461
10 9 8 7 6 5 4 3 2

Printed in the USA.

Contents

The Impossibility of Fulfilment: Power as Sum of Seductions

Survival and Its Pseudo-Negation

PART TWO Reversal of Perspective

Translator's Acknowledgements

Once again I am most grateful to Raoul Vaneigem for his unstinting help. My great thanks, too, to Jean-Marie Pierret and François Rabet for the cover art and cover design respectively, and to all at PM Press, especially for their patience. The eagle eyes of John McHale and Jim Brook must be credited for the elimination of many an error. I am indebted to T. J. Clark and Chris Winks for their encouragement. Mia Nadezhda Rublowska has contributed immeasurably to this new edition, and there is no way for me to thank her enough.

In memoriam Chris Gray (1942–2009), one of Raoul Vaneigem's earliest translators (in the broadest sense of the word).

D. N.-S., June 2012

Author's Preface to the Present Edition

Long known as the New World, the United States of America is now viewed by Europeans as a paradoxically archaic country. Its technological achievements would warrant only admiration were they not belied by a mental stagnation that allows the 'icy waters of egotistical calculation' to preside over an inhumanity cynically defended in the name of profit.

I am not speaking of the Americans themselves. It takes a repellent contempt and stupidity to place what are unique individuals under the abstract rubric of a national identity, no matter how prone those individuals may be to relinquishing their creative powers and embracing mass conformity. What I have in mind, rather, is the dismal succession of American administrations, all brought to power by plain old graft, which in their ever more risible arrogance care nothing for growing immiseration, know nothing of social solidarity, degrade the environment, destroy the earth for financial gain and, armed with an ignominiously clear conscience, promote a Calvinism that treats financial success as a divine dispensation.

Of course the Europeans, no less arrogant, have a grand old time pointing the finger at these would-be paragons of formal democracy who practise capital punishment, embrace the idiotic fad for creationism, tolerate a woefully inadequate social safety net that scorns workers' rights and skimps on unemployment benefits and pensions, and cede immense power to the military and to barbarity—in which last department they are indeed champions.

But so-called left-wing public opinion in France, as fond as it is of draping itself in the robes of the Revolution of 1789, even of the Paris Commune, and to citing those events as object lessons for others, has not only fallen over the years for every conceivable false vision of emancipation—liberalism, socialism, Stalinism, Trotskyism, Maoism, Castroism—but offers not the slightest objection to the reversal of progressive social gains: the slashing of social security and cultural budgets, the dismemberment of the health-care system, the reduction of education to a form of battery farming, and, in general, the growing impoverishment of existence—source of the despair from which the managers of economic collapse wring their last profits.

Ever since consumerism spread patronage everywhere and harnessed the lies of ideology to the needs of merchandising, the free-for-all of market democracy has obliterated any consciousness of the need to fight exploitation.

The crimes committed in the name of the liberation of the proletariat have helped in no small measure to spread a spirit of apathy and fatalism highly conducive to that suicidal impulse which, with or without religious buttressing, works for a universal and apocalyptic death. The plunder of existential and terrestrial resources carried on with impunity by state and private mafias fuels a creeping dread, a state of funk that is absurd inasmuch as Europeans no longer need to fear tanks in the streets or brutal and systematic police intrusion. This internalized terror is, quite simply, a fear of living, of autonomy, of self-creation.

But no matter how exhausted the life forces grow, a moment always comes when consciousness rouses itself, reasserting its rights and retrieving its outgoing exuberance. I have always wagered on a reversal of perspective which, razing a past dominated by contempt for human beings, will usher in a new society founded on the creative capacities of individuals and on an irrepressible desire to revel in oneself and in the world.

We are in the midst of a civilizational shift, one that the Occupations Movement of May 1968 in France illuminated in that it strove to accelerate it, thus hastening the collapse of consumer society and the emergence of a society committed to life.

Just as the agrarian economy of the *ancien régime* was an atrophied formation fated, thanks to the Revolution of 1789, to be swept away by the surging free-market system, so the investment-driven and speculative capitalism whose crisis we are now witnessing is about to give way to a newly dynamic form driven by the production of 'green', nonpolluting kinds of energy, by an appeal to use-value, by organic farming, by a hurried makeover of the public sector and by a spurious ethical reform of trade.

We are confronted not by an economic crisis but by a crisis of the economy as such. Strife rages between two forces within the capitalist system, the one moribund, the other still young: on the one hand a system dating back thousands of years whose basis is the exploitation of nature and of human beings; on the other a rejigged version seeking to establish itself by investing in natural forces and making us pay very dear (once new means of production have been put in place) for things hitherto free: wind, sun, water, and the energy that resides in the plant world and in the earth itself.

The *Traité de savoir-vivre* made no prophecies. It merely pointed out what many people, blinded by the past, refused to see. It sought to show how the will to emancipation, reborn with each succeeding generation, might take advantage of the seismic convulsions which under the impact of consumerism were shaking a supposedly eternal authoritarian power to its very foundations. And it demonstrated the irreversibility of the break with patriarchal values—with work, the exploitation of nature, exchange, predatory relationships, separation from the self, sacrifice, guilt, the renunciation of happiness, the fetishism of money and power, hierarchical authority, contempt for and fear of women, the corruption of childhood, intellectual pedigrees, military and police despotism, religion, ideology, and repression (and lethal ways of relieving repression).

By counting on the inevitable disintegration of the patriarchal order, the *Traité* was able to embody a commitment to life which, co-optation notwithstanding, has now become commonplace: women, children, animals, nature, desire, and the quest for happiness and gratification freed from fear and guilt—all now enjoy a status granted them never before in history. But the most radical part of my wager was confidence in the vital force that spreads surreptitiously from one individual to the next when the consciousness of the wish to live and of its possible fulfilment stymies the death reflex which is its reverse; when, throwing despair itself into despair, one finds oneself to be a human being capable of constructing one's own happiness while at the same time nourishing that of others.

It is my belief, despite all the dillydallying—as the barbarism of old continues, thanks to inertia, to tyrannize over the present—that a new society is being built in secret, that genuinely human relationships are coming into being—without replying to oppressive violence by a like violence (albeit directed at the oppressor)—relationships able to create zones of freedom where existence can free itself from the diktats of the commodity, banishing competition in the name of emulation and work in the name of creativity.

This is not a matter of observation but of continuing practical experience. All that is called for is more vigilance, greater consciousness, and firmer allegiance to the life forces. We must provide ourselves with a new, solid human foundation for the rebuilding of a world laid waste by the inhumanity of the cult of the commodity.

Failing to jettison economic reality and create a human reality means giving the commodity yet another chance to perpetuate its barbaric reign.

The *Traité* laid the groundwork for a project which most of my writings since have sought to refine and correct, even as changing political, social, economic and existential conditions have continued to demonstrate its pertinence. Amid the awful turbulence of the struggle between obscurantism and enlightenment, I persist (with an obstinacy likely to aggravate the resigned among us) in relying on the action of the life forces to smash the age-old rituals of death blow by blow.

It is now easier to see how vigorous still, despite the reversals inflicted upon it by ideologies and their military extensions, is the radical current that links the communalist uprisings of twelfth-century Europe to the libertarian communities of the Spanish Revolution; this is the current that likewise informed the French Revolution, the Paris Commune, and the Occupations Movement of May 1968.

I still think, despite the bewilderment of oppressors and oppressed alike in face of the collapse of the old world, that individual and social emancipation is the only way out. Identification with an ethnic or national community, with a religion, ideology, or any abstraction is nothing but a blood-soaked delusion. There is only one identity: that of men and women with what is most vital and human within them.

The future belongs to self-managed communities which, not content merely to place the production of goods at the service of the whole society, will decree that the happiness of all must depend on the happiness of each. This principle is the basis of a direct democracy that will put to rout those destructive shadows of tyranny and universal corruption which parliamentary democracy continues to spread—ever more visibly—across the globe.

R.V., 29 January 2010

The Revolution of
Everyday Life

Introduction

My aim is not to make the real experience contained in this book comprehensible to readers who have no real interest in reliving it. I fully expect this experience to be lost—and rediscovered—in a general alteration of consciousness, just as I am convinced that the present conditions of our lives will one day be no more than a memory.

The world is going to be remade, not reconditioned. All its would-be renovators are powerless to stop this. If these experts do not understand me, so much the better; I certainly have no desire to understand *them*.

As for my other readers, I beg their indulgence with a humility that should not be hard to see. I would have wished a book such as this one accessible to minds quite unschooled in the jargon of ideas. I hope I have not failed entirely. Out of this confusion will one day come formulations capable of firing point-blank on our enemies. In the meanwhile, let sentences remembered here or there have what effect they may. The path of simplicity is the most tortuous of all and, especially here, it seemed better not to wrench commonplaces from the many roots that make it possible to transplant them to other soils and cultivate them to our own profit.

I have never claimed to have anything new to say; I am not trying to launch novelties on the culture market. One tiny adjustment in what is essential has much greater import than a hundred incidental improvements. The only truly new thing here is the direction of the stream that carries commonplaces along.

Since humans came upon the earth, and read Lautréamont, everything has been said, yet few have taken advantage of it. Since all our knowledge is fundamentally banal, it can be of value only to minds that are not.

The modern world has to learn what it already knows, become what it already is, through a great exorcism of obstacles, through practice. We can escape the commonplace only by manipulating it, controlling it, thrusting it into our dreams or surrendering it to the free play of our subjectivity. I realize that I have given subjective will an easy time in this book, but let no one reproach me for this without first considering the extent to which the objective conditions of the contemporary world advance the cause of subjectivity day after day. Everything starts from subjectivity, but nothing stays there. Today less than ever.

The struggle between subjectivity and everything that corrupts it is widening the battleground of the old class struggle, revitalizing that struggle and making it more bitter. The desire to live is a political decision. Who wants a world where the guarantee of freedom from starvation means the risk of death from boredom?

The man of survival is a man ground up in the machinery of hierarchical power, caught in a net of crossed purposes, a chaos of oppressive techniques whose ordering awaits only patient programming by programmed minds.

The man of survival, however, is also the unitary man, the man of absolute refusal. Not a moment passes without each one of us experiencing, on every level of reality, the contradiction between oppression and freedom; without each one of us being caught up and weirdly twisted by two antagonistic perspectives simultaneously: the perspective of power and the perspective of supersession. So, although the two parts of this book deal in turn with each of these perspectives, they should not really be treated as separate. Instead the reader must imagine that they are synchronic; for description of the negative underpins the positive project, and the positive project attests to negativity. Ideally a book would have no order to it, and the reader would have to discover his own.

My shortcomings as a writer also reflect on the reader—as a reader and even more as a human being. If the element of boredom I experienced in writing finds an echo in the reader, here is but one more proof of our failure to live. For the rest, the gravity of the times must excuse the gravity of my tone. Levity always lies either before words or beyond them. For our purposes irony will consist in never forgetting this.

This work is part of a subversive current of which the last has not yet been heard. It constitutes one contribution among others to the reconstruction of the international revolutionary movement. Its significance should escape no one; in any case, as time will show, no one is going to escape its conclusions.

PART ONE
POWER'S PERSPECTIVE

I   The Insignificant Signified

Because of its increasing triviality, everyday life has gradually become our central preoccupation [1]. No illusion, sacred or secular [2], collective or individual, can now hide the poverty of our day-to-day actions [3]. The enrichment of life calls for an unblinking analysis of the new forms taken by poverty and the perfecting of old weapons of refusal [4].

1

The history of our time calls to mind those cartoon characters who rush madly over the edge of a cliff without seeing it: the power of their imagination keeps them suspended in midair, but as soon as they look down and see where they are, they fall.

Contemporary thought, like Bosustov's heroes, can no longer rest on its own delusions. What used to hold it up, today brings it down. It rushes full tilt in front of the reality that will crush it: the reality that is lived every day.

/////

Is this dawning lucidity essentially new? I don't think so. Everyday life always produces the demand for a brighter light, because of the need felt by all to walk in step with history. There are more truths in twenty-four hours of an individual's life than in all the philosophies. Even a philosopher cannot ignore it, for all his self-contempt—that same self-contempt that the very comfort of philosophy has taught him. After somersaulting onto his own shoulders to shout his message to the world from a greater height, the philosopher finishes by seeing the world upside down; and everything in it obligingly goes askew, and walks on its head, to persuade him that he is standing upright. But he is the centre of his delusional state, and struggling to contest it merely renders his delusion more uncomfortable.

The moralists of the sixteenth and seventeenth centuries presided over a vast stock of platitudes, but so active were their efforts to conceal this fact that a veritable stuccoed palace of speculation arose above it, an ideal palace to shelter and imprison real experience. From its gates emerged a conviction and sincerity quickened by a sublime tone and by the fiction of the 'universal man' but contaminated by a breath of permanent anxiety. The analytic approach of these philosophers sought to escape the gradual atrophying of existence by attaining some essential profundity; and the further into alienation their philosophy led them by embracing the age's dominant imagery (the feudal image in which God, monarchy, and the world are indivisibly united), the more their lucidity photographed the hidden face of life, the more it 'invented' everyday experience.

Enlightenment philosophy accelerated the descent into the concrete, for the concrete was in some ways brought to power along with the revolutionary bourgeoisie. From the ruins of Heaven, humanity fell into the ruins of its own world. What happened? Something like this: ten thousand people are convinced that they have seen a fakir's rope rise into the air, while so many cameras prove that it hasn't moved an inch. Scientific objectivity exposes mystification. Very good, but what does it show us? A coiled rope of absolutely no interest. I have little inclination to choose between the doubtful pleasure of being mystified and the tedium of contemplating a reality which does not concern me. A reality which I have no grasp of—isn't this just the old lie recycled, the highest stage of mystification?

From now on the analysts are in the streets. Lucidity is not their only weapon. Their thinking is no longer in danger of being imprisoned, either by the false reality of gods or by the false reality of technocrats.

2

Religious beliefs concealed humans from themselves, a Bastille walling them up in a pyramidal world with God at the summit and the king just below. Alas, there was not enough freedom to be found on that fourteenth of July among the ruins of unitary power to prevent those ruins themselves from becoming another prison. Behind the rent veil of superstition appeared, not naked truth, as Meslier dreamed, but the slime of ideologies. The prisoners of fragmented power have but a shadow of freedom as their only refuge from tyranny.

Today no action and no thought evades the web of received ideas. The slow fall-out of particles from the old myth, now exploded, spreads the dust of the sacrosanct everywhere, choking the spirit and the will to live. Constraints have become less occult, more blatant; less powerful, more numerous. Docility is no longer ensured by priestly magic; it results from a mass of minor hypnoses: news, culture, city planning, advertising, mechanisms of conditioning and suggestion ready to serve any order, established or to come. We are like Gulliver, stranded on the Lilliputian shore, with every part of his body tied down; determined to free himself, he looks keenly around him: the smallest detail of the landscape, the smallest contour of the ground, the slightest movement, everything becomes a sign on which his escape may depend. The surest chances of liberation lie in what is most familiar. Was it ever otherwise? Art, ethics, philosophy bear witness: under the crust of words and concepts, the living reality of maladjustment to the world is always crouched ready to spring. Since neither gods nor words can any longer decently cover it up, this commonplace creature roams naked in railway stations and vacant lots; it confronts you at each self-evasion, it grasps your shoulder, catches your eye, and the dialogue begins. You go down with it, or make your escape with it.

3

Too many corpses strew the paths of individualism and collectivism. These seemingly contrary principles cloak one and the same gangsterism, one and the same oppression of the isolated individual. The hand that smothered Lautréamont returned to strangle Sergei Esenin; one died in the lodging-house of his landlord Jules-François Dupuis, the other hanged himself in a nationalized hotel. Everywhere the same law holds good: 'There is no weapon of your individual will which, once appropriated by others, does not turn against you.' If anyone says or writes that practical reason must henceforth be based on the rights of the individual and the individual alone, he negates his own proposition if he does not incite his audience to make this statement true for themselves. Such a proof can only be lived, grasped from within. That is why everything in the notes that follow should be tested and corrected by everyone's immediate experience. Nothing is so valuable that it need not be started afresh, nothing is so rich that is it has no need of continual enrichment.

//////

Just as we distinguish in private life between what a man thinks and says about himself and what he really is and does, everyone has learned to distinguish the rhetoric and messianic pretensions of political parties from their organization and real interests; what they think they are, from what they are. A man's illusions about himself and others are not basically different from the illusions which groups, classes, and parties cultivate about themselves and within themselves. Indeed they come from the same source: the dominant ideas, which are the ideas of the dominant class, even when they take an antagonistic form.

The world of -isms, whether it envelops the whole of humanity or a single person, is never anything but a world drained of reality, a terribly real seduction by falsehood. The three crushing defeats suffered by the Commune, the Spartakist movement and Kronstadt-the-Red (1921) showed once and for all what bloodbaths could be precipitated by three ideologies of freedom, namely liberalism, socialism and Bolshevism. Before this was universally understood and admitted, however, bastard or hybrid forms of these ideologies had to vulgarize their initial atrocity with even weightier evidence: concentration camps, Lacoste's Algeria, Budapest. The great collective illusions, anaemic from shedding the blood of so many, have since given way to the thousands of prepacked ideologies sold by consumer society like so many portable brain-scrambling machines. Will it take as much bloodshed to prove that a hundred thousand pinpricks kill as surely as a couple of blows with a club?

//////

What could I possibly do in a group of militants who ask me to leave in the cloakroom, not a few ideas—for if anything ideas would be the reason for my signing up—but the dreams and desires which never leave me, the wish to live authentically and without restraint? What is the use of exchanging one isolation, one monotony, one lie for another? Once a change has been exposed as illusory, merely replacing it with another illusion is intolerable. Yet such is precisely our situation: the economy cannot stop making us consume more and more, and to consume without respite is to change illusions at an accelerating pace which eventually dissipates the illusion of change. We find ourselves alone, unchanged, frozen in the void created by the cascade of gimmick-objects, Volkswagens, and paperback books.

People without imagination are beginning to tire of the importance attached to comfort, to culture, to leisure, to all that destroys the imagination. This is not to say that people are tired of comfort, culture, and leisure, but merely of the use to which they are put, which is precisely what stops us enjoying them.

The affluent society is a society of voyeurs. To each his own kaleidoscope: a slight movement of the fingers and the picture changes. You can't lose: two fridges, a Renault Dauphine, a TV set, a free gift, time to kill . . . But then the monotony of the images we consume gets the upper hand, reflecting the monotony of the action which produces them, the slow rolling motion of finger and thumb that rotates the kaleidoscope. There was no Dauphine, only an ideology almost unconnected with automobiles. Flushed with Johnny Walker, whisky of the élite, we savour a strange cocktail of alcohol and class struggle. Nothing surprises us any more, there's the rub. The monotony of the ideological spectacle reflects the passivity of life, of survival. Beyond all the prefabricated scandals— Scandale girdles, scandal in high places—a real scandal appears, the scandal of actions drained of their substance to bolster an illusion that becomes more odious by the day as its attraction wanes; actions weakened and dulled by having had to nourish dazzling imaginary compensations, impoverished from enriching lofty speculations to which they play flunkey while being ignominiously categorized as 'trivial' or 'banal'; actions now freed up but feeble, prone to stray once more, or expire from sheer exhaustion. There they are, in every one of you: familiar, sad, newly returned to the immediate living reality which is their 'spontaneous' environment. And here you are too, bewildered and lost in a new prosaicness, in a perspective where near and far are one and the same.

4

In its concrete and tactical form, the concept of class struggle constituted the first marshalling of responses to the shocks and injuries which people experience as individuals; it was born in the whirlpool of suffering which the reduction of human relationships to the mechanisms of exploitation created everywhere in industrial societies. It issued from a will to transform the world and change life.

Such a weapon needed constant adjustment. Yet we see the First International turning its back on artists by making workers' demands the sole basis of a project which Marx had nevertheless shown to concern all those who sought, in the refusal to be slaves, a full life and a complete humanity. Lacenaire, Borel, Lassailly, Büchner, Baudelaire, Hölderlin— wasn't this also poverty and its radical refusal? Perhaps the mistake was excusable then: I neither know nor care. What is certain is that it is sheer madness a century later, when the economy of consumption is absorbing the economy of production and the exploitation of labour power is being subsumed by the exploitation of everyday creativity. A single energy, wrested from the workers as easily now during their leisure time as during their hours on the shopfloor, drives the turbines of Power which the custodians of the old theory blithely lubricate with their purely formal opposition.

Anyone who talks about revolution and class struggle without referring explicitly to everyday life—without grasping what is subversive about love and positive in the refusal of constraints—has a corpse in his mouth.

The Impossibility of Participation: Power as Sum of Constraints

The mechanisms of attrition and destruction: humiliation (II), isolation (III), suffering (IV), work (V), decompression (VI).

II   Humiliation

The economy of everyday life is based on a ceaseless exchange
of humiliations and aggressive attitudes. It conceals a technique
of attrition itself subject to the *gift* of destruction, which
paradoxically it provokes [1]. The more humans are treated as
objects, the more social they become [2]. Decolonization has
not yet begun [3]. It is about to give a new meaning to the old
principle of sovereignty [4].

1

Travelling through a busy village one day, Rousseau was mocked by a
yokel whose barbs delighted the crowd. Confused and discountenanced,
Jean-Jacques could not think of a word in reply and was forced to take
to his heels amid the jeers of the villagers. By the time he had finally
regained his composure and thought of a thousand possible retorts, any
one of which would have silenced the taunter at a stroke, he was two
hours' distance from the village.

What are most of the trivial incidents of everyday life but this misad-
venture writ small, in an attenuated and diluted form, reduced to the
duration of a step, a glance, a thought, experienced as a muffled impact, a
fleeting discomfort barely registered by consciousness and leaving in the
mind only a dull irritation at a loss to discover its own origin? The endless
minuet of humiliation and responses to it lends human interaction an
obscene hobbling rhythm. In the ebb and flow of crowds sucked up and
squashed together by shuttling commuter trains, then spewed out into
streets, offices and factories, there is nothing to be seen but cringing and
flinching, brutal aggression, smirking faces, and cat-scratches delivered
for no apparent reason. Soured by unwanted encounters, wine turns to
vinegar in the mouth. Don't talk to me about innocent and good-natured
crowds. Look how people bristle, threatened on every side, isolated deep
in enemy territory and far, very far, from themselves. Lacking knives,
they learn to use their elbows and their eyes as weapons.

There is no remission, no truce between attackers and attacked. A flux of barely perceptible signs assails the stroller, who is anything but solitary. Remarks, gestures, glances tangle and collide, miss their aim, ricochet like stray bullets, and kill just as surely by the unrelenting nervous tension they produce. All we can do is enclose ourselves in embarrassing parentheses, as witness these fingers of mine (I am writing this on a café terrace) slipping a tip across the table, and the fingers of the waiter which pick it up, while the faces of the two of us, as if anxious to conceal the infamy to which we have consented, maintain an expression of utter indifference.

From the point of view of constraint, everyday life is governed by an economic system in which the production and consumption of insults tend to balance out. The old dream of the theorists of free trade is thus fulfilled in the customs of a democracy granted a new lease on life by the lack of imagination of left-wing thought. Is it not strange, at first sight, to see the fury with which 'progressives' attack the ruined edifice of liberalism, as if the capitalists, its official demolition gang, had not themselves already planned liberalism's nationalized reconstruction? But it is not so strange, in fact, for the deliberate purpose of keeping all attention fastened on criticisms already overtaken by events—after all, anybody can see that capitalism is coming to maturity as a planned economy of which the Soviet model is nothing but a primitive form—is to conceal the fact that the only reconstruction of human relationships envisaged is one based precisely on an economic model which, being obsolete, is on offer at a knock-down price. Who can fail to notice the alarming persistence with which 'socialist' countries continue to organize life along bourgeois lines? Everywhere it's hats off to family, marriage, sacrifice, work, inauthenticity, while simplified and rationalized homeostatic mechanisms reduce human relationships to a 'fair' exchange of deference and humiliation. And soon, in the ideal democracy of the cyberneticians, everyone, without apparent effort, will earn their portion of indignity that they will be at leisure to share out in the most equitable possible way. Distributive justice will reach its apogee. Good luck to the old people who live to see that day!

For me—and for some others, I dare to think—there can be no real homeostasis in a pathological situation. Planning is merely the other face of the free market. The only thing planned is *exchange*—along with the mutual sacrifices it entails. But if the word 'innovation' means anything it means supersession—not camouflage. Indeed, a truly new reality can be founded only on the principle of the *gift*. In the historical experiment of workers' councils (1917, 1921, 1934, 1956), their errors and their slender means notwithstanding, and in the pathetic search for friendship and love, I see a single and inspiring reason not to despair over the circumstances of the present. Everything conspires to keep the positive character of such experiences secret; doubt is cunningly maintained as to their real importance, even their existence. By a strange oversight, no historian has ever taken the trouble to study how people actually lived during the most extreme revolutionary moments. At such times the will to make an end of free trade in human behaviour is spontaneously revealed, albeit in negative ways: pathology challenged by an even greater, more substantial pathology collapses under the onslaught.

In that negative sense, Ravachol's bombs or, closer to our own time, the epic of Caraquemada leave no possible doubt regarding the will—manifested in varying degrees, but manifested everywhere—to utterly reject relationships based on exchange and compromise. I am quite sure, having experienced it so many times, that anyone who passes a single hour in the cage of such constraining relationships must feel a deep empathy for Pierre-François Lacenaire and his passion for crime. I make no apology for anarchist terrorism, but it should be recognized as a form of action, at once pitiful and noble, with the power to sabotage and thereby expose the self-regulating mechanisms of a hierarchical social community. Murder is inherent in the logic of an unlivable society, and in this sense it invariably appears as the dark side of the gift: as that absence of a fiercely wished-for presence that Mallarmé spoke of—the same Mallarmé who at the Trial of the Thirty (1894) called the anarchists 'angels of purity'.

My sympathy for the solitary killer ends where tactics begins; but perhaps tactics needs scouts motivated by individual despair? However that may be, the new revolutionary tactics—which will be based indissolubly on historical tradition and on the techniques, so widespread and so disregarded, of individual self-fulfilment—will have no time for people who merely mimic the acts of a Ravachol or a Bonnot. All the same, tactics will be condemned to theoretical hibernation if it fails, using other means, to effect the *collective* seduction of individuals whom isolation and hatred for the collective lie have driven to the rational decision to kill and to kill themselves. No murderers—and no humanists either!

The former accept death, the latter impose it. Let ten people meet who are set on the lightning of violence rather than the agony of survival: that is precisely where despair ends and tactics begins. Despair is the infantile disorder of the revolutionaries of everyday life.

Today I still feel my adolescent admiration for outlaws, less out of a regressive romanticism than because they expose the justifications social power uses to avoid being *directly* implicated. Hierarchical social organization is like a gigantic racket whose secret, so clearly highlighted by anarchist terror, is to place itself out of reach of the violence it provokes by using up everybody's life forces in a host of dubious struggles. (A 'humanized' Power can no longer allow itself to rely on the old methods of war and genocide.) The witnesses for the prosecution here can hardly be suspected of anarchist tendencies. The biologist Hans Selye, for example, notes that, 'As specific causes of disease (microbes, malnutrition) disappear, a growing proportion of people die of what are called stress diseases, or diseases of degeneration caused by stress, that is, by the wear and tear resulting from conflicts, shocks, nervous tension, frustrations, debilitating routines, etc.' From now on, no one can escape the need to conduct their own investigation into the criminal racket that pursues them even into their thoughts, hunts them down even in their dreams. The smallest details take on a major importance. Irritation, fatigue, rudeness, humiliation . . . *cui bono?* Who profits by them? And who profits by the stereotyped answers—really just so many excuses—that Big Brother Common Sense peddles as reasonable? Why should I settle for explanations that kill me when I have everything to win at the very place where all the cards are stacked against me?

2

The handshake ties and unties the knot of encounters. A gesture at once curious and trivial which we quite accurately say is *exchanged*: is it not in fact the simplest expression of the social contract? What guarantees are they trying to seal, these hands clasped to the right, to the left, everywhere, with a liberality that seems like a compensation for a complete lack of conviction? That agreement reigns, that social harmony exists, that life in society is perfect? What could be more disturbing than this need to convince ourselves of these lies, to believe them out of habit, to reaffirm them with the strength of our grip? Our glances convey nothing of these accommodations, affecting not to see the exchange. When our eyes meet someone else's they become uneasy, as though discerning their own empty, soulless reflection in the other person's pupils. Hardly have they met than they slip aside and try to dodge the other's gaze; their fugitive sight lines intersect virtually at an angle whose width conveys nothing so much as the divergence, the deeply felt lack of harmony between us. Just occasionally unison is achieved and eyes connect: the beautiful parallel gaze of royal couples in Egyptian statuary or the misty, melting gaze, brimming with eroticism, of lovers: eyes devouring one another from afar. But most of the time eyes give the lie to the superficial agreement sealed by the handshake. All the backslapping that goes on could not be more phoney. Its commercial overtones are not hard to find, of course: the handshake clinches a deal. More important, though, is the fact that this energetically reiterated affirmation of social harmony is an attempt to trick our senses—to blunt our perception and habituate it to the emptiness of the spectacle. 'You have to face up to things', people used to say; the common wisdom of consumer society has given this sentiment a new force, for now *things* are the only reality we can see.

Become as insensitive (and hence as easy to handle) as a brick! That is what the social order benevolently asks everyone to do. The bourgeoisie has managed to mete out frustrations more fairly, allowing a greater number of people to suffer them according to 'rational' norms, in the name of concrete, specialized imperatives (economic, social, political, legal, etc.). Once split up in this way, constraints in turn fragment the cunning and energy customarily devoted to reversing or breaking them. The revolutionaries of 1793 were great because they dared to wrest the government of human beings from God's grip; the greatness proletarian revolutionaries struggled for, on the other hand, could scarcely have been wrested from their bourgeois adversaries, for their strength derived from themselves alone.

A whole ethic based on market value, the *utile dulci*, the dignity of labour, moderation of desire, and survival, and on their opposites, pure value, the gratuitous, parasitism, instinctive brutality, and death— such is the foul stew in which human faculties have been bubbling for nearly two centuries. From these ingredients—refined a little of course— the cyberneticians dream of cooking up the human being of the future. Can we even be sure that we have not already achieved the security of perfectly adapted beings, moving about as uncertainly and unconsciously as insects? For quite some time now experiments have been going on with subliminal advertising in which single frames (lasting one twenty-fourth of a second) are inserted into films; though seen by the eye, they are not registered by the conscious mind. The first slogans give more than a glimpse of what is to come: 'Don't drive too fast' and 'Go to church'. But what does a minor improvement like this represent in comparison with the whole immense conditioning machine, each of whose cogs—city planning, advertising, ideology, culture—is capable of hundreds of comparable improvements? Once again, knowledge of the conditions which will inevitably continue to be imposed on people if they do not take action is of less consequence than the actual experience of such degradation in the here-and-now. Huxley's *Brave New World*, Orwell's *1984* and Yves Touraine's *Cinquième Coup de Trompette* (The Fifth Trumpet Blast) all consign to the future the shudder which a single glance at the present can produce; but only the present nurtures consciousness and the will to refuse. Compared with my present incarceration the future holds no interest for me.

//////

The feeling of humiliation is simply the feeling of being an object. Once this is grasped, it can become the basis of an aggressive lucidity thanks to which the critique of the organization of life can no longer be detached from the immediate inception of the project of living otherwise. Construction can begin only on the foundation of individual despair and of its supersession: the very efforts made to disguise such despair and manipulate it under new packaging are sufficient proof of that.

What seductive illusion prevents me from seeing the collapse of values, the disintegration of the world, inauthenticity, nontotality? Could it be the belief that I am happy? Hardly! Such a belief withstands neither analysis nor the anxiety that assails me. No, I find rather that it is a belief in the happiness of others, an inexhaustible source of envy and jealousy, which gives me, in a negative way, the feeling that I exist. I envy therefore I am. To define oneself by reference to others is to perceive oneself as other. And the other is always object. So humiliation is the measuring-rod of life. The more you choose your own humiliation, the more you 'live': the more, that is to say, you live the orderly life of *things*. This is the cunning of reification, the way it passes undetected, like arsenic in the jam.

The predictable gentleness of such methods of oppression goes a long way to explaining the perverse attitude that prevents me from crying out, as in Andersen's tale, 'The emperor has no clothes' every time the wretchedness of my sovereignty over everyday life is exposed. Not that police brutality is on the wane. Far from it! Wherever it rears its head the kindly souls of the Left quite rightly condemn it. But what do they do about it? Do they urge people to arm themselves? To take appropriate reprisals? Do they encourage cop-hunts like the one which in 1956 decorated the trees of Budapest with the most loyal servants of the AVO, the Hungarian secret police? No: they organize peaceful demonstrations at which their trade-union police force treats anyone who questions their orders as an *agent provocateur*. Meanwhile the new-style police are already with us, waiting to take over. Social psychologists need no truncheons, no morgues. Oppressive violence is about to be transformed into a host of equitably distributed pinpricks. The same high-minded people who denounce police-state brutality would have us all live in a state of well-policed brutality.

Humanism upholsters the machine described in Kafka's 'In the Penal Colony'. Less grinding and shouting! You can't stand blood? Never mind: let humans be bloodless. The promised land of survival will be a land of peaceful death; the gentle death that the humanists are fighting for. No more Guernicas, no more Auschwitzes, no more Hiroshimas, no more Sétifs. Hooray! But what about the impossibility of living, this stifling mediocrity, this absence of passion? This jealous fury to which we are driven when the rankling of never being ourselves makes us imagine that others are happy? This feeling of never really being inside your own skin? Let nobody say these are minor details or secondary considerations. There are no benign irritants: gangrene can start in the slightest graze. The crises that shake the world do not differ fundamentally from the conflicts in which my actions and thoughts confront the hostile forces that entangle and deflect them. (How could what goes for my everyday life fail to apply to history when history, in the last reckoning, is only important to me insofar as it impinges on my own existence?) Sooner or later the continual division and redivision of aggravations will split the atom of unlivable reality and liberate a nuclear energy which nobody suspected behind so much passivity and gloomy resignation. That which produces the common good is always terrible.

3

From 1945 to 1960, colonialism was a sugar daddy to the Left. With this new enemy on the scale of fascism, the Left never had to define itself (there was nothing there); it could assert itself by merely negating something else, and thus accept itself as a thing within a system where things are at once all and nothing.

For a long time nobody dared hail the end of colonialism for fear that it would spring up again everywhere like a jack-in-the-box not properly shut. Once the collapse of colonial power revealed the colonialism of all power exercised over human beings, the issues of race and skin colour became about as significant as a crossword competition. What purpose was served, then, by all the Left's trotting about on its pet anti-racist and anti-antisemitic hobbyhorses? In the final analysis, all it did was smother the cries of all those who were not Jews or blacks—starting with the Jews and blacks themselves. Far be it from me to contest the spirit of generosity that inspired antiracism in times still not far distant. But since I cannot alter the past it holds scant interest for me. I am speaking in the here and now, and nobody can persuade me, in the name of Alabama or South Africa and their spectacular exploitation, to forget that the epicentre of such problems lies within me, and within every human being who is humiliated and scorned by every aspect of a society that prefers to think of itself as 'well policed' rather than as the police state that it clearly is.

I shall not relinquish my share of violence.

It is scarcely possible, when it comes to human relationships, to speak of more or less tolerable conditions or more or less acceptable indignities. Quantification does not add up in this context. Do insults like 'wog' or 'nigger' hurt more than a call to order? Does not everyone, when stopped, dressed down or ordered about by a policeman, a boss, or some other authority, feel deep down, in the clear light of a transient reality, like a yid, a darkie, or a chink?

The old colonials gave us a perfect identikit portrait of Power when they predicted a descent into bestiality and wretchedness for those who found their presence undesirable. Safety first and foremost, says the guard to the prisoner. The opponents of the colonialism of yesterday are now out to humanize the colonialism of Power in general: cleverly, they become its watchdogs by yapping against the effects of an inhumanity now past.

Before aspiring to a leadership role in Martinique, Aimé Césaire famously remarked that 'The bourgeoisie has found itself unable to solve the major problems which its own existence has produced: the colonial problem and the problem of the proletariat.' He forgot to add: 'For they are one and the same problem, a problem which anyone who separates them will fail to grasp.'

4

Gouy tells us that 'The slightest insult to the King meant immediate death' (*Histoire de France*). According to the American Constitution the people are sovereign. For Pouget's paper *Le Père Peinard*, 'Kings get fat off their sovereignty, while we are starving on ours'. Corbon's *Secret du peuple* notes that 'The people today means the mass of men to whom all respect is denied.' Here we have, in just a few lines, the vicissitudes of the principle of sovereignty.

Monarchism called the objects of its arbitrary will 'subjects'—clearly an attempt to disguise the radical inhumanity of its domination as the humanity of idyllic bonds. The respect due to the King's person cannot in itself be criticized. It is odious only because it is based on the right to humiliate others by subordinating them. Contempt was what caused the thrones of kings to rot. But what about the sovereignty of citizens, meaning rights multiplied by bourgeois vanity and jealousy, sovereignty distributed like a dividend to each individual? What happens when the principle of monarchy is shared out democratically?

Today France contains twenty-four million mini-kings, of which the greatest—the bosses—are great only in their absurdity. The sense of respect has degenerated to the point where humiliation is all it requires. Democratized into public functions and roles, the monarchical principle floats belly up, like a dead fish: only its most repulsive aspect is visible. Its will to be unrestrictedly and absolutely superior has disappeared. Instead of basing our lives on our sovereignty, we now try to base our sovereignty on other people's lives. Such are the manners of slaves.

III   Isolation

Para no sentirme solo
Por los siglos de los siglos

All we have in common is the illusion of being together. Against the illusory official remedies for isolation the only countervailing force is a general will to break its bonds [1]. Neutral relationships are the no-man's-land of isolation. Isolation is a death sentence signed and passed by the present organization of society on itself [2].

1

It was as if they were in a cage whose door might as well have been wide open, for they could not escape. Nothing outside the cage had any significance, for nothing else existed any more. They stayed in the cage, estranged from everything except the cage, without so much as a flicker of desire for anything outside the bars. It would have been peculiar—indeed impossible—to break out into a place with neither reality nor significance. Absolutely impossible. Inside the cage, in which they had been born and in which they would die, the only tolerable framework of experience was the real, which amounted to an irresistible instinct to act so that things should have significance. Only if things had significance could one breathe, and suffer. It was as though there was an understanding between things and the silent dead that it should be so, for the habit of acting so that things should be significant had become a human instinct, and a seemingly eternal one. Life was the important thing, and the real was part of the instinct that gave life some slight meaning. The instinct did not try to imagine what might lie beyond the real, because there was nothing beyond it. Nothing significant. The door stayed open and the cage became more and more painful in its reality, which was significant for countless reasons and in countless ways.

We have never left the age of the slave traders.

On public transport, where they are thrown against one another with statistical indifference, people assume an unbearable expression of disillusion, pride, and contempt—an expression much like the natural effect of death on a toothless mouth. The atmosphere of false communication makes everyone the policeman of their own encounters. The fight-or-flight response haunts the knights-errant of wage-labour, who now depend on rapid transit and suburban trains for their pitiful wanderings. If human beings have mutated into scorpions who sting themselves and each other, is it not really because nothing has happened, and human beings with empty eyes and flabby brains have 'mysteriously' become mere shadows of humans, ghosts of humans, and are now in some ways no longer human save in name?

All we have in common is the illusion of being together. Certainly the seeds of an authentic collective life lie dormant within that illusion itself—there is no illusion without a real basis—but real community has yet to be created. The power of the lie sometimes manages to erase the bitter reality of isolation from our minds. In a crowded street we can occasionally forget that suffering and separation are still in force. And since it is only the lie's power that makes us forget, suffering and separation are thus reinforced; but in the end the lie is hoisted by its own petard, for a moment comes when no illusion can match the enormity of our distress.

The malaise assails me as the crowd around me grows. The concessions I have made to stupidity, under the pressure of circumstances, rush to meet me, surging around me in hallucinatory waves of faceless heads. Edvard Munch's famous picture *The Scream* gives me a feeling I experience ten times a day. Carried along by a crowd which only he can see, a man suddenly screams out in an attempt to break the spell, to call himself back to himself, to get back inside his own skin. All the tacit compliance, all the fixed smiles, lifeless words, cowardice and humiliation strewn along his path suddenly coalesce and possess him, driving him out of his desires and his dreams and exploding the illusion of 'being together'. People rub shoulders without meeting; isolation accumulates but is never totalized; emptiness pervades people as their density increases. The crowd drags me out of myself and allows thousands of tiny surrenders to colonize my empty presence.

Everywhere neon signs blink out the dictum of Plotinus: *All beings are together though each remains separate*. But we only need to hold out our hands to touch one another, raise our eyes to meet one another, and thanks to such simple actions everything will become at once close and far away, as if by magic.

//////

Like the crowd, like drugs or love, drink has the special power to bewitch the most lucid mind. It can make the concrete wall of isolation seem like the kind of paper curtain that actors can tear open at will, for alcohol places everything on the stage of a private theatre. A generous illusion—and all the more deadly for that.

In a gloomy bar where everyone is bored to tears, a drunken young man breaks his glass, then picks up a bottle and smashes it against the wall. Nobody gets excited; disappointed in his expectations, the young man lets himself be thrown out. Yet everyone there was in silent sympathy with his gesture. He alone made the thought concrete, crossing the first radioactive belt of isolation, namely inner isolation, the inward-looking separation between self and outside world. Nobody responded to a sign which he thought was explicit. He remained alone like the hooligan who burns down a church or kills a policeman, at one with himself but condemned to exile as long as other people remain exiled from their own existence. He has not escaped from the magnetic field of isolation; he is suspended in a zone of zero gravity. All the same, the indifference which greets him allows him to hear the sound of his own cry; and even if this revelation torments him, he knows that he will have to start again in another register, more loudly—more *coherently*.

A common doom will be the only thing people share so long as isolated human beings refuse to understand that a free gesture, however weak and clumsy, always embodies an authentic communication, an adequate personal message. The repression that comes down on the anarchist comes down on everyone: the blood of all flows with the blood of a murdered Durruti. When freedom retreats an inch, there is a hundred-fold increase in the weight of the order of *things*. Excluded from authentic participation, human actions are waylaid either by the fragile illusion of being together, or else by its opposite, a brutal, total refusal of all social life. They swing from one to the other like a pendulum turning the hands on the clock-face of death.

//////

As for love, it too fertilizes the illusion of unity. In general it miscar-
ries or sinks into triviality. Fear of taking the well-trodden and only too
familiar path to solitude, whether as a couple or as a small group, casts a
chilling pall over love's symphonies. What drives us to despair is not the
immensity of our unsatisfied desires, but the moment when our fledg-
ling passion discovers its own emptiness. Insatiable desire for passionate
knowledge of one pretty girl after another stems from anxiety and from
fear of love, so afraid are we of never encountering anything but *objects*.
The dawn when lovers leave each other's arms is the same dawn that
breaks on the execution of revolutionaries without a revolution. Isolation
à deux cannot prevail over the isolation of all. Pleasure is broken off
prematurely and lovers find themselves naked in the world, their actions
suddenly ridiculous and feeble. No love is possible in an unhappy world.

The boat of love breaks up on the reefs of ordinary life (Mayakovsky).
Are we ready, so that our desire may never come to grief—are we ready to
breach the reefs of the old world? Lovers must love their pleasure with
more earnestness, and with more poetry. It is said that Prince Shekur
captured a city and presented it to his favourite in exchange for a smile.
A few of us at least have fallen in love with the pleasure of loving without
reservations—passionately enough to offer love the sumptuous bed of a
revolution.

2

Adapting to the world is a trick coin-toss where heads always comes up: it
is decided a priori that the negative is positive and that the impossibility
of living is a prerequisite of life. Alienation never takes such firm root as
when it passes itself off as an inalienable good. In its positive disguise, the
consciousness of isolation is simply the private consciousness, the unfor-
sakable shard of individualism that respectable people drag around like a
piece of cumbersome but cherished property. A sort of pleasure-anxiety
prevents us from settling thoroughly into the illusion of community yet
keeps us locked up in the dungeons of isolation.

The no-man's-land of neutral relations is the territory between
the blissful acceptance of bogus communities and the total rejection
of society. Its moral principles are those of the shopkeeper: 'One hand
washes the other'; 'There are good people everywhere'; 'Things are not
too bad. Not too good either. It's up to us.' In short, politeness—the art-
for-art's-sake of noncommunication.

Let's face it: human relationships being what social hierarchy has made of them, neutrality is the least tiring form of contempt. It allows us to pass without needless friction through the hopper of daily contacts. But it does not prevent us from dreaming—far from it—of such superior forms of civility as the courtliness of Lacenaire, on the eve of his execution, urging a friend: 'Above all, please convey my gratitude to Monsieur Scribe. Tell him that one day, suffering from the pangs of hunger, I presented myself at his house to worm some money out of him. He complied with my request with admirable deference; I am sure he will recall. Tell him that he acted wisely, for I had in my pocket, ready to hand, the means of depriving France of a dramatist.'

The innocuousness of neutral relations, however, offers no more than a moment of dead time in the ceaseless battle against isolation, a brief stopping-place on the road that seems to lead towards communication but that in fact leads far more often to the illusion of community. Which probably explains my reluctance to stop a stranger for the time of day, for directions, or simply to exchange of couple of words, for I am loath to seek contact in this dubious fashion. The pleasantness of neutral relations is built on sand, and empty time never does me any good.

Living is made impossible with such cynicism that even the balanced pleasure-anxiety of neutral relations may function as a cog in the machinery that destroys people. It seems better in the end to go straight to a radical and tactically worked-out rejection rather than knock politely on every door looking to swap one kind of survival for another.

'It would irk me to die so young,' wrote Jacques Vaché two years before his suicide. If the desperation of survival fails to join forces with a new consciousness and transform the years ahead, only two 'options' will be left for the isolated individual: the potty-chair of political parties and pataphysico-religious sects, or immediate death with *Umour*. A sixteen-year-old murderer recently explained: 'I did it because I was bored.' Anyone who has felt the drive to self-destruction welling up inside him knows with what jaded insouciance he might just happen to kill the organizers of his boredom. One day. If he was in the mood.

After all, if individuals refuse either to adapt to the violence of the world or to embrace the violence of the maladapted, what path is still open to them? Unless they elevate their will to achieve perfect union with the world and with themselves to the level of consistent theory and practice, the vast silence of social space will surely confine them to a palace of solipsism and delusion.

From the depths of their prisons those who have been convicted of mental illness add the screams of their strangled revolt to the sum of negativity. What a Fourier *in potentia* was consciously destroyed in a patient described by the psychiatrist Volnat: 'He began to lose all capacity to distinguish between himself and the external world. Everything that happened in the world also happened in his body. He could not put a bottle between two shelves in a cupboard because the shelves might come together and break the bottle. And that would hurt inside his head, as if his head was wedged between the shelves. He could not shut a suitcase, because pressing the effects in the case would exert pressure inside his head. If he walked into the street after closing all the doors and windows of his house, he felt uncomfortable, because his brain was compressed by the air, and he had to go back home to open a door or a window. "For me to be at ease", he would say, "I must have wide open space in front of me. . . . I have to be *free in my space*. It's a battle with the *things* all around me."'

The Consul paused, turning. He read the inscription: '*No se puede vivir sin amar*' (Lowry, *Under the Volcano*).

IV   Suffering

The suffering of natural alienation has given way to that of social alienation, while remedies have become justifications [1]. Where there is no justification, exorcism takes its place [2]. But no subterfuge can now hide the fact that suffering is organized, and as such contributes to a social organization based on the distribution of constraints [3]. Consciousness reduced to the consciousness of constraints is an anteroom to death. The despair of consciousness makes murderers in the name of order; the consciousness of despair makes murderers in the name of disorder [4].

1

A symphony of spoken and shouted words animates the urban landscape. Against a *basso continuo*, dark or light themes develop from raucous or singsong voices and endless evocative fragments of speech. A sonorous architecture thus overlays the web of streets and buildings, reinforcing or counteracting the attractive or repellent feel of a particular district. But from the Place de la Contrescarpe to the Champs-Élysées the basic chords are the same: their sinister resonance has sunk so deeply into everyone's mind that it no longer surprises us. 'That's life', 'You can't change human nature', 'That's the way it goes', 'You have to take the rough with the smooth', 'Every day can't be a holiday'—this lament whose weft unites the most diverse conversations has so perverted our sensibility that it passes for the commonest of human attitudes. Where despair is not acknowledged, it disappears from view. Nobody seems concerned that joy has been absent from European music for nearly two centuries— which says everything. Consume, consume—in both senses of the word: we take ashes for fire.

What is the origin of the significance now claimed by suffering and its rites of exorcism? Its roots probably lie in the harsh conditions of survival imposed on the first humans by a hostile nature permeated by cruel and mysterious forces. In the face of such danger, social bonds offered vulnerable early mankind not only protection but also a way of cooperating with nature, of making a truce with it and even transforming it. In the course of the struggle against natural alienation—against death, sickness and suffering—alienation became social. And hence, strange as it may seem to some, death, sickness and suffering likewise became social. We escaped the rigours of exposure, hunger and discomfort only to fall into the trap of slavery. We were enslaved by gods, by human beings, by language. And that slavery had its positive side: there was a kind of grandeur about living in terror of a god who also made one invincible. This mixture of human and inhuman might, it is true, suffice to explain the ambiguity of suffering, its way of appearing throughout human history as at once a shameful ill and a salutary one—as a good thing, after a fashion. But this would be to overlook the ignoble slag of religion, especially Christian mythology, which devoted all its genius to perfecting a morbid and depraved precept: protect yourself against mutilation by mutilating yourself!

'Since Christ's coming, we are delivered not from the evil of suffering but from the evil of suffering uselessly', writes Father Charles of the Society of Jesus. How right he is: Power's problem has never been to abolish itself but rather to resign itself not to oppress 'uselessly'. By marrying humanity to suffering, whether on grounds of divine grace or of natural law, Christianity, that pathological therapy, contrived its masterstroke. From prince to manager, from priest to expert, from father confessor to social worker, it is always the principle of useful suffering and willing sacrifice that forms the most solid basis for hierarchical power. Whatever reason is invoked—a better world, the next world, a socialist world, or pie in the sky—suffering willingly accepted is always Christian—*always*. Today the clerical vermin have made way for the missionaries of a Christ dyed red. Everywhere official pronouncements bear as their watermark the disgusting image of the crucified Christ, everywhere the comrades are urged to sport the idiotic halo of the martyr-militant. But their blood will serve the kitchen-hands of the Good Cause well as they knead the sausage-meat of the future: less cannon-fodder, more dogma-fodder!

//////

At first, bourgeois ideology seemed determined to go after suffering as relentlessly as it went after the religions it so hated. Infatuated with

progress, comfort, profit, well-being, reason, it had enough weapons—
if not real weapons, then at least the weapons of illusion—to convince
everyone of its will to put an end, with the help of science, to the evil
of suffering and the evil of faith. As we know, all it did was invent new
analgesics and new superstitions.

With God gone, suffering became 'natural'—inherent in 'human
nature'; an end was put to this notion, but only at the cost of more,
compensatory suffering: martyrs of science, victims of progress, lost
generations. But this very tendency exposed the social origin of the
idea of natural suffering. With Human Nature gone, suffering became
social, inherent to 'being-in-society'. Revolutions, of course, proceeded
to demonstrate that social evil was not a metaphysical principle: that
a form of society could exist from which the ills of life were banished.
History shattered the social ontology of suffering, but suffering, far
from disappearing, found new pretexts for its existence in the requirements of history, itself suddenly trapped in its famous one-way street.
China prepares children for the classless society by teaching them love
of country, family and work. Historical ontology gathers up the dregs
of all the metaphysical systems, all the *an sich*, of the past: God, Nature,
Man, Society. From now on, people will have to make history by fighting
History itself, because History has become the last ontological bulwark
of Power, the last ruse whereby, behind the promise of a long weekend, it
conceals its will to endure until a Saturday that will never come. Beyond
this fetishized history, suffering may be seen to derive from the hierarchical organization of society. And when the will to put an end to hierarchical power has sufficiently aroused human consciousness, everyone will
have to admit that armed freedom and the burden of constraints have
nothing metaphysical about them.

2

Even as it placed happiness and freedom on the agenda, technological
civilization was inventing the *ideology* of happiness and freedom. It thus
doomed itself to creating no freedom save the freedom of apathy, no
happiness save that of passivity. But at least these inventions, perverted
though they were, gave the lie on a universal scale to the notions that
suffering was an intrinsic aspect of the human condition and that such
an *inhuman* condition had anything eternal about it. That is why bourgeois thought fails when it tries to provide consolation for suffering; none

of its justifications are as powerful as the hope aroused by its initial wager on technology and well-being.

Desperate fellowship in sickness is the worst thing that can befall a civilization. It is not so much death that terrifies twentieth-century humanity as the absence of real life: the lifeless gestures, the mechanized, specialized gestures that steal portions of life hundreds, thousands of times a day until mind and body are exhausted, until an end comes that is less the end of life than an absence at saturation point. This is what lends such a dangerous allure to apocalypse, vast destruction, complete annihilation, and brutal death, hygienic and total. Auschwitz and Hiroshima are indeed the 'solace of nihilism'. Let impotence in the face of suffering become a collective feeling, and the demand for suffering and death can sweep a whole community. Consciously or not, most people would rather die than live a life forever unfulfilled. On anti-nuclear marches, for instance, all I ever see—aside from an active minority of radicals—are penitents trying to exorcise their desire to disappear along with the rest of humanity. They would deny it, of course, but their miserable expressions betray them. The only real joy is revolutionary.

Perhaps it is to ensure that a universal desire to perish does not take hold of humanity that such a production is made of particular sufferings and misfortunes. A kind of philanthropy, presumably in the public interest, urges each of us to find consolation for our own woes in the contemplation of the woes of others.

Manifestations of this phenomenon range from disaster photographs, sagas of cuckolded singers, catchy tunes in the manner of a Berthe Sylva, and all the pathetic bilge that fills the pages of *France-Soir*, to the spectacle of hospitals, asylums and prisons—real museums of suffering for those whose fear of being confined there makes them rejoice to be on the outside. I sometimes feel such a diffuse pain everywhere in me that I find relief in the chance misfortune that can concretize and justify it, offering it a legitimate outlet. Nothing will dissuade me of one thing: the sadness I feel after a break-up, a failure, a bereavement does not reach me from the outside like an arrow, but wells up from inside like a spring freed by a landslide. There are wounds that let the spirit utter a long-stifled cry. Despair never lets go its prey; it is just that the prey seizes upon a love lost or a child's death to see despair in what is really but despair's cast shadow. Mourning is a pretext, a convenient way of ejaculating nothingness in small drops. The tears, the cries and howls of childhood remain imprisoned in the hearts of human beings. Forever? In you too the emptiness continues to grow.

3

Another word about the rationales of Power. Suppose a tyrant took pleasure in throwing prisoners, who had been flayed alive, into a small cell; suppose that to hear their screams and see them scramble each time they brushed against one another amused him no end, while prompting him to meditate on human nature and the curious behaviour of human beings. Suppose that at the same time and in the same country there were philosophers and wise men who explained to the worlds of science and art that suffering had to do with the collective life of human beings, with the inevitable presence of Others, with society as such—would we not be right to look upon these people as the tyrant's henchmen? A brand of existentialism, by underwriting such claims, has killed two birds with one stone, paradoxically exposing not only the collusion of left intellectuals with Power, but also the crude trick whereby an inhuman social organization ascribes responsibility for its cruelty to its victims. A nineteenth-century commentator noted that 'Throughout contemporary literature we find the tendency to regard individual suffering as a social evil and to make the organization of our society responsible for the misery and degradation of its members. This is a profoundly new idea: suffering is no longer treated as a matter of destiny.' This 'new' and viable idea seems to have given startlingly little pause to certain respectable thinkers imbued with fatalism, as witness Sartre's hell-is-other-people, Freud's death instinct or Mao's historical necessity. What is the difference, when all is said and done, between these doctrines and a stupid tag such as 'It's just human nature'?

Hierarchical social organization is like a system of hoppers equipped with sharp blades. While it flays us alive, Power makes a point of persuading us that we are flaying each other. It must be granted that merely *writing* these words is to court a new fatalism; but I certainly intend in writing them that nobody should merely *read* them.

//////

Altruism is simply the reverse of 'hell-is-other-people', though here the mystification occurs in its positive form. It is high time to jettison this boy-scout mentality. For other people to interest me I must first find in

myself the energy for such an interest. What binds me to others must
stem from what binds me to the richest and most demanding part of my
will to live—not the other way round. It is always myself that I seek in
other people—my enrichment, my fulfilment. Once everyone grasps this,
the logic of 'every man for himself', carried to its logical conclusion, will
be transformed into the logic of 'all for each'. The freedom of one will be
the freedom of all. A community not grounded in individual demands
and their dialectic must needs reinforce the oppressive violence of Power.
The Other in whom I do not recognize myself is nothing but a thing, and
altruism clearly leads me to love things—and to love my isolation.

The viewpoint of altruism—or of solidarity, which is what the Left
calls it—turns the meaning of equality on its head. Equality becomes
nothing but the common distress of social isolates humiliated, fucked
over, beaten down, betrayed—and contented: the distress of monads
aspiring to join together not in reality but in a mystical unity. Anything
will do: the Nation, the workers' movement—no matter what, so long as
it purveys that drunk-Saturday-night feeling of 'we are all brothers and
sisters'. Equality in the great family of man reeks of incense, of religious
mystification. You would need a stuffed-up nose not to be sickened by it.

For myself, I recognize no equality except that which my will to
live according to my desires recognizes in the will to live of others.
Revolutionary equality will be inseparably individual and collective.

4

From Power's perspective there is but one horizon: death. And life goes
so often to this well of despair that eventually it drowns. Wherever the
running water of everyday life begins to stagnate, the features of the
drowned reflect the faces of the living: the positive, looked at closely,
turns out to be negative, the young are already old, and everything we
are building is already a ruin. Under the sway of despair, lucidity blinds
as easily as falsehood. We may die of not knowing, struck down from
behind. Foreknowledge of the death that awaits us merely increases the
torture and hastens the agony. The erosive effect of the continual slowing,
shackling and prohibition of our acts eats away at us more surely than
a cancer, but nothing spreads the disease like a keen awareness of the
process. I am convinced that nothing can save someone continually
confronted by the question: do you see the hand that, ever so courte-
ously, is killing you? Gauging the impact of every tiny insult, resorting

to Artaud's *pèse-nerfs* to weigh each constraint, is enough to consign the hardiest individual to a single overwhelming feeling of horrible weakness, utter powerlessness. The plague of constraints arises from the very depths of the mind; nothing human can resist its onslaught.

Sometimes I feel as if Power is imparting its traits to me: a great force on the point of collapsing, a rage unable to explode, a yearning for wholeness suddenly calcified. An impotent order can survive only by ensuring the impotence of its slaves. Franco and Batista demonstrated this with brio by castrating captured revolutionaries. As for those regimes jokingly referred to as democratic, they merely humanize castration. At first sight, to hasten the onset of old age might seem less feudal than the use of knife and ligature. But only at first sight—for once a lucid mind grasps the fact that that powerlessness stems from the mind itself, it is very tempting to throw in the towel.

There is a kind of consciousness that Power allows because it serves its ends. To see things in the light of Power reveals only the darkness of despair, and amounts to nourishing one's truth with lies. In aesthetic terms the choice is clear: death against Power or death in Power's bosom. On the one hand Arthur Cravan or Jacques Vaché; on the other, the SS, the French paratrooper in Algeria, or the hired killer. For all of them death is a logical and natural outcome, proof supreme of a permanent state of affairs and end-point of a lifeline upon which, ultimately, nothing was written. All who fail to resist Power's well-nigh universal attraction meet the same fate: the stupid and confused always, the intelligent very often. The same chasm confronted Drieu La Rochelle and Jacques Rigaut, but they came down on different sides: the impotence of the first was moulded by submission and servility; the rebellion of the second ran straight into the brick wall of impossibility. The despair of consciousness makes murderers in the name of order; the consciousness of despair makes murderers in the name of disorder. The relapse into conformity of the so-called anarchists of the Right parallels and obeys the same gravitational pull as the fall of archangels into the iron jaws of suffering. The crypt of despair resounds with the croaking call of counterrevolution.

Suffering is the malady that constraints bring on. Yet a single moment of unalloyed joy, no matter how fleeting, can keep it at bay. Stoking real joy and festivity is tantamount to fomenting a general uprising.

These days people are urged to engage in a gigantic search-and-destroy operation aimed at myths and received ideas. But make no mistake, they are sent out unarmed—or worse, armed only with the paper weapons of pure speculation—into the swamp of constraints, ever ready to swallow them up. Which is why a foretaste of pleasures to come will perhaps be achieved by pushing the ideologues of demystification ahead of us, to see how they fare, and either exploiting their success or advancing over their dead bodies.

As Rosanov says, people are crushed under the wardrobe. If the wardrobe it not lifted it will be impossible to deliver whole peoples from endless and unbearable suffering. It is terrible that just one person should be crushed under such a weight: that they should want to breathe, and not be able to. The wardrobe weighs down on everyone, and everyone tries to raise it, but not all with the same conviction, not all with the same strength. An odd, groaning civilization.

Thinkers ask themselves: 'What? People under the wardrobe? How ever did they get there?' But get there they did. And if someone comes along and proves in the name of objectivity that the burden can never be removed, their every sentence, their every word adds to the weight of the wardrobe—the object that they claim to *describe* thanks to the universality of their 'objective consciousness'. And the whole Christian spirit is here, has made sure to be here, fondling suffering like a good dog and handing out photographs of crushed but smiling people. 'The logic of the wardrobe is always the best', proclaim the thousands of books published every day and duly placed in the wardrobe. And all the while everyone wants to breathe and no one can breathe, and many say 'We will breathe later', and most do not die because they are already dead.

It is now or never.

V   The Decline of Work

The obligation to produce alienates the passion to create.
Productive labour is a function of law and order. Work time
diminishes as conditioning tightens its grip.

In an industrial society that conflates work and productivity, the need
to produce has always stood opposed to the desire to create. What spark
of humanity, which is to say possible creativity, can remain alive in a
being dragged from sleep at six every morning, jolted about in commuter
trains, deafened by the racket of machinery, bleached and steamed by
speed-up and meaningless gestures and production quotas, and tossed
out at the end of the day into great railway-station halls—temples of
arrival and departure for the hell of weekdays and the nugatory paradise
of the weekend, where the masses commune in brutish weariness? From
adolescence to retirement age, relentlessly, every twenty-four-hour cycle
helps lengthen all the cracks—like those in a broken window pane—that
work inflicts in the shape of mechanical repetition, time-that-is-money,
submission to bosses, boredom, exhaustion, and so on. From the shattering of youthful vitality to the yawning chasm of old age, life splinters
in every direction under the blows of forced labour. Never has a civilization achieved such a degree of contempt for life; never, though, has
a generation, overwhelmed by revulsion, experienced such a wild urge
to live. Those threatened by slow-motion murder in labour's mechanized slaughterhouses are suddenly debating, singing, drinking, dancing,
making love, taking to the streets, picking up weapons, and inventing a
new poetry. Already the front against forced labour is forming; already
its acts of refusal are shaping the consciousness of the future. Every call
for productivity under the conditions imposed by capitalist and Soviet
economies alike is a call to slavery.

Arguments for the necessity of producing are so easy to find that even
a hack like Jean Fourastié can fill a dozen tomes with them. Unfortunately
for the economism of such neotheorists, their justifications date from

the nineteenth century, harking back to a time when the poverty of the working classes made the right to work analogous to the right to slavery claimed at the dawn of history by prisoners about to be massacred. A time when the main thing was to avoid physical elimination—simply to survive. The imperatives of productivity are the imperatives of survival; but now people want to live, not just survive.

The *tripalium* is an instrument of torture. The Latin word *labor* means 'suffering'. We do well to bear in mind these origins of the words *'travail'* and 'labour'. It must be said for the nobles that they never forgot either their dignity or the lack thereof that characterized their bondservants: the aristocratic contempt for work reflected the master's contempt for the subject classes; work was the expiation to which serfs were condemned for all eternity by the divine decree which, for impenetrable reasons, had willed their inferiority. Work had its place, among the sanctions of Providence, as the punishment for poverty, and because it determined future salvation such a punishment could paradoxically take on a joyful aspect. At bottom, though, work was less important than submission.

The bourgeoisie for its part does not dominate. It exploits. It does not *subject* people so much as *wear them out*. Why has nobody noticed that the principle of productivity was simply a replacement for the principle of feudal authority? Why has nobody wanted to understand this?

Is it because work improves the human condition and saves the poor, at least illusorily, from eternal damnation? Very likely so, but today it would seem that the carrot of happier tomorrows in this world has readily replaced the carrot of salvation in the next. In either case the *present* lies under the heel of oppression.

Is it because work transforms nature? Perhaps, but what good to me is a nature ordered according to profits, a world where an inflation of technology masks a deflation in the use-value of life? Besides, just as the sexual act is not intended to procreate, but makes children by accident, work as organized at present transforms the face of continents not intentionally but as a spin-off effect. Work to transform the world? What nonsense! The world is being transformed as a function of the existence of forced labour, not vice versa—which is why it is being transformed so badly.

Could humanity ever find fulfilment through forced labour? In the nineteenth century the connotations of work still included vestiges of creativity. Zola describes a nailsmiths' contest in which workers applied their skill to the making of tiny masterpieces. Love of craft and the now daunting challenge of deploying some measure of creativity certainly helped people to endure ten- or fifteen-hour days—which would surely have been impossible had not some sort of pleasure entered into them. The survival of the craft approach gave workers a chance to contrive a precarious comfort for themselves in the hell of the factory. But Taylorism dealt the death-blow to attitudes carefully fostered by early forms of capitalism. It is vain to expect even a caricature of creativity from work on the conveyor belt. Today the love of a job well done and belief in the rewards of hard work signal nothing so much as spineless and stupid submission. And wherever submission is required, the stink of ideology hangs in the air, from the *Arbeit Macht Frei of* the concentration camps to the homilies of Henry Ford and Mao Tse-tung.

So what is the function of forced labour? The myth of power exercised jointly by the master and by God drew its coercive force from the unity of the feudal system. Destroying the unitary myth, the fragmented power of the bourgeoisie, flying the flag of crisis, ushered in the reign of ideologies, which can never, separately or in combination, achieve a fraction of the effectiveness of myth. The dictatorship of productive work stepped conveniently into this breach. Its mission was to weaken the majority of people physically, to castrate and stupefy them collectively and to make them receptive to the least significant, least vital, most senile ideologies in the history of falsehood.

At the beginning of the nineteenth century most of the proletariat had been physically diminished, systematically broken by the torture of the workshop. Revolts arose among small craftspeople or among privileged or unemployed workers rather than among workers demolished by fifteen-hour days. It is surely rather disturbing to note that the reduction of working hours eventually came just as the ideological variety show devised by consumer society was ready to provide an effective replacement for the feudal myths destroyed by the ascendant bourgeoisie. (People have worked really hard for a refrigerator, a car, a television set. Many still do—'invited' as they are to consume the passivity and the empty time that the 'necessity' of production 'offers' them.)

Statistics published in 1938 indicated that the use of the most modern technology would reduce necessary working time to three hours a day. Not only are we very far from that with our seven hours, but after wearing out generations of workers by promising them the happiness sold to them today on the instalment plan, the bourgeoisie (and its Soviet counterpart) now pursue the destruction of workers beyond the shop-floor. Tomorrow they may be expected to suffer five hours of necessary wear and tear with 'creative time', which is bound to increase as fast as they can fill it with the impossibility of creating anything (this is what is meant by the 'planning of leisure').

It has been pointed out, correctly, that 'China faces gigantic economic problems; for her, productivity is a matter of life and death'. Nobody would dream of denying it. What I find troubling is not economic imperatives but the manner of responding to them. The Red Army of 1917 was a new kind of organization. The Red Army of the 1960s is an army just like any army in a capitalist country. Events have shown that its effectiveness falls far short of that of revolutionary militias. In the same way, the planned Chinese economy, by refusing to allow federated groups to organize their work autonomously, has doomed itself to become just another example of the perfected form of capitalism called socialism. Has anyone bothered to study the approaches to work of primitive peoples, the importance of play and creativity, the incredible yield obtained by methods which the application of modern technology would make a hundred times more efficient? Apparently not. Every appeal for productivity comes from above, but only creativity is spontaneously rich. Productivity can never ensure a rich life, nor can it ever power an enthusiastic collective response to economic demands. One is at a loss for words in face of the cult of work in Communist countries from Cuba to China. How perfect the virtuous pages of a Guizot would sound if read at a May Day parade!

To the extent that automation and cybernetics foreshadow the massive replacement of workers by mechanical slaves, forced labour is exposed as simply one belonging purely to the barbaric practices needed to maintain order. Power manufactures the dose of fatigue necessary for the passive assimilation of its televised diktats. What carrot is worth working for, at this point? The game is up; there is nothing more to lose, not even illusion. The organization of work and the organization of leisure are the twin blades of castrating shears whose job is to improve the race of fawning dogs. One day, perhaps, we shall see strikers demanding automation and a ten-hour week, and deciding, instead of picketing, to make love in the factories, offices and cultural centres. Only programmers, managers, union bosses and sociologists would be surprised—and worried. For good reason: their hides will be on the line.

VI   Decompression and the Third Force

> Until now tyranny has merely changed hands. By virtue of their like respect for the principle of the ruler, antagonistic powers have always contained the seeds of their future coexistence. (When the organizer of the game assumes the power of a leader, the revolution dies along with the revolutionaries.) Unresolved antagonisms fester, hiding real contradictions. Decompression is the permanent control of antagonists by a ruling caste. The third force radicalizes contradictions, and leads towards their supersession in the name of individual freedom and against all forms of constraint. Power has no recourse but to smash or co-opt the third force without acknowledging its existence.

Let us take stock. A few million people lived in a huge building with no doors or windows. The feeble light of countless oil lamps vied with the ever-present obscurity. As had been the custom since Antiquity in its wisdom, the upkeep of the lamps was the duty of the poor, so the oil supply rose and fell in precise accord with the ups and downs of calm and rebellion. One day a general insurrection broke out, the most violent that this people had ever known. The rebel leadership demanded a fair allocation of the costs of lighting; a large number of revolutionaries said that what they considered a public utility should be free; a few extremists went so far as to clamour for the destruction of the building, which they claimed was unhealthy, even unfit for human habitation. As usual, the more reasonable elements found themselves helpless in face of the violence of the conflict. During a particularly lively clash with law enforcement, a stray projectile breached the thick wall, creating a gap through which daylight streamed in. After a moment of stupefaction, this flood of light was greeted with cries of victory. The solution had been found: all that was needed was to make more openings. The lamps were thrown away or put in museums, and power fell to the window-makers. The partisans of complete destruction were forgotten, and even their discreet liquidation seemingly went unnoticed. (Everyone was arguing about the number and placing of the windows.) Then, a century or two later, their names were remembered when the people, that eternal malcontent, having grown accustomed to large picture-windows, took to asking extravagant questions: 'To drag out your days in an air-conditioned greenhouse,' they began to ask, 'you call that living?'

//////

In our time consciousness fluctuates between that of someone completely walled up and that of a prisoner in a cell. For each of us this fluctuation takes the place of freedom: we go back and forth between the blank wall of our cell and the barred window that bespeaks escape. Any chink that is opened lets in not only light but also hope. The hope of escape, which prisons deliberately foster, can ensure good behaviour from convicts. By contrast, an individual facing a wall with no exit can only feel a raging impulse to knock it down or smash his head against it, which is inevitably undesirable from the point of view of efficient social control. (This is true even if the suicide, failing to emulate the admirable example of the Oriental prince who immolates all his slaves along with himself, does not resolve to take a few others with him from the ranks of judges, bishops, generals, policemen, psychiatrists, philosophers, managers, experts and cyberneticians.)

Someone walled up alive has nothing to lose; the prisoner still has hope to lose. Hope is the leash of the submissive. Whenever Power is in danger of exploding, it opens a safety-valve to lower the pressure. At such times it is said to have changed hands, but in fact it has merely adapted, thus resolving its difficulties.

Against any established power another always arises that is similar but flies the flag of opposition. Nothing is more threatening to the principle of hierarchical government, however, than merciless confrontation between two opponents each driven by a like rage for the total annihilation of the other. In such a conflict, the tidal wave of fanaticism sweeps away the most stable values, turning the entire territory in dispute into a no-man's-land and ushering in everywhere the interregnum of 'nothing is true, everything is permitted'. History, be it said, offers not a single instance of a titanic conflict of this kind not defused in good time and turned into a comic-opera battle. What is the origin of this process of decompression? It stems from a tacit agreement of principle between the belligerents.

The principle of hierarchy is indeed espoused by the true believers on both sides. Conflicts are never unleashed with impunity, nor are they ever innocent. The capitalism of Lloyd George and the Krupps was challenged by the anticapitalism of Lenin and Trotsky. From the mirror of the masters of the present, the masters of the future are already smiling back. As Heinrich Heine wrote:

> Lächelnd scheidet der Tyran
> Denn er weiss, nach seinem Tode
> Wechselt Willkür nur die Hände
> Und die Knechtschaft hat kein Ende.

The tyrant dies smiling, for he knows that after his death tyranny will merely change hands, and slavery will never end. Leaders differ just as the ways they dominate differ, but they are always leaders—proprietors of a power exercised as a private entitlement. (Lenin's greatness certainly has to do with his romantic refusal to assume the position of absolute master implied by the ultrahierarchical organization of his Bolsheviks; it is this same greatness, be it said, that the workers' movement has to thank for Kronstadt 1921, for Budapest 1956, and for *Batiuchka* Stalin.)

The common ground of the opponents thus becomes the site of decompression. To identify the enemy with Evil and crown one's own side with the halo of Good has the strategic advantage of ensuring unity of action by channelling the energy of the combatants. But such a strategy calls for the enemy's annihilation. Moderates baulk at such a prospect, especially inasmuch as the *radical* destruction of the enemy would include the destruction of what their own side has in common with that enemy. The logic of Bolshevism demanded the heads of the leaders of Social Democracy; those leaders hastily sold out, and they did so qua leaders. The logic of anarchism demanded the liquidation of Bolshevik power, which rapidly crushed the anarchists, and did so qua hierarchical power. The same predictable sequence of betrayals delivered Durruti's anarchists to the rifles of the Republican alliance of Socialists and Stalinists.

As soon as the organizer of the game turns into a leader, the principle of hierarchy is preserved, and the revolution, now in power, can preside over the execution of the revolutionaries. We must never forget that the insurrectionary project belongs to the masses alone; organizers help it—leaders betray it. The real struggle occurs, to begin with, between organizers and leaders.

The revolutionary careerist measures the balance of forces in quantitative terms, just as any soldier gauges an officer's rank by the number of men under his command. The leaders of insurrectionary parties real or supposed abandon qualitative criteria on the grounds that quantitative ones are more realistic. But had the 'Reds' been blessed with half a million more troops and modern weaponry, the Spanish Revolution would still have been lost. It died under the heel of the People's Commissars. The speeches of La Pasionaria already sounded like funeral orations; pathos-laden cries drowned out the language of deeds, the spirit of the collectives of Aragon—the spirit of a radical minority determined to cut off at a single stroke not just the Fascist head but all the heads of the hydra.

Never, and for good reason, has an absolute confrontation been fought through to the end. So far, the 'last fight' has had only false starts. Everything must be begun afresh. History's only justification is to help us do so.

//////

Once subjected to decompression, seemingly irreconcilable opponents grow old side by side, becoming frozen in a purely formal antagonism, losing their substance, neutralizing each other and mouldering away together. Who could discern the Bolshevik with a knife between his teeth in the Gagarinism of a doting Moscow? Today, by some ecumenical miracle, the slogan 'Workers of the World, Unite' cements the union of the world's bosses. What a charming picture: what the antagonists had in common—the seeds of a power that radical struggle would have rooted out—has matured to the point of reconciling the warring brothers.

Could it really be so simple? Of course not—the farce would lose its bounce. On the international stage, those two old hams, capitalism and anticapitalism, continue with their repartee. How the spectators shudder at the prospect of a falling-out, how they stamp with glee when peace blesses the loving pair! Is interest flagging? A brick is added to the Berlin Wall; or the awful Mao gnashes his teeth against the backdrop of a Chinese children's choir singing paeans to fatherland, family and work. Patched up like this, the old Manichaeanism continues on its merry way. To keep current, the ideological spectacle is continually launching new pseudo-antagonisms: are you for or against Brigitte Bardot, Johnny Hallyday, Citroën 3CVs, young people, nationalization, spaghetti, old people, the United Nations, miniskirts, Pop Art, thermonuclear war, hitch-hiking? There is no one who is not accosted at some moment of the day by an advertisement, a news item or a stereotyped image that summons them to take sides over one or other of the prefabricated trifles that work relentlessly to obstruct all sources of everyday creativity. Under the sway of Power's icy fetishism, particles of antagonism form a magnetic field whose function is to distort the individual's compass, to abstract individuals from themselves and scramble all their points of reference.

Decompression, in short, is the manipulation of antagonisms by Power. The opposition of two terms is usually made meaningful by the intervention of a third. As long as there are only two poles, they cancel each other out, since each derives its significance from the other; and since it is impossible to choose between them, we are led into the realm of tolerance and relativity that is so dear to the bourgeoisie. How easy it is to understand the importance for the apostolic Roman hierarchy of the dispute between Manichaeanism and Trinitarianism. In the wake of a true fight to the death between God and Satan, what would be left of ecclesiastical authority? Nothing—as the millenarian crises clearly showed. That is why the secular arm performed holy offices, why the pyres crackled alike for God-loving and devil-loving mystics, as for any theologian rash enough to question the principle of the Three in One. The temporal masters of Christianity were determined that they alone should adjudicate the struggle between the Master of Good and the Master of Evil. They were the great intermediaries through which the choice of one side or the other had to pass; they controlled the paths of salvation and damnation, a control more important to them than salvation and damnation themselves. On earth, they set themselves up as judges without appeal, while submitting themselves to judgement solely in an afterlife whose laws were of their own devising.

The Christian myth defanged the bitter Manichaean conflict by offering believers the chance of individual salvation; this was the breach opened up by the Hairy Man of Nazareth. In this way mankind escaped the rigours of a clash that would lead inevitably to the destruction of values, to nihilism. But by the same token it lost the chance to reclaim itself by means of a general upheaval, the chance to take its proper place in the universe by chasing out the gods and the afflictions they brought. The essential function of decompression would therefore appear to be the shackling of humanity's deepest desire, the desire to be itself and itself alone.

In all conflicts pitting two antagonistic forces against each other, an intractable upsurge of individual demands comes into play and often succeeds in imposing its dangerous requirements. So much so, in fact, that one may reasonably speak of a *third force*. This force is to the individual perspective what the force of decompression is to the perspective of Power. A spontaneous by-product of every struggle, the third force radicalizes insurrections, exposes false problems, and threatens Power in its very structure. Its roots are omnipresent in everyday life. It is what Brecht was referring to in one of his Mr Keuner stories: 'When a proletarian was brought to court and asked if he wished to take the oath in the ecclesiastical or the lay form, he replied "I'm out of work".' The third force initiates not the withering away of constraints but rather their supersession. If prematurely crushed or co-opted, its energy can be turned in the opposite direction and enlisted by decompression. The salvation of the soul is thus nothing but the will to live co-opted by myth, mediated, and emptied of its real content. By contrast, their peremptory demand for a full life explains the hatred incurred by certain Gnostic sects or by the Brethren of the Free Spirit. During the decline of Christianity, the struggle between Pascal and the Jesuits mobilized the reformist doctrine of individual salvation and compromise with heaven against the project of achieving godliness through the nihilistic destruction of the world. Once rid of the dead wood of theology, the third force went on to inspire Babeuf's struggle against the *million doré*, the Marxist project of the whole man, the dreams of Fourier, the unleashing of the Paris Commune, and the violence of the anarchists.

/ / / / / /

Individualism, alcoholism, collectivism, activism—the very variety of -isms shows that there are a hundred ways of being on the side of Power. There is only one way to be radical. The wall to be knocked down is immense, but it has been breached so many times that before long a single cry will be enough to bring it crashing to the ground. May the formidable reality of the third force—all the individual passions that have fuelled the insurrections of the past—emerge at last from the fog of history. It will then become clear that everyday life embodies an energy which can move mountains and abolish distances. The long revolution will soon make its mark on reality, tossing its unknown or nameless authors pell-mell into the ranks of Sade, Fourier, Babeuf, Marx, Lacenaire, Stirner,

Lautréamont, Léhautier, Vaillant, Henry, Villa, Zapata, Makhno, of the Communards, the insurrectionaries of Hamburg and Kiel, Kronstadt and Asturias—in short, of all those precursors who have not yet played their last cards in a game that we have only just joined: the great gamble on freedom.

The Impossibility of Communication: Power as Universal Mediation

Under Power's sway, mediation is the fake necessity that teaches human beings how to lose themselves in a rational way. This alienating capacity of mediations is strengthened, yet at the same time brought into question by the dictatorship of consumption (VII), by the priority of exchange over gift (VIII), by the application of cybernetics (IX), and by the reign of the quantitative (X).

VII The Age of Happiness

In anachronistic fashion, the modern welfare state provides the guarantees of survival once demanded by the disinherited members of the former production-based society [1]. Affluent survival means the impoverishment of life [2]. Purchasing power is a licence to purchase power, to become an object in the order of things. Oppressor and oppressed alike fall prey—albeit at different rates— to the self-same dictatorship of consumption [3].

1

The face of happiness ceased to appear like a watermark in works of art and literature the moment it began to be reproduced endlessly, as far as the eye could see, on walls and hoardings, offering each individual passer-by universal images with which to identify.

With Volkswagen your problems are over! Live worry-free with Balamur! The man with good taste is savvy too: he chooses Mercedes-Benz!

Three cheers for Adam Smith and Jeremy Bentham! Happiness is not a myth! 'The more we produce, the better we shall live', writes the humanist Jean Fourastié, and another genius, General Eisenhower, takes up the refrain: 'To save the economy we must buy—buy anything, but buy!' Production and consumption are the tits of modern society. Thus suckled, humanity grows stronger and more beautiful. A higher standard of living, countless conveniences, entertainment galore, culture for all— in short, a once undreamt-of level of comfort. Meanwhile, on the horizon of the Khrushchev Report, the rosy dawn of Communism is breaking at last, a new age heralded by two revolutionary decrees: the abolition of taxes and free transport for all. Yes, the golden age is in sight—indeed within spitting distance.

Conspicuously absent from this picture of transformation is the proletariat. Could it have vanished into thin air? Taken to the hills? Been put in a museum? *Sociologi disputant.* Some say that in the advanced industrial countries the proletarian is no more, as witness an

avalanche of fridges, TVs, Renault Dauphines, public housing develop-
ments, and people's theatres. Others denounce all this as hocus-pocus
and point meaningfully to a few remaining workers whose low wages
and wretched conditions indisputably evoke the nineteenth century.
'Backward sectors,' comes the retort. 'Pockets still in the process of integration. Surely you won't deny that the trend of economic development
is towards Sweden, Czechoslovakia, the welfare state, and not towards
India?'

The black curtain rises: the search for the hungry, for the last of the
proletarians, is on. Hurrah for whoever sells him a car and a blender, a
basement bar or a home library; for whoever teaches him to see himself
in the smiling character in the ever so reassuring ad: 'Happiness is a
Lucky Strike.'

And happy, happy humanity, so soon to receive the care packages
addressed to it at such great cost by the rebels of the nineteenth century!
How very lucky the insurgents of Lyons and Fourmies have turned out
to be—albeit posthumously! The millions of human beings shot, imprisoned, tortured, starved, brutalized and systematically humiliated must
surely be at peace, in their cemeteries and mass graves, to know how
history has made sure that the struggle in which they died has enabled
their descendants, isolated in their air-conditioned apartments, to learn
from their daily dose of TV how to repeat that they are happy and free.
'The Communards went down, fighting to the last man, so that you too
could buy a Philips hi-fi.' A fine legacy indeed—one that must surely
warm the cockles of all those revolutionaries of the past.

Only the present is short-shrifted in this accounting. Ungrateful
and uncouth, the younger generation cares nothing for a glorious past
offered as a free gift to every consumer of Trotskyoid-reformist ideology.
They claim that making demands means making demands for the here
and now. They insist that the sense of past struggles was rooted in the
present of those who fought them—a present, however, which despite
changed historical circumstances they themselves still inhabit. In short,
if we are to believe them, a single unchanging project underlies all radical
revolutionary currents, namely the project of the whole human being,
powered by that *will to total life* which Marx was the first to equip with
a scientific tactical plan. But these are pernicious theories which the
holy churches of Christ and Stalin have never missed an opportunity to
stigmatize. Higher wages, more refrigerators, more holy sacraments and

more National Popular Theatres—surely these should suffice to quell the revolutionary hankerings of today?

Is the welfare state inevitable? Naturally, right-thinking people are bound to deplore the forms taken by opposition to an agenda approved by everyone from Khrushchev to Albert Schweitzer, from the Pope to Fidel Castro, from Louis Aragon to the late Mr Kennedy. In December 1956, for example, a thousand young people ran wild in the streets of Stockholm, setting fire to cars, demolishing neon signs, slashing advertising posters, looting department stores. At Merlebach, during a strike called to force owners to bring up the bodies of seven miners killed by a cave-in, the workers directed their fury at the cars parked at the pit-head. In January 1961, strikers in Liège burned down the Guillemins railway station and destroyed the premises of the newspaper *La Meuse*. Concerted onslaughts on seaside resorts on the English and Belgian coasts were mounted by hundreds of juvenile delinquents in March 1964. In Amsterdam in 1966 the workers held the streets for several days. Not a month goes by without a wildcat strike pitting workers against employers and union bosses alike. Welfare state? The people of Watts have given their answer.

The words of a worker in Espérance-Longdoz encapsulate the clash between his point of view and that of such sociological watchdogs of our future as Jean Fourastié, Peter Berger, Louis Armand and Abraham Moles: 'Since 1936 I have been fighting for higher wages. My father before me fought for higher wages. I've got a TV, a fridge and a VW. If you ask me, it's been a dog's life from start to finish.'

The words and deeds of the new poetry have no room for the welfare state.

2

The nicest radios *within everyone's reach* (a). You too can join the *great family* of DAF drivers (b). Carven means quality. Choose *freely* from our product range (c).

In the kingdom of consumption the citizen is king. A democratic monarchy: equality in consumption (a), fraternity via consumption (b), liberty as per consumption (c). The dictatorship of consumption has completed the abolition of barriers of blood, lineage and race; this would be great cause for celebration were it not for the fact that consumption, with its logic of *things*, prohibits all qualitative differentiation and permits only quantitative differences between values and human beings.

The distance between those who possess the most and those who possess a small (if ever-increasing) amount has not shrunk; but the intermediate levels have multiplied, and so to speak brought the two extremes, rulers and ruled, closer to the same mediocrity. To be rich nowadays means to possess a large number of impoverished objects.

Consumer goods tend to lose all use-value. Their nature is to be consumable at all costs, as witness the recent American fad for the 'nothing box'—an object with no conceivable utility. And as General Eisenhower explained in all candour, the present economic system can be rescued only by turning human beings into consumers, conflating them with the largest possible number of consumable values—which is to say nonvalues, empty, fictitious, abstract values. After being 'the most precious kind of capital', in Stalin's happy phrase, human beings must now become the most highly prized of consumer goods. Stereotyped images—movie star, poor person, Communist, murderer-out-of-love, law-abiding citizen, rebel, bourgeois—are about to replace humanity with a punch-card system of categories arranged in accordance with an irrefutable robotic logic. Already the idea of 'teenager' tends to identify buyers and what they buy, reducing their real variety to a still varied but circumscribed range of commodities (records, guitars, Levis, etc.). You are no longer as old as you feel or as old as you look, but as 'old' as what you buy. The time of production, of 'time is money', is giving way to the time of consumption (in both the figurative and the material senses of the word), a time measured in terms of products bought, worn out and thrown away—the time of that premature old age which is the eternal youth of trees and stones.

The theory of pauperization is strikingly confirmed today—not, as Marx expected, in terms of goods necessary for survival, since these, far from becoming scarce, have become more and more abundant, but rather in terms of survival itself, which is ever the enemy of real life. Modern comforts seemed at first to promise everyone a life richer even than the *dolce vita* of the feudal aristocracy. But in fact they turned out to be mere offshoots of capitalist productivity, offshoots doomed to premature old age as soon as the distribution system transformed them into nothing but objects of passive consumption. Working to survive, surviving by consuming and for the sake of consuming: the hellish cycle is complete. According to the logic of the-economy-rules, survival is both necessary and sufficient. This is the basic reality of the bourgeois era. But it is also true that a historical period based on such an antihuman reality must needs be a period of transition, an intermediate stage between the life genuinely lived, if less than transparently, by the feudal masters and the life that will be constructed rationally and passionately by masters without slaves. We have only thirty-odd years left in which to prevent this transitional period of slaves without masters from reaching its bicentennial.

3

From the point of view of everyday life, the bourgeois revolution has not a few counterrevolutionary aspects. Rarely, on the market of human values, has the conception of existence suffered such a sharp devaluation. Proclaimed so defiantly to the whole universe, the bourgeoisie's pledge to usher in the reign of liberty and well-being served merely to underscore the mediocrity of a life which the aristocracy had managed to fill with passion and adventure but which, once made accessible to all, resembled nothing so much as a palace split up into servants' quarters. Thereafter hate would give way to contempt, love to attachment, the ridiculous to the stupid, passion to sentimentality, desire to envy, reason to calculation, and lust for life to desperation to survive. The utterly despicable ethos of profit replaced the utterly detestable ethos of honour; the mysterious and perfectly ridiculous power of birth and blood gave way to the perfectly Ubuesque power of money. The inheritors of the formal abolition of feudalism on 4 August 1789 elevated bank balances and turnover figures to the status of coats of arms, transforming the mystery of nobility into the mystery of the account book.

What is the mystery of money? The clear answer is that money represents a sum of beings and things that can be appropriated. The nobleman's heraldic shield expresses God's choice and the real power exercised by his chosen; money is no more than a sign of what might be acquired: a draft on power, a possible choice. The feudal God, apparently the foundation of the social order, was really only the pretext for it, its glorious rationale. Money, that odourless god of the bourgeois, is likewise a mediation, a social contract. A god swayed no longer by prayers or oaths but by specialized science and technology. A deity whose mystery resides no longer in a dark, impenetrable totality but rather in the sum of an infinite number of partial certainties; no longer in the unique value of lordship but rather in the value of all the beings and venal things that a million dollars, say, puts within reach of its possessor.

In an economy driven by the production requirements of free-trade capitalism, wealth alone confers power and honour. As master of the means of production and of labour power, wealth ensures by extension, thanks to the development of productive forces and of consumer goods, that its owners enjoy a wealth of choice among the fruits of never-ending progress. But to the extent that this form of capitalism is transformed into an antithetical form, namely a state-planned economy, the prestige of the capitalist playing the market with his millions fades away, and with it the caricature of the pot-bellied, cigar-puffing merchant of human flesh. Today's managers draw their power from their organizing skills—even if computer technology already holds them up to ridicule by providing a model that they can never emulate. They are rich in their own right, certainly, but can they vaunt their wealth by having it signify the potential choices available to them? Can they build a Xanadu, maintain a harem, or cultivate *filles-fleurs*? Alas, no—for how could money retain its symbolic force when it is continually solicited and hampered by the imperatives of consumption? Under the dictatorship of consumption money melts away like snow in the sunshine, its significance passing to objects with more representational value—more tangible objects better adapted to the welfare state and its spectacle. The function of money has surely already been sidelined by the market in consumer goods, which, duly wrapped in ideology, have become the true signs of power. Before long, money's only remaining justification will be the quantity of objects and useless gadgets it enables one to acquire and wear out at an ever-accelerating pace; only the quantity and the pace matter, for mass distribution and standardization automatically wipe out quality and rarity. The ability to consume faster and faster, to change your car, your drink, your house, your TV or your girlfriend ever more frequently, is now the only index of how much power you can lay claim to in the social hierarchy. From the preeminence of blood to the power of money, from the preeminence of money to the power of novelties, Christian and socialist civilization has now attained its highest stage: a civilization of the prosaic and the trivial. The perfect dwelling-place for Nietzsche's 'little man'.

Purchasing power is a licence to purchase power. The old proletariat sold its labour power in order to subsist; what little leisure time remained proletarians spent as best they could in conversation, arguments, tavern games, country matters, going on the tramp, festivity and riot. The new proletariat sells its labour power in order to consume. When they are not too busy working themselves to death in hopes of a promotion, workers are invited to buy objects—a car, a suit and tie, some culture—that will signal their social rank. We have reached the point where the ideology of consumption becomes the consumption of ideology. Never underestimate the importance of East-West exchanges! In the West, *homo consumator* buys a bottle of whiskey and receives the lie that comes with it; in the East, Communist man buys ideology and gets a bottle of vodka for free. Paradoxically, Soviet and capitalist regimes are on the same path, the one by virtue of a production-driven economy, the other by virtue of a consumption-driven one.

In the USSR, the surplus labour of a worker does not, strictly speaking, enrich the comrade-manager of the enterprise. It merely increases that manager's power as organizer and bureaucrat. The surplus value here is a surplus value of power. (But this new-fangled surplus value is nevertheless subject to the tendency for the rate of profit to fall: Marx's laws of economic life are now borne out in the economy of life.) The manager earns his surplus power not from money-capital, but from a primitive accumulation of confidence-capital generated thanks to the passive absorption of ideology. The car and the dacha thrown in as a bonus to reward services to country, proletariat, output and the Cause clearly prefigure a form of social organization in which money will indeed have disappeared, giving way to honorific distinctions, ranks, a mandarinate of muscle and specialization. (Think of the privileges granted to Stakhanovites, to 'heroes of space', to scrapers of violin strings and champions of the production quotas.)

In capitalist countries, meanwhile, the material profit reaped by the employer from both production and consumption remains distinct from the ideological profit which the employer is not alone in deriving from the organization of consumption. This is all that prevents us from reducing the difference between a manager and a worker to the difference between a new Ford every year and a Dauphine lovingly maintained for five. The fact remains that planning—towards which, no matter how confusedly, everything now points—serves to quantify social differences in terms of ability to consume and make others consume. As differences grow in number and shrink in significance, the real distance between rich and poor diminishes, and mankind is levelled into mere variations on poverty. The logical culmination of this process would be a cybernetic society composed of specialists ranked hierarchically according to their aptitude for consuming—and having others consume—the doses of power necessary for the functioning of a gigantic social apparatus of which they themselves would be at once the programme and the outcome. A society of exploiters/exploited where some slaves would be more equal than others.

This leaves the 'third world'. The old forms of oppression. That the serfs of the *latifundia* should be the contemporaries of the new proletariat seems to me a perfect formula for an explosive mix from which total revolution will emerge. Who would seriously suggest that the peons and Indians of South America will be satisfied with land reform and fully equipped kitchens and lay down their arms when the best paid workers in Europe are demanding a radical change in their way of life? No, the revolt against the welfare state will set the *minimum* demands for revolutions worldwide. Those who forget this will learn the hard way what Saint-Just meant when he observed that 'those who make revolutions by halves will have merely dug their own graves'.

VIII Exchange and Gift

Both the nobility and the proletariat conceive human relationships on the model of the *gift*, but the proletarian way of giving supersedes the feudal. The bourgeoisie, the class of *exchange*, is the lever which enables the feudal project to be overthrown and superseded in the long revolution [1]. History is the continuous transformation of natural alienation into social alienation, and also, paradoxically, the continuous strengthening of a countervailing movement which is destined to overcome all alienation. The historical struggle against natural alienation transforms natural into social alienation, but the disalienating movement of history eventually affects social alienation itself, and reveals that it is based on magic. This magic has to do with privative appropriation. It is expressed through sacrifice. Sacrifice is the archaic form of exchange. The extreme quantification of exchange reduces human beings to objects. From this rock bottom a new type of human relationship, involving neither exchange nor sacrifice, can arise [2].

1

The bourgeoisie presides over a precarious and none-too-glorious inter-regnum between the sacred hierarchy of feudal lords and the anarchistic order of the classless societies of the future. The bourgeois no-man's-land of exchange is the uninhabitable region separating the old, unhealthy pleasure of giving oneself, in which the aristocrats indulged, from the pleasure of giving out of self-love, which new generations of proletarians are little by little beginning to discover.

That there is no such thing as something for nothing is a mantra for both capitalism and its seemingly antagonistic progeny. When the USSR 'donates' hospitals and technicians, or the USA 'donates' investments and good offices, they do so in the same sense that breakfast cereals offer free gifts in every box.

The fact is that the meaning of the gift has been uprooted from our minds, our feelings and our actions. Think of André Breton and his friends handing out roses to the pretty girls on the Boulevard Poissonnière and immediately arousing the suspicion and hostility of the public.

The blighting of human relationships by exchange and compensation is obviously tied to the existence of the bourgeoisie. The fact that exchange persists in a part of the world where society is said to be classless suggests at the very least that the bourgeoisie continues to rule even under the red flag. Meanwhile, wherever industrial working classes are to be found, the pleasure of giving marks a clear dividing-line between a world of calculation and a world of exuberant festivity. The proletarian way of giving is radically at odds, too, with the nobility's bestowing of prestige, hopelessly compromised by the notion of sacrifice. The proletariat is the genuine bearer of the project of human fulfilment, the project of total life; a project which the aristocracy failed—though in the most magnificent way—to realize. To give the devil his due, it was the historical presence and mediation of the bourgeoisie that opened this future up to the proletariat. After all, it is thanks to the technical progress and the productive forces developed by capitalism that the proletariat is now poised, armed with a scientifically designed plan for a new society, to actualize egalitarian visions, utopian dreams of omnipotence and the desire to live without dead time. Today everything points up the mission, or rather the historical opportunity, of the proletariat: the destruction and supersession of feudalism. This it will achieve by trampling the bourgeoisie underfoot. The bourgeoisie is fated to have embodied no more than a transitional phase in the development of humanity, albeit one without which no supersession of the feudal project would have been conceivable—an essential phase, therefore, constituting the lever needed to topple unitary power, or more specifically to invert and redirect it in accordance with the project of the whole human being. The system of unitary power was already a world made for the whole human being—as the invention of God demonstrates—but for a whole human being standing on his head. Humanity had merely to be set back on its feet.

No liberation was possible prior to the reign of the economic; yet under this reign the only economy possible is the abstract economy of survival. Spurred by these two truths the bourgeoisie is leading mankind on towards the supersession of the economy, towards a point beyond history. Putting technology at the service of poetry will not have been the meanest of the bourgeoisie's achievements. This class will never have been so great as at the moment of its disappearance.

2

Exchange is bound up with the survival of primitive hordes in the same way as privative appropriation: together, these two factors are the bedrock of the history of mankind up to now.

When the first humans found that it afforded them greater security in face of a hostile nature, the marking off of hunting grounds laid the foundation for the social arrangements that have held us captive ever since (see Raoul and Laura Makarius, *The Origin of Exogamy and Totemism*). Early mankind's unity with nature was essentially magical. Humanity truly separated itself from nature only by transforming it technologically, and thus deconsecrating it. But the use of technology is subordinate to social organization. The advent of tools marked the birth of the social, indeed social organization itself was the first viable tool in the struggle against nature. Hierarchical in character because it was based on privative appropriation, social organization gradually destroyed the magical bond between humanity and nature, but it deployed magic for its own purposes, creating a mythical unity between itself and humanity modelled on humanity's earlier participation in the mystery of nature. Constrained by the 'natural' relations of prehistoric times, human social organization slowly dissolved this defining and confining framework. Seen in this light, history is simply the transformation of natural alienation into social alienation—a process of disalienation transformed in its turn into social alienation: a movement of liberation checked, then completely arrested, until such time as the human will for emancipation mounts an attack on the entire edifice of paralysing mechanisms, that is to say on social organization founded on privative appropriation. This new disalienating movement is destined at once to undo history and to realize it in new forms of social life.

The bourgeoisie's rise to power heralded humanity's victory over the forces of nature. But by the same token hierarchical social organization, made necessary by the struggle against hunger, sickness and want, lost all justification, and must be held fully responsible for the malaise of industrial civilization. Today human beings no longer blame their woes on the hostility of nature, but on the tyranny of a perfectly inadequate and perfectly anachronistic social system. By destroying the magical power of the feudal lords, the bourgeoisie passed judgement on the magic of hierarchical power as such. The proletariat will carry out the sentence. What the bourgeoisie began in accordance with history will now be completed in a way quite at odds with that class's narrow conception of history. But it will once again be a historical struggle, a class struggle, that realizes history.

The principle of hierarchy is the spell that has blocked humanity's path to emancipation and hexed its historical struggles for freedom. Henceforward, no revolution will be worth the name if it does not at the very least imply the radical elimination of all hierarchy.

//////

As soon as a band of humans marked out a hunting ground and claimed exclusive ownership of it, they found themselves confronted by a hostility which was no longer that of wild animals, harsh weather, inhospitable territory, or disease, but rather that of other human groups now deprived of the use of the preserve. The law of the animal kingdom—destroy the rival group or be destroyed by it—was successfully circumvented by human genius. The chance of survival for primitive communities came to depend on pacts, contracts and exchange. Between the 'hunting and gathering' stage and the coming of agriculture, human clans were of necessity beholden to three kinds of exchange: the exchange of women, the exchange of food, and the exchange of blood. This system involved magical thinking, for the invocation of a supreme planner, a master of exchange, a power beyond and beneath the contracting parties. The birth of gods coincided with the twin birth of sacred myth and hierarchical power.

Of course the exchange was never of equal benefit to the two clans. The problem, after all, was to ensure the neutrality of the excluded clan without actually giving it access to the hunting preserve. Agricultural societies refined these tactics. The excluded, tenants before being enslaved, were allowed into the landowning group not as landowners, but as their degraded reflection (as witness the notorious myth of the Fall), as a mediation between the land and its masters. Their submission was obtained through the consistent hold over them of a myth. This myth masked not a deliberate intention of the masters (to say so would be to credit those masters with a rationality still foreign to them), but rather the cunning of exchange—the imbalance in the sacrifice which each side agreed to make. To the landowners the excluded made a *real* sacrifice of a significant part of their lives, accepting the owners' authority and labouring for them. To the dominated group the masters for their part made a *mystical* sacrifice of their authority and their power as owners: they were ready to pay for the well-being of their people. God was the underwriter of the transaction and the guardian of the myth. He punished those who broke the contract, while those who kept to it he rewarded with power: mythical power for those who *really* sacrificed themselves, real power for those who did so *mythically*. (History and mythology both show that the master could go so far as to sacrifice his own life to the mythical principle. Paying the price for the alienation that he imposed on others indeed strengthened his divine aspect. Before long, however, a make-believe execution, or one in which he was replaced by a surrogate, released the master from such a hard bargain. When the God of the Christians delegated his son to the human world, he supplied generations of bosses with a perfect model with which to authenticate their own supposed sacrifice.)

Sacrifice is the archaic form of exchange. It is a magical exchange, neither quantified nor rational. It held increasing sway over human relations, including commercial ones, until market capitalism with its money as measure-of-all-things had carved out such a large sphere of influence in the contexts of slavery, feudalism and ultimately bourgeois society that the economy emerged as an autonomous zone, a domain split off from life. The element of exchange in the feudal gift prevailed with the rise of money. The sacrifice-gift or potlatch—the *game* of exchange or loser-takes-all, in which the size of the gift determines the prestige of the giver—had barely any place in a rationalized trading economy. Driven out of sectors ruled by economic imperatives, the gift found refuge in values such as hospitality, friendship and love—oases doomed to disappear as the dictatorship of quantified exchange (market value) colonized everyday life and turned that too into a market.

Mercantile and industrial capitalism accelerated the quantification of exchange. The feudal gift was rationalized strictly according to the model of commerce. Exchange-as-gamble was replaced by calculation. The Roman pledge to sacrifice a cock to the gods in exchange for a safe voyage was based on a playful principle. Market logic could never grasp such disparity in the things being exchanged. Small wonder that the age in which a man like Fouquet could ruin himself in order to shine more brightly in the eyes of his contemporaries (and to outshine Louis XIV) was able to produce a poetry that has disappeared from our times, whose model of a human relationship is the exchange of 12.80 francs for 750 grams of meat.

So sacrifice came to be quantified, rationalized, weighed and quoted on the stock market. But what became of the magic of sacrifice in a world of market values? And what became of the magic of power, the sacred terror that still impels the model employee to tip his hat to the office manager?

In a society where the accumulation of novelties and ideologies reflects quantities of power consumed, assumed and used up, magical relations evaporate and leave hierarchical power as the sole target of opposition. The fall of the last bastion of the sacred will mean the end of a world—or else the end of the world. That bastion must be brought down before it takes humanity down with it in its collapse.

Systematically quantified (first by money and then by what might be called 'sociometric units of power'), exchange corrupts all human relationships, feelings and thoughts. Wherever exchange rules, only *things* remain in a world of human objects frozen in place in the organigrams of the cybernetic powers-that-be: a world of reification. Yet paradoxically this world can become the launching pad of a complete restructuring of all our patterns of life and thought: a zero point whence *everything* can truly begin.

//////

The feudal mind apparently conceived of the gift as a sort of haughty refusal to exchange—a will to deny interchangeability. This attitude went hand in hand with a contempt for money and for any common measure. True, the principle of sacrifice excluded the pure gift, yet the appeal of play, of the gratuitous, of humanity was so powerful that inhumanity, religion and solemnity often took second place when it came to such preoccupations as war, love, friendship, or hospitality.

By virtue of the gift of self, the nobility firmly hitched their power to the totality of cosmic forces while simultaneously claiming hegemony over the totality hallowed by myth. The bourgeoisie for its part bartered *being* for *having*, destroying the mythical unity of being and the world as the basis of Power; the totality fell to pieces. Quasi-rational exchange under a production-driven system implicitly equated creativity, reduced to labour power, with an hourly wage-rate; quasi-rational exchange under the consumption-driven system implicitly equates consumable life—life reduced to the activity of consumption—with the quantity of power needed to lock consumers into their places in the org charts. The sacrifice of the masters was therefore followed by the last stage in the history of sacrifice: the sacrifice of experts. In order to consume, the expert has others consume according to a cybernetic programme whose hyperrational system of exchange will abolish sacrifice—and humanity to boot. The day pure exchange comes to regulate the modes of existence of the robotic citizens of a cybernetic democracy, sacrifice will cease to exist. Objects need no justification to make them obedient. Sacrifice is no more part of the programme of machines than it is of the diametrically opposed project of the whole human being.

//////

The crumbling of those human values for which the mechanisms of exchange are responsible leads to the crumbling of exchange itself. The inadequacy of the feudal gift means that new human relationships must be built on the principle of the pure gift. We need to rediscover the pleasure of giving: giving out of a surfeit of riches, a superabundance of possessions. What magnificent potlatches the affluent society will witness once the exuberant younger generation discovers the pure gift! (The growing passion for stealing books, clothes, food, weapons or jewellery for the sheer pleasure of giving them away offers a glimpse of what the will to live has in store for consumer society.)

Prefabricated needs call forth the unitary demand for a new way of life. Art, which is an economy of lived moments, has been absorbed by business. Desires and dreams are now the raw material of marketing. Everyday life has disintegrated into a succession of instants as interchangeable as the gadgets that define them: mixers, stereos, diaphragms, euphorimeters, sleeping pills. Everywhere equal particles shimmer in the equitably distributed light of Power. So much for equality and justice. An exchange of nullities, of restrictions and prohibitions. Nothing happens; dead time passes.

We must renew our acquaintance with the shortcomings of feudalism—not to correct them but to supersede them. We need to rediscover the harmony of unitary society while stripping it of its divine phantom and its sacrosanct hierarchy. What I call the new innocence (see Chapter xxiv) is not so very far removed from God's ordeals and judgements; and the inequality of bloodlines is closer to the equality of free individuals, irreducible to one another, than to bourgeois equality. The cramped style of the aristocracy was nothing but a crude sketch of the grand style to be invented by masters without slaves—yet what a world away it was from the wretched survival that ravages so many lives today!

IX   Technology and Its Mediated Use

Contrary to the interests of those who control its use, technology deconsecrates. The democratic reign of consumption strips gadgetry of all magical force. Similarly, the reign of the technological organization of technology strips the new productive forces of their ability to transform and seduce. Organization in this sense is thus manifestly nothing but the organization of authority [1]. Alienated mediations weaken humanity by making themselves indispensable. A social mask conceals people and things, transforming them, under the present conditions of privative appropriation, into dead things—into commodities. Nature is no more. Nature cannot be rediscovered—only reinvented as a worthy adversary thanks to the construction of new social relations. The pathological growth of material paraphernalia bursts the shell of the old hierarchical society [2].

1

The same shortcomings affect nonindustrial civilizations where people still die of hunger and automated civilizations where people already die of boredom. Every paradise is artificial. The life of a Trobriand Islander, rich in spite of ritual and taboo, is at the mercy of a smallpox epidemic; the average Swede's life, impoverished in spite of its creature comforts, is at the mercy of suicide and survival sickness.

Rousseauism and pastoral dreams accompanied the first throbbings of the industrial machine. The ideology of progress of an Adam Smith or a Condorcet stemmed from the old myth of the four ages. Just as the iron age was thought to lead back into the golden age, it seemed 'natural' that progress too should embody a recurrence—the return to a prelapsarian state of innocence.

Belief in the magical power of technology coexisted not infrequently with its opposite, the tendency towards deconsecration. The machine was the model of intelligibility: there was no mystery, nothing obscure in its drive-belts, cogs and gears, and everything about it could be explained perfectly. But the machine was also the miracle supposed to transport humanity into a realm of happiness and freedom. This ambiguity, moreover, was useful to the machine's masters: mystical claims about glorious tomorrows served in various ways to rationalize the exploitation of human beings in the present. Thus it was less a desanctifying logic that shook people's faith in progress than the inhuman application of technological possibilities and the cheap mystique surrounding it. So long as the labouring classes and underdeveloped peoples presented the spectacle of a material poverty gradually being relieved, the enthusiasm for progress continued to draw ample fodder from the troughs of liberal ideology and its extension, socialism. But a century after the spontaneous demystification effected by the loom-breaking workers of Lyons, a general crisis erupted, springing this time from the problems of large-scale industry. This was the regression known as fascism, with its asinine fantasies of a return to craft production and corporatism and its Ubuesque notion of an Aryan 'noble savage'.

What was once promised by a production-driven society now rains down on us in a torrent of consumer goods that nobody is likely to mistake for manna from heaven. To hail the magic of gadgetry as formerly the magic of productive forces was hailed is a hopeless enterprise. There is something of a laudatory literature on the steam-hammer. It is hard to imagine much of the kind on the cake-mixer. The mass production of labour-saving devices—all equally revolutionary, according to the ad-men—has given even the most unsophisticated person the right to pass judgement on the marvels of technological innovation in a way as casually appreciative as a man's pat on a willing girl's backside. The first landing of humans on Mars will barely distract the attention of people at a village fair.

True, the yoke and harness, the steam engine, electricity, or the advent of nuclear energy all disturbed and altered the infrastructure of society (even if they were discovered, when all is said and done, almost by chance). But today it would be futile to expect the new productive forces to transform the mode of production. The blooming of technology has given rise to a synthesizing supertechnology which may prove as significant as that first technological synthesis, the social community, achieved at the dawn of human history. Even more significant, perhaps—for, once wrested from its present masters, cybernetics might well be capable of liberating human societies from labour and from social aliena-tion. Capable, in other words, of fulfilling the project of Charles Fourier, conceived in an age when utopia was still feasible.

But the gap between Fourier and the cyberneticians in operational control of the organization of technology is the gap between freedom and slavery. Naturally the cyberneticians will claim that their science is already sufficiently developed to solve all the problems raised by any new technology. Nothing is less certain.

In the first place, nothing is to be expected from the ever-evolving productive forces, nor from the ever-proliferating mass of consumer goods. We hear no dithyrambs to musical air-conditioners, no cantatas to the latest solar-powered oven. A fatigue is already setting in, a lassi-tude that will obviously, sooner or later, evolve into a critical challenge to technological organization itself.

Secondly, for all its flexibility, the cybernetic synthesis will never succeed in hiding the fact that it synthesizes and supersedes nothing save all previous forms of authority over human beings—that it is in fact merely the highest stage of such authority. How could it ever conceal an inherent alienation that no power has ever managed to protect from the arms of criticism and the criticism of arms? The relative intelligence of the crocodiles in the water makes no difference to the canoeist under attack. In seeking to perfect Power, the cyberneticians will only encour-age competition among those set on perfecting the rejection of that Power. Their programming of new technology will come to grief when that technology is repurposed by another kind of organization. A revo-lutionary organization.

2

Technocratic organization elevates technological mediation to its most coherent form. It has long been known that masters appropriate the objective world thanks to their slaves, and that tools alienate workers only so long as they belong to the bosses. Similarly, in the realm of consump-tion, it is not goods per se that alienate but the conditioning that leads buyers to choose them, and along with them the ideology in which they are packaged. The tool in the case of production and the conditioning of choice in that of consumption are the mainstays of deception—the mediations which entice humans as producers or consumers into illu-sory action and real passivity, so transforming them into essentially dependent beings. Commandeered mediations separate individuals from themselves, their desires, their dreams and their will to live, nourishing the legend that no one can do without them—or without the Power that controls them. Where Power fails to paralyse by constraint, it does so by suggestion, forcing everyone to use crutches of which it is the sole owner and purveyor. As the sum of alienating mediations, Power is counting on baptism by the cyberneticians to promote it to the status of a totality. But there is no such thing as total Power; there are only totalitarian powers. Nor could this system ever be consecrated by such risible priests.

Held captive as it is by alienated mediations (tools, thoughts, false needs), the objective world—or nature, if you prefer—is now surrounded by a sort of screen which paradoxically makes it more alien to human beings even as they transform it—and themselves. The natural world is inextricably veiled by social relations. What we call natural today is about as natural as 'natural' foundation cream. The instruments of praxis do not properly belong to the agents of praxis, namely the workers, which clearly explains why the opaque zone that separates humanity from itself and from nature is itself part of humanity and nature. There is no nature waiting to be rediscovered, merely a nature to be remade, reconstructed.

The quest for a true nature, for a natural life diametrically opposed to the lies of social ideology, is one of the most touching naiveties of a good part of the revolutionary proletariat, of the anarchists and even of such remarkable thinkers as the young Wilhelm Reich.

So long as exploitation of man by man endures, any real transformation of nature presupposes a real transformation of the social lie. At no point in their conflict have mankind and nature ever been truly face to face. Instead, they have been at once bound together and kept apart by the mediation of hierarchical social power and its organization of appearances. Transforming nature meant socializing it, but it was badly socialized. If all nature is social, it is because history has never known a society without Power.

Is an earthquake a natural phenomenon? It affects people, but it affects them only as alienated social beings. What is an earthquake-in-itself? What if at this moment, as I write, a seismic tremor alters the surface of Sirius but will remain forever unknown to us? What can I do with this question except leave it to the doddering metaphysicians in the academy or other centres of pure thought?

And consider death, which likewise strikes people socially. This is not just because all the energy and resources swallowed up by military debacles and by the general anarchy of capitalist and bureaucratic systems could meet the desperately needed requirements of the scientific struggle against death. It is also—and above all—because the death-nurturing cauldron of culture is kept on the bubble, with science's blessing, in society's vast laboratory (stress, nervous tension, social conditioning, mystification, toxic therapies, etc.). Only animals are still entitled to die a natural death—some of them, at least.

Could it be that, having detached themselves from the higher animal world by virtue of history, humans might actually come to envy animals' closeness to nature? Such is, I think, the rather puerile idea underlying the current quest for the 'natural'. Once refined and redirected, however, the basic wish expressed here is for the positive supersession of thirty thousand years of history.

The challenge is to join battle with a nature newly conceived as a worthy adversary, or in other words to resocialize nature by liberating technology from the toils of alienation, by wresting it from the grip of leaders and experts. Only at the end of a process of social disalienation will nature become that worthy opponent, in a civilization 'a thousand times superior', where human creativity no longer runs up against humanity itself as the first obstacle to its growth.

//////

Technological organization will not succumb to external forces. Its collapse will result from inner decay. So far from being punished for its Promethean aspirations, it is dying for never having surpassed the master-slave dialectic. Even if the cyberneticians should ever come to power, their rule would be far too precarious. Their rosiest vision of their own prospects already brings to mind these words from a black worker to a white boss: 'When we first saw your trucks and planes we thought you were gods. Then, after a few years, we learnt how to drive your trucks, just as we shall soon learn how to fly your planes, and we realized that your main concern was manufacturing trucks and planes and making money. For us the main thing is using them. Now you are just our blacksmiths.' (*Présence Africaine*, 1956)

X   The Reign of Quantity

Economic imperatives seek to impose the standardized measuring system of commodities on the whole of human activity. Very great quantity ought to generate quality, but now even quantity is relativized and rationed. Myth is based on quality, ideology on quantity. Ideological saturation means an atomization into small antagonistic quantities which can no more avoid destroying one another than being smashed by the qualitative negativity of popular rejection [1]. The quantitative and the linear are inseparable. A line and measure of time and a line and measure of life define survival: a succession of interchangeable instants. These lines are part of the ambiguous geometry of Power [2].

1

The system of commercial exchange has now come to govern all of people's everyday relations with themselves and with their fellows. Every aspect of public and private life is dominated by the quantitative.

The Merchant in Brecht's *The Exception and the Rule* confesses: 'I don't know what a man is. Only that every man has his price.' To the extent that individuals accept Power and enable it to exist, Power applies its own measure to them: it reduces and standardizes them. What is the individual to an authoritarian system? A point duly located in its perspective. A point that it recognizes, certainly, but recognizes only in mathematical terms, in terms of its exact position as plotted relative to x- and y-axes.

The calculation of a human's capacity to produce or make others produce, to consume or make others consume, is the perfect concrete expression of the idea so dear to the philosophers (and so revealing as to their function) of *the measure of man*. Even the simple pleasure of a drive in the country is widely assessed in terms of miles on the clock, speeds reached and petrol consumed. Given the rate at which economic imperatives gobble up feelings, desires and needs, and pay cash to corrupt them, people will soon be left with nothing but the memory of having once existed. History, in which we shall live retrospectively, will be our sole consolation for our condition of survival. How can real joy exist in a space-time that is measurable and continually measured? Not so much as a hearty laugh. At best, the dull satisfaction of the person-who's-got-his-money's-worth, and who exists by that standard. Only objects can be measured, which is why all exchange reifies.

/////

Any remnants of passionate tension between sexual pleasure and the adventurous quest for it are fast disintegrating into a panting succession of mechanically repeated gestures whose rhythm offers no hope of approaching so much as a semblance of orgasm. The quantitative Eros of speed, rapid change, and love-against-the-clock everywhere disfigures the face of real pleasure.

The qualitative is slowly taking on the aspect of a quantitative infinity, an endless continuum any temporary interruption of which is always a negation of pleasure, the fundamental lack of satisfaction of a Don Juan. What if, *per mirabile*, our society were actively to foster such dissatisfaction, giving full rein to the insatiable appetite for complete licence and allowing it to run riot and exert its wild appeal? Who could fail to see a certain charm in the life of the idler, a trifle cynical perhaps, but enjoying at his leisure everything that can make passivity sweet: a *seraglio* of beautiful women, witty and sophisticated friends, refined drugs, exotic meals, fiery liquors and sultry perfumes? The style of someone, in other words, less inclined to change life than to take refuge in its greatest attractions: a sensualist in the grand tradition (as opposed to pigs, who merely give the outward appearance of gratification). But not so fast! Today no one at all has any such option, for both Eastern and Western societies ration quantity itself. Many a captain of industry given just a month to live would still refuse to sink his entire fortune into a huge orgy. The morality of exchange and profit does not easily release its prey. Capitalist economics, even in a jumbo-size package, means parsimony.

What a stroke of good fortune for mystification that quantity could be dressed as quality, and the shining illusion sustained that the construction of a multidimensional world was of the order of the possible. But to let exchange be subsumed by the gift, to open all doors between heaven and earth to every kind of adventure (from that of a Gilles de Rais to that of a Dante) was precisely what the bourgeoisie was forbidden to do. Precisely what it destroyed in the name of industry and commerce. But what an immense nostalgia it thus condemned itself to! A poor yet vital catalyst—at once everything and nothing—thanks to which a classless, nonauthoritarian society will realize the dreams of an aristocratic childhood.

In the act of faith, the unitary societies of tribal and feudal times possessed a qualitative element of myth and mystification of the greatest import. No sooner had the bourgeoisie shattered the unity of Power and God than it set about striving to drape in unity's raiment what in its hands was no longer anything but fragments and crumbs of power. Without unity, alas, there can be no quality. The triumph of democracy meant social atomization. Democracy is the limited power of the greatest number—and the power of the greatest number limited. The great ideologies quickly abandon faith for numbers. What is the nation? Today it amounts to a few thousand war veterans. And what is what Marx and Engels used to call 'our party'? A few million voters and a few thousand bill-posters: a mass party.

In fact ideology's essence is drawn from quantity: ideas reproduced again and again in time (Pavlovian conditioning) and in space (once consumers take up the refrain). Ideology, the news media, and culture—all tend gradually to shed their content and become pure quantity. The less importance a news item has, the more it is repeated, and the more it distracts people from their real problems. We are a long way from the Big Lie of which Goebbels said that it was the easiest to swallow. Ideological hyperbole evinces equal conviction to pitch a hundred books, a hundred washing powders, a hundred political ideas, each of which it promotes in turn as far and away the best. Even in the ideological realm quantity is destroyed by quantity itself: conditioning is inevitably eroded by its self-contradictions.

Could this possibly open an avenue back to power of the qualitative, a power that can move mountains? Far from it: self-contradictory conditioning is prone to produce trauma, inhibition, or a radical refusal to be brainwashed further. True, ideology can parry this by leaving conditioned individuals choices between lies, by raising spurious questions, false dilemmas. But such feeble distractions count for precious little in view of the survival sickness to which consumer society exposes its members.

At any instant boredom can breed an unanswerable rejection of uniformity. Recent events in Stockholm, Amsterdam, and Watts have shown how the merest pretext can precipitate salutary uprisings. What an immense quantity of oft-repeated lies can be swept away by a single burst of revolutionary poetry! From Villa to Lumumba, from Stockholm to Watts, qualitative agitation—agitation that radicalizes the masses because its source is the radicalism of the masses—effectively pushes back the frontiers of submission and brutishness.

2

In unitary regimes the sacred was the mortar of a social pyramid in which each particular being, from lord to serf, had their assigned place in accordance with the will of Providence, the order of the world and the King's pleasure. The cohesion of this structure was doomed to disappear, dissolved by the corrosive criticism of the youthful bourgeoisie, but as we know the shadow of the divine hierarchy lingered on. The dismantling of the pyramid, so far from eliminating inhumanity, merely fragmented it. A myriad of diminutive beings emerged, each seemingly absolute: little 'citizens' set in motion by the process of social atomization. An inflated egocentric imagination turned the substance of a single point into a universe in its own right, likewise thousands of other points, loose monads, all free, equal and fraternal, scurrying hither and thither like so many ants whose elegant labyrinthine nest has been overturned. There were severed lines everywhere, haywire since the disappearance of God deprived them of a point of convergence, lines getting entangled or breaking up in apparent disorder; but apparent only, for, make no mistake, despite the anarchy of competition and individualistic isolation, class and caste interests soon solidified and framed a new geometry able to rival the old divine one and chafing to achieve a like coherence.

But the coherence of unitary power, while based on the divine principle, is a palpable one, experienced intimately by each individual. Paradoxically, the material principle of fragmentary power can support only an abstract coherence. How could the organization of economic survival possibly be a seamless replacement for an immanent, omnipresent God incessantly called upon to vet acts as trivial as breaking bread or sneezing? Even if we grant that a secular government, with some help from the cyberneticians, might vie with the omnipotence (in any case quite relative) of the feudal mode of domination, what could replace (and how?) the mythic and poetic ambience that once enveloped the life of socially cohesive communities, providing them in some sense with a third dimension? No, the bourgeoisie is well and truly caught in the trap of its own semirevolution.

//////

The quantitative and the linear are inseparable. Quality is polyvalent, quantity unequivocal. The life we have now is broken up—a broken line.

The radiant ascent of the soul towards heaven has given way to a ridiculous preoccupation about the future. No moment radiates now as moments did in the cyclical time of earlier societies. Time for us is a thread: from cradle to grave, from memories of the past to anticipations of the future, an endless survival strings out its succession of instants and hybrid presents, all gnawed at by the time that slips away and the time yet to come. The feeling of living in symbiosis with cosmic forces—a sense of simultaneity—vouchsafed joys to our forebears that our way of passing through the world can scarcely provide. What remains of such a joy? All we have is the headiness of our transit, of our efforts to keep in step with the times. You must move with the times—or so we are told by those who profit if we do.

Not that we should lament the cyclical time of old, which emanated from a mystical source. Rather, we should refocus it: centre it in the human being, not in the Divine Animal. At present man is not the centre of time, but merely a point in it. Time is made up of a succession of such points, each taken, independently of all the others, as an absolute, but an absolute endlessly repeated and rehashed. Because they are located along the same line, all actions and all moments assume equal importance. An epitome of the prosaic. Under the reign of quantity, everything is much of a muchness. These absolutized fragments are all quite interchangeable. Detached from one another—and hence separated from human beings themselves—the moments of survival follow and resemble one another just like the specialized attitudes that correspond to them, namely roles. Making love or riding a motorcycle—it's all the same. Each moment follows a stereotype, and fragments of time carry off fragments of human beings into an unalterable past.

What is the good of stringing pearls to make a necklace of memories? If only the weight of the pearls would snap the thread! But no: moment by moment, time deepens its pit; everything is lost, nothing is created . . .

What I want is not a succession of instants but one huge moment. A totality that is lived, and lived in innocence of duration. Time in which I merely endure is no more than the time of my growing old. And yet, since one must survive in order to live, virtual moments, possibilities, are necessarily rooted in that time. By striving to federate moments, to invest them with pleasure, to release their promise of life, we are already learning to 'construct situations'.

//////

Individual survival-lines cross, collide and cut one another off. Each imposes its limits on the freedom of others; projects cancel one another out in the name of their autonomy. Such is the basis of the geometry of fragmentary power.

We think we are living in the world, when in fact we are taking our place in a perspective: no longer the simultaneous perspective of primitive painters, but that of the rationalists of the Renaissance. It is hardly possible for looks, thoughts and gestures to resist the attraction of the distant vanishing point which orders and alters them, situating them in its spectacle. Power is the great city planner. It lets off survival in public and private parcels, buys up cleared lots cheap, and permits no construction that does not meet its standards. Its own constructions are designed to strip individuals of everything. Its monolithic style is the envy of its actual builders of cities, who ape it assiduously as they replace the old mumbo-jumbo architecture of the sacred hierarchy with stockbroker belts, white-collar districts and workers' housing projects (like Mourenx).

The reconstruction of life and the rebuilding of the world: the self-same quest.

XI   Mediated Abstraction and Abstracted Mediation

Reality is imprisoned in metaphysics today just as it was once imprisoned in theology. The way of seeing which Power imposes 'abstracts' mediations from their original function, which is to extend the requirements of lived experience into the real world. But mediation never completely loses contact with direct experience: it resists the magnetic pull of the authoritarian principle. The point where resistance begins is the look-out post of subjectivity. Until now, metaphysicians have merely organized the world in various ways; our problem is to change it in opposition to them [1]. The reign of guaranteed survival is slowly undermining belief in Power's necessity [2]. This signals a growing rejection of the forms which govern us, a rejection of their ordering principle [3]. Radical theory, which is the only guarantee of the coherence of such a rejection, penetrates the masses by extending their spontaneous creativity. 'Revolutionary' ideology is radical theory co-opted by the rulers. Words lie at the frontier between the will to live and its repression; their meaning is determined by the way they are employed; the way they are employed is governed by history. The historical crisis of language foreshadows its supersession by the poetry of action, by the great game over signs [4].

1

What is it that diverts me when, in search of myself, I end up losing my way? What is this supposedly protective screen that separates me from myself? And how can I ever find myself in the mass of fragments of which I am composed? I am beginning to experience some kind of doubt that I shall ever properly grasp my own self. It is as though my path were already marked out in front of me, as though my thoughts and feelings were cleaving to the forms of a mental landscape which they fancy they are creating, but which is in fact moulding them. An absurd force—all the more absurd for being part of the rationality of the world and hence seemingly incontestable—obliges me to leap continually for a solid ground that my feet have never left. And this vain reaching for myself effectively robs me of my present: for the most part I live out of step with what I am, in harmony only with a dead time.

People are far too unperturbed, it seems to me, by the way in which the world, in certain periods, assumes the *forms* of the prevailing metaphysics. No matter how bizarre belief in God and the Devil may be, this phantom pair become a living reality the moment a social group deems them sufficiently present to inspire the text of its laws. In the same way, the obtuse distinction between cause and effect has been able to govern societies where human behaviour and phenomena in general are analysed in such terms. Even now nobody should underestimate the power of the misbegotten dichotomy between thought and action, theory and practice, real and imaginary . . . Such ideas have organizational force. The world of falsehood is a real world; people kill and get killed there, and we had best not forget it. Scoff as we may at the degeneration of philosophy, the philosophers of today can continue to smirk at us from behind their mediocre ideas, secure in the knowledge that the world is still a philosophical construction, a huge ideological junk-room. We *survive* in a metaphysical landscape. The abstract, alienating mediation that estranges me from myself is terribly concrete.

Grace, a feature of God bestowed upon man, has outlived God himself. Secularized, metaphysical now rather than theological, it is still implanted in the individual like a guiding spirit, an internalized government agency. By hanging the monstrous Superego above the doorway of the ego, Freudian imagery fell prey less to oversimplification than to a refusal to look further and identify the social origin of constraints. (Reich for his part understood this well.) Oppression rules because humans are divided not only among themselves but also within themselves. What separates us from our selves and weakens us attaches us artificially to Power, which, taken as protector and as *father*, is much reinforced.

'Mediation', says Hegel, 'is nothing other than self-moving identity with self.' But self-movement can also mean self-loss. And when he adds, 'It is the moment of dying and becoming', not a word needs changing for the formulation to have radically different meanings depending on the perspective in which it is placed: that of totalitarian Power or that of the whole human being.

No sooner does mediation escape my control than steps I had felt to be mine lead me into strange and inhuman territory. Engels discerningly showed that a stone, a fragment of nature alien to man, became human as soon as it extended the hand by serving as a tool (and the stone in its turn humanized the hand of the hominid). Yet, once appropriated by a master, an employer, a planning commission or a governing body, the tool's meaning is changed: it deflects the action of its user towards other purposes. And what holds for tools holds for all mediations.

Just as God served as a looking-glass for human beings, the magnetism of the principle of authority succeeds in capturing the largest possible number of mediations. Power is the sum of alienated and alienating mediations. It fell to science (*scientia theologiae ancilla*) to convert the divine illusion into operational information, into organized abstraction— thus underscoring the etymology of the word: *ab-trahere*, to draw out of.

The energy expended by individuals in pursuit of self-fulfilment, as they seek to project themselves into the world according to their desires and dreams, is suddenly braked, suspended, switched onto other tracks, co-opted. The normal stage of accomplishment is forced onto another plane, out of the realm of lived experience into that of the transcendental.

But the mechanism of abstraction is never purely and simply compliant with the principle of authority. However diminished humans may be by the theft of their mediations, they still enter the labyrinth of Power armed with the aggressive will of a Theseus. If they lose their way, it is because they have already lost the sweet Ariadne's thread that attaches them to life, to the will to be oneself. Only a continuous relationship between theory and living praxis can sustain the hope of ending all dualities, ushering in the era of totality, and abolishing the power exercised by man over man.

The human course is not diverted towards inhumanity without resistance, without a fight. As for the field of combat, it is always to be found where direct experience is extended in the immediate—in spontaneity. I am not saying that the 'abstraction' of mediations must be countered by some wild or so to say 'instinctive' spontaneity; that would be merely to reproduce on a higher level the fatuous choice between pure speculation and mindless activism, the disjunction of theory and practice. Rather, the appropriate tactical response is to attack at the precise spot where the plunderers of lived experience lie in wait, at the frontier between the initiation of the act and its perverted outcome, at the very moment when spontaneous action is gobbled up by misinterpretation and misunderstanding. At such moments the briefest imaginable overview is opened up, a crystallization of consciousness that illuminates both the demands of the will to live and the fate that social organization has in store for them: lived experience and its co-optation by the authoritarian machine. The point where resistance begins is the look-out post of subjectivity. For identical reasons, my knowledge of the world exists effectively only from the moment when I transform that world.

2

Power's mediation bludgeons the immediate continually. Of course, the idea that an act cannot be carried through in the totality of its implications faithfully reflects the reality of a deficient world, a world of nontotality; but at the same time it strengthens the metaphysical view of the facts—i.e., the official misrepresentation of them. Common sense has embraced such claims as 'You have to have leaders', 'Without authority mankind would sink into barbarism and chaos', and so on and so forth. So thoroughly, indeed, has habit mutilated human beings that they mistake self-mutilation for obedience to a law of nature. And perhaps the suppression of the memory of self-loss is what clamps them most tightly into the pillory of submission. At all events, it befits the slave mentality to equate Power with the only possible form of life, namely survival. And naturally it suits the masters' purposes to encourage such sentiments.

In mankind's struggle for survival, hierarchical social organization unquestionably marked a decisive step forward. At one point in history human groups secured their best, perhaps their only prospect of self-preservation by cohering around a leader. But survival was ensured only at the price of a new alienation: the safeguard was a prison, preserving life but preventing growth. Feudal regimes displayed this contradiction with brutal clarity: serfs, half-human and half-beast, existed side by side with a privileged caste a handful of whose members aspired as individuals to a genuinely exuberant and vigorous life.

The feudal worldview cared little about survival as such: famines, plagues and massacres swept millions of beings from that best of all worlds without unduly disturbing generations of literati and refined hedonists. For the bourgeoisie, by contrast, survival is the raw material of its economic interests. Nourishment and material subsistence are the inevitable drivers of trade and industry. Indeed it is not excessive to view the primacy of the economy—that axiom of bourgeois thought—as the very source of that class's renowned humanism. If the bourgeoisie prefers human beings to God, it is because only human beings produce and consume, supply and demand. The divine universe, which is preeconomic, has as much reason to incur bourgeois disapprobation as the posteconomic world of the whole human being.

By sating survival needs, however, and even artificially inflating them, consumer society awakens a new appetite for life. Once both survival and work are guaranteed, the old safeguards become obstacles. Not only does the struggle to survive prevent us from living, but once it becomes a struggle without real demands it begins to challenge survival itself: what was paltry becomes precarious. Survival has grown so fat that if it doesn't shed its skin it will be asphyxiated, and smother us all in the process.

The protection once guaranteed by feudal lords lost its *raison d'être* as soon as the mechanical solicitude of gadgetry brought the necessity for slavery, at least theoretically, to an end. The deliberately fostered terror of a thermonuclear apocalypse is the *ultima ratio* of today's leaders. Peaceful coexistence underwrites *their* existence, but the existence of the rulers by no means guarantees the continued existence of humanity. Power no longer protects the people; rather, it protects itself against each and every individual. A spontaneous creation of inhumanity by human agency, Power is now nothing more than an inhuman barrier to creativity.

3

Whenever the total and immediate consummation of an action is deferred, Power is confirmed in its function of grand mediator. Spontaneous poetry, on the other hand, is antimediation *par excellence*.

Broadly speaking, it is true to say that the characterization of the bourgeois or Soviet forms of fragmentary power as a 'sum of constraints' is becoming less and less apt as these systems come to depend increasingly upon alienating mediations. Ideological hypnosis is replacing the bayonet. This perfected mode of government bears a marked resemblance to the computers of the cyberneticians. Following the prudent directives of the Left's technocrats and specialists, an electronic Argus is doing away with small-time intermediaries—with spiritual leaders, putschist generals, Stalino-Francoists and other descendants of Ubu—as it plans and constructs its absolutism of well-being. But the more mediations are alienated, the more the thirst for immediacy rages—and the more the savage poetry of revolution tramples down frontiers.

At its highest stage, authority will achieve the union of abstract and concrete. The guillotine may still be at work, but Power is already busy abstracting. The very face of the world, as illuminated by Power, is being reorganized according to a metaphysics of reality; and what manna from heaven for Power to have the ever-dutiful philosophers lining up in their new uniforms as technocrats, sociologists, and experts in this or that.

The pure form haunting social space is the now clear prospect of the death of humanity. This is the neurosis before necrosis, survival sickness spreading slowly as lived experience is replaced by images, forms, objects—as alienated mediations reify lived experience like madrepores building a reef. It is a man or a tree or a stone—to borrow Lautréamont's prescient words.

Gombrowicz for his part pays well-deserved homage to Form, Power's old procuress, now promoted to the place of honour among agencies of government: '. . . you have never managed properly to appreciate, or to make others appreciate, the role, and the important role, of form in your own lives. Even in psychology you have not given form the place to which it is entitled. Hitherto we have always considered the feelings, instincts, or ideas which govern our conduct, and regarded form as at the most a harmless, ornamental accessory. When a widow weeps behind her husband's hearse, we think she does so because she feels her loss so keenly. When an engineer, doctor, or lawyer murders his wife, his children, or a friend, we think that he was driven to it by violent and bloodthirsty instincts. When a politician in a public speech expresses himself stupidly, deceitfully, or pettily, we say he is stupid because he expresses himself stupidly. But the real situation is this: a human being does not externalize himself directly and immediately in conformity with his own nature; he invariably does so by way of some definite form; and that form, style, way of speaking and responding, do not derive solely from him, but are imposed on him from without—and the same man can express himself sometimes wisely, sometimes foolishly, bloodthirstily or angelically, maturely or immaturely, according to the form, the style presented to him by the outside world, the pressure put on him by other men . . . The time has come, the hour has struck on the clock of ages. Try to set yourself against form, try to shake free of it. Cease to identify yourself with that which defines you.' (*Ferdydurke*)

4

In his *Critique of Hegel's Philosophy of Right*, Marx writes that 'theory also becomes a material force as soon as it has gripped the masses. Theory is capable of gripping the masses as soon as it demonstrates *ad hominem*, and it demonstrates *ad hominem* as soon as it becomes radical. To be radical is to grasp the root of the matter. But, for man, the root is man himself.'

In short, radical theory grips the masses because it emanates from them in the first place. As a repository of spontaneous creativity, its task is to ensure the striking power of that creativity: revolutionary technique at the service of poetry. Any analysis of insurrections past or present that does not incorporate a will to resume the struggle more coherently and more effectively plays willy-nilly into the hands of the enemy, joining forces with the dominant culture. Talk of revolutionary moments that does not help generate more such moments in short order is simply not pertinent—a criterion well worth applying, incidentally, to the wandering bellringers of the 'planetary' Left led by the likes of Kostas Axelos and company.

Those who call a halt to revolutions are always the first in line to explain why to revolution's architects. They have reasons for explaining themselves just as good, to put it mildly, as their reasons for aborting the process. When theory escapes the makers of a revolution, it ends up barring their way. Instead of gripping them, it dominates and conditions them. Whatever the people fail to advance by force of arms advances the forces of those who disarm them. The revolution as 'explained' by gunfire to the Kronstadt sailors or the followers of Makhno—that too was Leninism. Not theory but ideology.

Whenever leaders monopolize theory, it changes in their hands into ideology, into an *ad hominem* argument against mankind itself. Radical theory stems from the individual, in being qua subject, gripping the masses through what is most creative in each person, through subjectivity, through the will to self-fulfilment. Ideological conditioning, by contrast, is the technical manipulation of the inhuman, of the weight of *things*. It turns human beings into objects with no meaning external to the Order in which they have their place. It assembles them in order to isolate them, making the crowd into a multiplicity of solitudes.

Ideology is false language, radical theory true language. The conflict between them—the conflict between humans and the element of inhumanity that humanity secretes—presides over the transformation of the world into human reality but also over its transmutation into metaphysical reality. Everything that human beings do and undo passes through the mediation of language. The semantic realm is one of the main battlefields in the struggle between the will to live and the spirit of submission.

//////

The fight is unfair. Words are better servants of Power than human beings are users of words; words serve Power more faithfully than most humans, and more scrupulously than other mediations—space, time, technology and so on. For all supersession depends on language and develops as a system of signs and symbols (words, dance, ritual, music, sculpture, architecture, etc.). When a half-completed action which has suddenly been obstructed seeks to proceed in a new form that should sooner or later eventuate in its completion and realization—rather as a generator transforms mechanical energy into electrical energy that will then be reconverted into mechanical energy by a motor miles away—at this very moment language swoops down on lived experience, takes it captive, robs it of its substance: in sum, it *abstracts* it. And language always has categories ready and waiting to render incomprehensible and nonsensical whatever does not fit into them and to usher whatever resides in the void, because it still has no place in the reigning Order, into existence under Power's aegis. The repetition of familiar signs is the foundation of ideology.

At the same time, nonetheless, people strive to use words and signs to complete their aborted actions. Because they do so, there is such a thing as poetic language: a language of lived experience which, for me, is inseparable from the radical theory which grips the masses and becomes a material force. Even co-opted and turned against its initial aims, poetry finds sooner or later finds its way to fulfilment. The watchword 'Workers of the World Unite!' may have helped construct the Stalinist state, yet one day it will underpin the classless society. No poetic sign is ever definitively commandeered by ideology.

The language that diverts radical actions, creative actions—human actions *par excellence*—from their fulfilment becomes antipoetry, which defines Power's linguistic function, its information technology. The information produced in this way is a model of false communication, the communication of the inauthentic, the nonlived. We may safely say, it seems to me, that the moment language fails to obey the push towards fulfilment it falsifies communication, no longer communicating anything save the false promise of truth that we call a lie. But this lie is the truth of what destroys me, infects me with its virus of submission. Signs are the vanishing points of the two opposed perspectives which carve up the world and define it: the perspective of power and the perspective of the will to live. Each word, idea or symbol is a double agent. Some, like the word 'fatherland', or the policeman's uniform, usually work for authority; but make no mistake, when ideologies clash or simply begin to wear out, the most mercenary sign can become a good anarchist (think of the splendid title that Bellegarigue chose for his newspaper: *L'Anarchie, Journal de l'Ordre*).

For the dominant semiological system—which is that of the dominant castes—all signs are mercenary signs, and, as Humpty Dumpty says, when the master makes a word do a lot of work he pays it extra. But, deep down, every mercenary dreams of killing the King some day. Condemned as we are to a diet of lies, let us learn to spike them with a drop of acid truth. Let our model be the agitator, who invests his words and signs so forcefully with living reality that all the others are pulled along in their wake: an exemplary repurposing of language.

In a general way, the fight for language is the fight for the freedom to live. For a reversal of perspective. The battle is between metaphysical facts and real facts, which is to say between facts conceived of as static, as part of a system of interpretation of the world, and facts grasped in their unfolding by a praxis that transforms them.

Power cannot be overthrown as a government is overthrown. A united front against authority covers the whole spectrum of everyday life and enlists the vast majority of people. *Savoir-vivre* means knowing how not to give an inch in the struggle against renunciation. Let nobody underestimate Power's ability to force-feed its slaves with words to the point where they become slaves to those words themselves.

What weapons does each of us have at our disposal to defend our freedom? Here are three:

(a) 'Information' revised, converted into poetry: the news decoded, official terminology translated (so that 'society', in the anti-Power perspective, becomes a 'racket' or a 'zone of hierarchical power'); this might eventually give rise to a glossary or encyclopaedia—Diderot was well aware of the value of such a project, as were the Situationists.

(b) Free dialogue, which is the language of the dialectic: open-ended and all nonspectacular kinds of discussion.

(c) What Jakob Boehme called 'sensual speech' (*sensualische Sprache*), because it was 'an unclouded mirror of the senses'. The author of *The Way to Christ* goes on: 'Spirits speak to each other only in sensual speech, and have no need for any other form of speech, because this is the Speech of Nature.' In the context of what I have called the re-creation of nature, the language Boehme talks of may clearly be seen as the language of spontaneity, of 'doing', of individual and collective poetry; language centred on the project of self-fulfilment, leading lived experience out of the 'caverns of history'. There is a connection here too with what Paul Brousse and Ravachol meant by 'propaganda by the deed'.

//////

There is a silent communication; it is well known to lovers. In this arena language seems to lose its importance as essential mediation, thought is no longer a distraction (in the sense of leading us away from ourselves), and words and signs become a sort of bonus, a luxury, an extravagance. Think of lovers billing and cooing, of the baroque quality of their cries and caresses—so absurd to those who do not share the intoxication. Léhautier was also referring to a sort of direct communication when the judge asked him which anarchists he knew in Paris: 'Anarchists', he replied, 'don't need to know one another to think the same thing.' In radical groups able to reach the highest level of theoretical and practical consistency, words will, just occasionally, come to operate as they do in play or in lovemaking, suggesting an identity between the erotic and communication.

An aside. It has often been noted that history sometimes proceeds backwards, and this is confirmed once more when words become superfluous, as in language-play. A baroque current runs through the history of thought, making fun of words and signs with the subversive intention of disturbing the semiological order and indeed Order in general. The tradition of assaults on language which stretches from the *fatraisies* of the Middle Ages to Jean-Pierre Brisset by way of the iconoclast hordes was most fully epitomized by the Dadaist explosion. In 1916, the desire to have it out with signs, thought and words catalysed a real crisis of communication for the first time. The liquidation of language, so often undertaken in a speculative way, now at last found the way to its historical realization.

So long as the age kept a solid faith in the transcendent force of language and in God, master of all transcendence, any doubt raised over signs was tantamount to terrorism. But once the crisis in human relations shattered the unitary web of mythical communication, the attack on language took on a revolutionary cast. So much so that it is tempting to say, as Hegel might have, that the degeneration of language chose Dada as the medium through which to reveal itself to human consciousness. Under unitary regimes the self-same desire to play with signs had had no repercussions; it was betrayed, so to speak, by history. By denouncing the falsity of communication, Dada opened the era of language's supersession in the quest for poetry. Today both the language of myth and the language of spectacle are surrendering to the reality which underlies them: the language of facts. This language, embodying the critique of all modes of expression, also embodies its own self-criticism. Pity the poor sub-Dadaists! Because they have not understood the supersession that Dada necessarily implies, they continue to complain that we are engaged in a dialogue of the deaf. (Naturally, their complaining guarantees them a well-filled trough in the spectacle of cultural degeneration.)

//////

The language of the whole man will be a whole language: perhaps even the end of the old language of words. Inventing such a language means reconstructing human beings right down to their unconscious. The totality is hacking its way through the fractured nontotality of thoughts, words and actions towards itself. But we shall have to go on speaking until facts allow us to be silent.

The Impossibility of Fulfilment: Power as Sum of Seductions

As constraint breaks people, and mediation makes fools of them, the seduction of Power makes their wretchedness attractive. In consequence people forgo their true riches (a) for a cause that cripples them (XII); (b) for a fictitious unity that fragments them (XIII); (c) for appearances that reify them (XIV); for roles that wrest them from authentic life (XV); and for a time that slips away, taking them with it (XVI).

XII   Sacrifice

There is such a thing as a reformism of sacrifice that is really just a
sacrifice to reformism. Humanist self-mutilation and fascist self-
destruction both leave us nothing—not even the option of death.
All *causes* are equally inhuman. But the will to live raises its voice
against this epidemic of masochism wherever there is the slightest
pretext for revolt: beneath what appear to be partial demands,
that will is at work preparing a nameless revolution, the revolution
of everyday life [1]. The refusal of sacrifice is the refusal to be
bartered: human beings are not exchangeable. As of now, three
areas have been prepared as fall-back positions for the defence
of voluntary self-sacrifice, namely art, grand human virtues of the
past, and the present [2].

1

Where people are not broken—and broken in—by force and fraud, they are
seduced. As a means of seduction Power deploys internalized constraints
based on lies and cloaked in a clear conscience: the masochism of the
model citizen. To this end castration had perforce to be called selflessness,
and a choice of servitudes freedom. The feeling of 'having done one's
duty' makes everyone into their own honourable executioner.

As I showed in 'Basic Banalities' (*Internationale Situationniste* 7–8,
1962–63), the master-slave dialectic implies that the mythical sacrifice
of the master subsumes the real sacrifice of the slave: masters makes a
spiritual sacrifice of their real power to the general interest, while slaves
make a material sacrifice of their real life to a Power of which they
partake in appearance only. The framework of *generalized appearances*
or, if you prefer, the essential lie required initially for the development
of privative appropriation (the appropriation of things by means of the
appropriation of beings) is an intrinsic aspect of the dialectic of sacrifice, and the root of the notorious separation that it entails. The mistake
of the philosophers was that they built an ontology and the notion of

an unchanging human nature on the basis of a mere social accident, a purely contingent necessity. History has been seeking to eliminate privative appropriation ever since the conditions which called for it ceased to exist. But the metaphysical maintenance of the philosophers' error continues to work to the advantage of the masters, the 'eternal' ruling minority.

//////

The misfortune of sacrifice is inseparable from that of myth. Bourgeois thought exposes the materiality of myth, deconsecrating and fragmenting it. It does not abolish it, however, for otherwise the bourgeoisie would cease to exploit—and hence to exist. The fragmentary spectacle is simply one phase in the disintegration of myth, a process accelerated today by the dictatorship of the consumable. Similarly, the old sacrifice-gift ordained by cosmic forces has shrivelled into a sacrifice-exchange minutely metered in terms of social security and social-democratic justice. And sacrifice attracts fewer and fewer devotees, just as fewer and fewer people are seduced by the miserable show put on by ideologies. The fact is that today's tiny private masturbations are a feeble replacement indeed for the orgiastic heights offered by eternal salvation. How could hoping for a promotion conceivably vie with the wild dream of life everlasting! Our only gods are heroes of the fatherland, heroes of the shop-floor, heroes of the Frigidaire, heroes of fragmented thought. How are the mighty fallen!

Nevertheless. The knowledge that an ill's end is in sight is cold comfort when you still have to suffer it in the moment. And the praises of sacrifice are still sung on every side. The air is filled with the sermonizing of red priests and ecumenical bureaucrats. Vodka mixed with holy water. Instead of a knife between our teeth we have the drool of Jesus Christ on our lips. Sacrifice yourselves joyfully, brothers and sisters! For the Cause, for Order, for the Party, for Unity, for Meat and Potatoes!

The old socialists were wont to say, 'You think you are dying for your country, but really you are dying for Capital'. Today their heirs are berated in similar terms: 'You think you're fighting for the proletariat, but really you die for your leaders'. 'You are not building for the future; men and steel are the same thing in the eyes of the Five-Year Plan.' And yet, what do today's Young Turks of the Left do after chanting such slogans? They enter the service of a Cause—the 'best' of all Causes. The time they have for creative activity they squander handing out leaflets, sticking up posters, demonstrating, or heckling local politicians. They become militants, fetishizing action because others are doing their thinking for them. Sacrifice has an endless succession of tricks up its sleeve.

The finest Cause is one in which individuals can lose themselves body and soul. The principles of death are just the denial of the principles of the will to live. But either death or life must prevail. There is no middle way, no possibility of compromise between them on the level of consciousness. One must be entirely for the one or entirely for the other. The fevered supporters of an absolute Order—Chouans, Nazis, Carlists—have always shown with unwavering consistency that they are on the side of death. As a party line, the slogan *¡Viva la Muerte!* could hardly be clearer. By contrast, our reformists of death in small doses—our ennui-promoting socialists—cannot even claim the dubious honour of an aesthetic of total destruction. All they can do is mitigate the passion for life, stunting it to the point where it turns against itself and changes into a passion for destruction and self-destruction. They oppose concentration camps, but only in the name of moderation—moderate power and moderate death.

Great scorners of life that they are, the partisans of absolute self-sacrifice to State, Cause or Führer do have one thing in common with those whose passion for life challenges the ethos and techniques of renunciation: though antithetical, their sense of jubilation is equally acute. For them it is as though life, being so festive in its essence but tormented by a monstrous asceticism, resolves to end it all by distilling all the splendour of which it has been robbed into a single instant: legions of puritans, mercenaries, fanatics, death squads—all experience a moment of bliss as they die. But this is a *fête macabre*, frozen, caught for eternity in a camera flash, aestheticized. The paratroopers that Marcel Bigeard speaks of leave this world through the portal of aesthetics: they are statue-like figures, mineralized, conscious perhaps of their ultimate hysteria. For aesthetics is carnival paralysed, petrified, as cut off from life as a Jibaro head: the feast of death. The aesthetic element here, moreover, the element of *pose*, corresponds to the element of death secreted by everyday life. Every apocalypse is beautiful, but this beauty is dead. Remember the Song of the Swiss Guard that Louis-Ferdinand Céline taught us to love.

The end of the Commune was no apocalypse. The difference between the Nazis dreaming of bringing the world down with them and the

Communards leaving Paris to the flames is the difference between total death brutally affirmed and total life brutally denied. The Nazis merely activated a mechanism of logical annihilation already set up by humanists preaching submission and abnegation. The Communards knew that a life once constructed with passion cannot be reduced piece by piece; that there is more satisfaction in destroying such a life than in seeing it mutilated; and that it is better to go up in flames with a glad heart than to give an inch, when giving an inch is the same thing as complete surrender. 'Better die on our feet than live on our knees!' Despite its repulsive source—the lips of the Stalinist Ibarruri—it seems to me that this cry eloquently expresses the legitimacy of a particular form of suicide, a good way of taking leave. And what was right for the Commune holds good for individuals.

Let us have no more suicide from weariness, which comes like a final sacrifice crowning all those that have gone before. Better one last laugh *à la* Cravan, or one last song *à la* Ravachol.

//////

Revolution ceases to exist from the moment one must sacrifice oneself for it. From the moment one must lose oneself in it and fetishize it. Revolutionary moments are carnivals in which the individual life celebrates its unification with a regenerated society. The call for sacrifice in such a context is a death knell. Jules Vallès was unworthy of himself when he wrote: 'So long as the submissive live no longer than the rebellious, one might as well rebel in the name of an idea.' For a militant can only be a revolutionary *in spite of* the ideas he has agreed to serve. The real Vallès was the Vallès who fought for the Commune the sometime child, sometime student making up in one long Sunday for the endless weeks of his past. Ideology is the rebel's tombstone. Its purpose is to prevent his coming back to life.

When rebels start believing that they are fighting for a higher good the authoritarian principle is bolstered. Humanity has never been short of justifications for giving up the human. In fact some people possess a veritable reflex of submission, an irrational terror of freedom; this masochism is everywhere visible in everyday life. With what galling ease we give up a wish, a passion, the most essential parts of ourselves. With what passivity, what inertia, we accept living or acting for something, or rather some *thing*—a word whose dead weight seems to prevail everywhere. It is hard to be oneself, so we give up readily, seizing on whatever pretext we can: love of children, of reading, of artichokes, etc, etc. The wish for a remedy evaporates in face of the abstract generality of the ill.

And yet the impulse to freedom also knows how to make use of pretexts. Even a strike for higher wages or a riot in the streets can awaken the carnival spirit. As I write, thousands of workers around the world are downing tools or picking up guns, ostensibly in obedience to directives or principles, but actually, at the profoundest level, in response to their passionate desire to change their lives. The unstated agenda of every insurrectionary movement is the transformation of the world and the reinvention of life. No theorist formulates these demands; rather, they are the sole foundation of poetic creativity. Revolution is made every day despite, and indeed in opposition to the specialists of revolution. This revolution is *nameless*, like everything that springs from lived experience. Its explosive integrity is forged continuously in the everyday clandestinity of acts and dreams.

No problem bothers me so much as an issue I confront all day long: how can I invent a passion, fulfil a wish or construct a dream in the daytime in the way my mind does spontaneously as I sleep? What haunts me are my unfinished actions, not the future of the human race, nor the state of the world in the year 2000, nor the future conditional, nor polishing up abstractions. If I write, it is not, as they say, 'for others'; nor is it to be exorcised of others' demons. I string words together as a way of getting out of the well of isolation, because I need others to pull me out. I write out of impatience, and with impatience. I am seeking to live without dead time. I want to know nothing of others save that which concerns me directly. Let them free themselves of me just as I free myself of them. We have a common project. But it is out of the question that the project of the whole human being should require individuals to be diminished. There are no gradations in castration. The apolitical violence of the younger generation, and their contempt for the interchangeable goods on offer in the supermarkets of culture, art and ideology, are a concrete confirmation of the fact that individual fulfilment depends on the application of the principle of 'every man for himself', although this has to be understood in collective terms—and above all in *radical* terms.

At that stage in a piece of writing where we used to look for explanations, I would like us from now on to find a settling of scores.

2

The refusal of sacrifice is the refusal to be bartered. There is nothing in the world of things, exchangeable for money or not, that is equivalent to a human being. The individual is irreducible: subject to change but not to exchange. The scantest examination of movements for social reform shows that they have never demanded anything beyond a purification of exchange and sacrifice, making it a point of honour to humanize inhumanity and make it attractive. But whenever slaves try to make their slavery more bearable they come to the rescue of their masters.

The 'road to socialism' consists in this: as people become more and more tightly shackled by the sordid relations of reification, the pressure from humanitarians to cripple them in an *egalitarian* fashion grows ever more insistent. And while the deepening crisis of the virtues of self-abnegation and dedication spurs us on towards radical refusal, there are sociologists—those policemen of modern society—eager to erect a barrier in the shape of a subtler kind of sacrifice, namely art.

//////

The great religions succeeded in turning people's wretched earthly existence into a time of voluptuous expectation: at the end of this valley of tears lay life eternal in God. Art, in the bourgeoisie's conception of it, is more entitled than God to bestow eternal glory. The art-in-life-and-in-God of unitary social systems (Egyptian statuary, African art, etc.) was succeeded by an art which complemented life and sought to make up for the absence of God (fourth-century Greece, Horace, Ronsard, Malherbe, the Romantics, etc.). The builders of cathedrals cared no more for posterity than did Sade. Their salvation was guaranteed by God, as Sade's was guaranteed by himself: neither needed a place in the museum of history. Both strove for a supreme state of being, not for the temporal survival of their work or for the admiration of centuries to come.

History is the earthly paradise of bourgeois spirituality. This realm is reached not through commodities but through apparent gratuity, through the sacrifice attending the work of art, through activity not constrained by any immediate need to increase capital. The philanthropist does good works; the patriot performs heroic deeds; the soldier contrives victory; the poet or scholar creates works of literary or scientific value; and so on. But there is an ambiguity in the very idea of 'creating a work of art', for it embraces both the lived experience of the artist and

the abandonment of this experience to an abstraction of substantial creation, namely the aesthetic form. The artist sacrifices the lived intensity
of the creative moment in exchange for the durability of what he creates,
so that his name may live on in the funereal glory of the museum. But
is not the desire to produce a durable work the very thing that prohibits
the creation of imperishable instants of life?

As a matter of fact, setting aside strictly academic art, artists never
fall entirely prey to aesthetic co-optation. Though they may abdicate
their immediate experience for the sake of beautiful appearances, all
artists (and anyone who tries to live is an artist) are driven by the desire
to increase their tribute of dreams to the objective world of others. In this
sense they entrust the thing they create with the mission of completing
their personal fulfilment within their social group. And in this sense
creativity is revolutionary in its essence.

The function of the ideological, artistic and cultural spectacle is to
turn the wolves of spontaneity into the sheepdogs of knowledge and
beauty. Literary anthologies are replete with insurrectionary writings,
the museums with calls to arms. So thoroughly does history pickle them
in durability, however, that we omit to see or hear them. But in this area
consumer society has abruptly stepped in to perform a salutary task of
dissolution. Today art can construct only plastic cathedrals. The dictatorship of consumption ensures that every aesthetic collapses before it can
produce any masterpieces. Premature demise is fundamental to consumerism; the imperfection of an automobile ensures its rapid replacement.
For art work to be a sudden aesthetic sensation, it has merely to offer
some transient novelty to the spectacle of artistic disintegration. Bernard
Buffet, Georges Mathieu, Alain Robbe-Grillet, Pop Art, pop music—all are
available for casual purchase in the department stores. Betting on the
perennial value of an art work is much like betting on the eternal value
of stock in Standard Oil.

When the most forward-looking sociologists finally grasped the fact
that the worth of the art object was now nothing but its market price, and
that the once vaunted creativity of the artist was now beholden to the
norms of profitability, they decided that we should return to the source of
art, to everyday life—not in order to change it, of course, for such was not
their mandate, but rather to make it the raw material for a new aesthetic
that would defy packaging techniques and so remain independent of
buying and selling. As though there were no such thing as consuming

on the spot! The result? Sociodramas and happenings which supposedly allow spectators to participate in an unmediated way. All they participate in, however, is an aesthetic of nothingness. The only thing that can be expressed in the mode of the spectacle is the emptiness of everyday life. And indeed, what better commodity than an aesthetic of emptiness? Has not the accelerating disintegration of values itself become the only available form of entertainment? The trick is that the spectators of the cultural and ideological vacuum are here enlisted as its organizers, thus filling the spectacle's vacuousness by forcing its spectators—passive agents *par excellence*—to play their part. The ultimate logic of the happening and its derivatives is to supply the society of masterless slaves which the cyberneticians have planned for us with the spectatorless spectacle it will require. For artists in the strict sense, the road to complete co-optation is well posted: they have merely to follow Georges Lapassade and his ilk into the great corporation of specialists. They may be sure that Power will reward them well for applying their talents to the job of dressing up the old conditioning to passivity in seductive new colours.

From Power's perspective, everyday life is just a latticework of renunciations and mediocrity. A true void. An aesthetic of everyday life would make us all into artists responsible for organizing this nothingness. The final spasm of official art will be the attempt to lend therapeutic features to what Freud, in a dubious simplification, referred to as the death instinct—in other words rapturous submission to authority. The crucified Toad of Nazareth casts his shadow wherever the will to live fails to spring spontaneously from individual poetry. Regression to artistic forms defined by the spirit of sacrifice can never awaken the artist in every human being. Everything has to be begun again from the beginning.

//////

The Surrealists—or some of them at any rate—understood that the only genuine supersession of art lay in direct experience, in works that no ideology could assimilate into its internally consistent lie. They came to grief, of course, precisely because of their complaisant attitude towards the cultural spectacle. Admittedly, the current decay of thought and art has made the danger of aesthetic co-optation much less than it was in the 1930s. The present state of affairs can only favour Situationist agitation.

Much wailing has gone on—since Surrealism's demise, in fact—over the disappearance of idyllic relationships such as friendship, love and hospitality. But make no mistake: all this nostalgia for the more human virtues of the past answers to one thing and one thing only, namely the impending need to revive the idea of sacrifice, which has been coming under too heavy a fire. The fact is that there will never be any friendship, or love, or hospitality, or solidarity, so long as self-abnegation rules—and enhances the attraction of inhumanity. Here is an anecdote of Brecht's that makes the point perfectly. To illustrate the proper way of doing a service for friends, and to entertain his listeners, Herr K. used to tell the following story. Three young men once came to an old Arab and said: 'Our father is dead. He left us seventeen camels, but he laid down in his will that the eldest son should have a half, the second son a third, and the youngest a ninth part of his possessions. Try as we might, we cannot agree on how to divide up the camels. So we should like to leave it up to you to decide.' The old man thought it over before replying: 'I see that you need another camel before you can share them out properly. I have mine, just one, but take it, divide the beasts up, and bring me back whatever you have left over.' The young men thanked him for his kind offer, took his camel and divided up the eighteen animals as follows: the eldest took a half, which was nine camels, the second son took a third, which was six, and the youngest took his ninth, which was two. To everyone's surprise, there was still one camel remaining, and this they promptly returned with renewed thanks to their old friend. According to Herr K., this was the perfect example of the correct way to do a friend a service, because nobody had to make a sacrifice. Here is a model which should be made axiomatic and strictly applied to everyday life as a whole.

It is not a question of opting for the art of sacrifice as opposed to the sacrifice of art, but rather of putting an end to sacrifice as art. The triumph of an authentic *savoir-vivre* and of the construction of authentically lived situations exists everywhere as a potentiality, but everywhere these tendencies are perverted by distortions of the human.

//////

The sacrifice of the *present* may well turn out to be the last stage of a rite that has maimed humanity since its beginnings. Our every moment crumbles into bits and pieces of past and future. We never really give ourselves over completely to what we are doing, except perhaps in orgasm. Our present is defined by what we are going to do and what we have done: we construct it against a background of endless dissatisfaction.

In collective as in individual history, the cult of the past and the cult of the future are equally reactionary. Everything that has to be built has to be built in the present. According to a popular belief, the drowning man relives his whole life at the instant of his death. For my part I am convinced that we have intense flashes of lucidity which distil and remake our entire lives. Future and past are docile pawns of history which merely cover up the sacrifice of the present. I want to exchange nothing—not for a thing, not for the past, not for the future. I want to live intensely, for myself, grasping every pleasure firm in the knowledge that what is radically good for me will be good for everyone. And above all I would offer one watchword: 'Act as though there were no tomorrow.'

XIII Separation

Privative appropriation, the basis of social organization, keeps individuals separated from themselves and from others. Artificial unitary paradises seek to conceal this separation by more or less successfully co-opting people's prematurely shattered dreams of unity. To no avail. Between the pleasure of creation and the pleasure of destruction there is nothing but an oscillation that destroys Power.

People live separated from one another, separated from what they are in others, and separated from themselves. The history of humanity is the history of one basic separation which precipitates and determines all the others: the social distinction between masters and slaves. By means of history human beings strive to join together and achieve unity. The class struggle is but one stage, though a decisive one, in the struggle for the whole human being.

Just as the ruling class has every reason in the world to deny the existence of the class struggle, so the history of separation is necessarily indistinguishable from the history of its concealment. This mystification results less from a deliberate intent than from a long-drawn-out and confused battle in which the desire for unity is transformed more often than not into its opposite. Whatever fails to end separation completely reinforces it. When the bourgeoisie came to power, it shed fresh light on the factors which divide humanity in this most essential way by laying bare separation's social and material character.

//////

What is God? The guarantor and quintessence of the myth that justifies the domination of man by man. This repellent invention has no other *raison d'être*. As myth disintegrates and gives way to the stage of the spectacle, what Lautréamont called the Great External Object is shattered by the forces of social atomization and degenerates into a God-for-intimate-use-only—a sort of salve for social diseases.

At the high point of the crisis brought on by the end of classical philosophy and of the ancient world, Christianity's genius successfully subordinated a newly conceived mythic system to one fundamental principle: the doctrine of the Trinity. What is the meaning of this dogma of the Three in One, which caused so much ink and blood to flow?

In soul man belongs to God, in body to the temporal authority, and in mind or spirit to himself. His salvation depends on his soul, his freedom on his mind, and his earthly existence on his body. The soul envelops body and mind, and without the soul these are as nothing. This surely seems on closer inspection to be an analogy for the union of master and slave under the principle of man envisaged as a divine creature. The slave is the body, the labour-power appropriated by the lord; the master is the mind, which as governor of the body invests it with a small part of its higher essence. The slave sacrifices himself in body to the power of the master, while the master sacrifices himself in spirit to the community of his slaves (the king serves his people: de Gaulle serves France: the Church washes the feet of the poor). The slave abdicates his earthly life in exchange for the feeling of being free, that is, for the spirit of the master come down into him. Consciousness mystified is consciousness of myth. The master makes a notional gift of his master's power to all those whom he governs. By drowning the alienation of bodies in the subtler alienation of the spirit, he economizes on the amount of violence needed to maintain servitude. Thus the slave identifies in spirit, or at least he may, with the master to whom he gives up his life force. But whom can the master identify with? Not with his slaves qua possessions, qua bodies, certainly: rather, with his slaves qua emanation of the spirit of mastery itself, of the master supreme. Since the individual master must sacrifice himself on the spiritual plane, he must find something within the coherent mythic system to serve as recipient of his sacrifice, an idea of mastery-in-itself of which he partakes and to which he submits. The historically contingent class of masters had thus to create a God to bow down to spiritually and with whom to identify. God validated both the master's mythic sacrifice to the public good and the slave's real sacrifice to the master's private and privative power. God is the principle of all submission, the night which makes all crimes lawful. The only truly illegal crime is the refusal to accept a master. God is a harmony of lies, an ideal form uniting the slave's voluntary sacrifice (Christ), the consenting sacrifice of the master (the Father; the slave as the master's son), and the indissoluble link between them (the Holy Spirit). The same tripartite model underlies the ideal picture of man as a divine, unitary and mythic creature with which humanity is supposed to identify: a *body* subordinated to a guiding *spirit* working for the greater glory of the *soul*—the soul being the all-embracing synthesis.

We thus have a type of relationship in which two terms derive their meaning from an absolute principle, from an obscure and inaccessible norm of unchallengeable transcendence (God, blood, holiness, grace, etc). Innumerable dualities of this type were kept bubbling for century after century like a good stew on the fire of mythic unity. Then the bourgeoisie took the pot off the fire and was left with nothing but a vague nostalgia for the warmth of the unitary myth and a set of cold and flavourless abstractions: body and spirit, being and consciousness, individual and society, private and public, general and particular, etc., etc. Paradoxically, driven by its class interests, the bourgeoisie destroyed the unitary myth and its tripartite structure to its own detriment. The aspiration to unity, so cleverly fobbed off by the mythic thinking of unitary regimes, did not disappear along with those regimes: on the contrary, it became all the more urgent as the material nature of separation became clearer and clearer in people's consciousness. By laying bare the economic and social foundations of separation, the bourgeoisie supplied the arms destined to end separation once and for all. At the same time, the end of separation means the end of the bourgeoisie along with all hierarchical power. This is why no ruling class or caste finds it possible to effect the transformation of feudal unity into real unity, into genuine social participation. This mission can be accomplished only by the new proletariat, which must forcibly wrest the *third force* (spontaneous creation, poetry) from the gods, and keep it alive in the everyday life of all. The transient period of fragmentary power will then be seen in its true light as a moment of insomnia in a long slumber, as the zero point prerequisite to the reversal of perspective, as the purchase needed for the leap of supersession.

//////

History bears witness to the struggle waged against the unitary principle and to the ways in which a dualistic reality began to emerge. The challenge was voiced to begin with in a theological language, the official language of myth. Later the idiom became that of ideology, the idiom of the spectacle. In their preoccupations, the Manichaeans, the Cathars, the

Hussites, the Calvinists and all the rest have much in common with such figures as Jean de Meung, La Boétie or Vanino Vanini. We find Descartes desperately locating the soul, for want of any better place, in the pineal gland. The Cartesian God is a funambulist balancing for some perfectly unaccountable reason atop a perfectly intelligible world. Pascal's, by contrast, hides himself from view, so depriving humanity and the world of a foundation without which they are reduced to meaningless confrontation, each being gauged by reference to the other, or in other words by reference to nothing.

By the close of the eighteenth century the fabric was rending in all directions as the process of disintegration began to speed up. This was the beginning of the era of 'little men' in competition. Fragments of human beings claimed the status of absolutes: matter, mind, consciousness, action, universal, particular—what God could mend all this broken crockery?

The spirit of feudal lordship found an adequate justification in transcendence. But a capitalist God is an absurdity. Whereas lordship implied a trinitarian system, capitalist exploitation is dualistic. Moreover, it cannot be severed from the material nature of economic relations. The economic realm is no mystery: the nearest things to miracles here are the element of chance in the functioning of the market and the perfect agency of computerized planning. Calvin's rational God has far less drawing power than the loans with interest that Calvinism authorizes so readily. As for the God of the Anabaptists of Münster and of the revolutionary peasants of 1525, he was a primitive expression of the irrepressible thrust of the masses towards a society of whole human beings.

The mystical leader did not simply turn into a factory owner; the feudal lord did not mutate into a boss. Once the mysterious superiority of blood and lineage was abolished, nothing remained but a mechanics of exploitation and a race for profit with no justification but themselves. Boss and worker are separated not by any qualitative distinction of birth but merely by quantitative distinctions of money and power. Indeed, what makes capitalist exploitation so repulsive is the very fact that it occurs between 'equals'. The rule of the bourgeoisie—quite unintentionally, needless to say—justifies every kind of revolution. People no longer mystified no longer obey.

//////

Fragmented Power separates to the point where even the human beings over which it holds sway are split asunder. Simultaneously the unitary lie breaks down. The death of God democratizes the consciousness of separation. What was the despair of the Romantics if not an agonized outcry against this rift? Today we see it in every aspect of life: in love, in the human gaze, in nature, in our dreams, in reality. The tragedy of consciousness evoked by Hegel would be more accurately described as a consciousness of tragedy. We find such a consciousness in revolutionary form in Marx. Far less dangerous, from Power's point of view, is Peter Schlemiel going in search of his own shadow so as to forget that he is really a shadow in search of a body. The bourgeoisie's invention of artificial unitary paradises is a more or less successful defensive reflex meant to retrieve the old enchantment and revive prematurely shattered dreams of unity.

Thus in addition to the great collective onanisms—ideologies, illusions of being together, herd mentalities, opiums of the people—we are offered a whole range of marginal solutions lying in the no-man's-land between the permissible and the forbidden: individualized ideology, obsession, monomania, unique (and hence alienating) passions, drugs and other highs—alcohol, the cult of speed and rapid change, of rarefied sensations, etc. All these pursuits allow us to lose ourselves completely while preserving the impression of fulfilment; their corrosiveness stems above all from their partial character. The passion for play is no longer alienating if the person who gives himself up to it seeks play in every aspect of life—in love, in thought, or in the construction of situations. In the same way, the wish to kill is no longer megalomania if it is combined with revolutionary consciousness.

Unitary palliatives thus entail two risks for Power. In the first place they fail to satisfy, and in the second they tend to foster the will to build a real social unity. Mystical elevation towards unity led only to God; by contrast, horizontal historical progression towards a dubious spectacular unity is infinitely finite. It creates an unlimited appetite for the absolute, yet its quantitative nature is limiting by definition. Its mad rush, therefore, must sooner or later debouch into the qualitative, whether in a negative way or—should a revolutionary consciousness prevail—through the transformation of negativity into positivity. Granted, the negative road does not lead to self-fulfilment: rather, it plunges us into self-dissolution. Madness deliberately sought, the voluptuousness of crime and cruelty, the convulsive lightning of perversity—such are the enticing paths open to those prepared to embrace self-destruction unhesitatingly. To take them is to align oneself with unusual zeal to the gravitational pull of Power's own tendency to dismember and destroy. But if it is to *endure*, Power must shackle its destructiveness: a good general may lead his men towards annihilation, but not the whole way. It remains to be seen whether nothingness can be doled out drop by drop. Rationing the pleasure to be derived from self-destruction bids fair to bring down the very Power that sets the limits. We have only to consider Stockholm or Watts to see that negative pleasure is forever on the point of tipping over into total pleasure—a little shove, and negative violence *releases its positivity*. I firmly believe that all pleasure embodies the search for total, unitary satisfaction, in every sphere—a fact which I doubt Huysmans had the humour to see when he solemnly described a man with an erection as 'insurgent'.

The complete unchaining of pleasure is the surest route to the revolution of everyday life, to the construction of the whole human being.

XIV The Organization of Appearances

> The organization of appearances is a system for shielding the facts. A racket. It represents the facts in a mediated reality to prevent immediate reality from presenting them. Unitary power organized appearances as myth. Fragmentary power organizes appearances as spectacle. Under fire, the coherence of myth became the myth of coherence. Worsened by history, the incoherence of the spectacle turned into the spectacle of incoherence [thus Pop Art is at once a current example of consumable degeneracy and the expression of the current degeneration of consumption] [1]. The poverty of 'the drama' as a literary genre goes hand in hand with the colonization of social space by theatrical attitudes. Enfeebled on the stage, theatre battens on everyday life and attempts to dramatize everyday behaviour. Roles are moulds into which lived experience is poured. The job of enhancing roles is assigned to specialists [2].

1

According to Nietzsche, the 'ideal world' is a construct based on a lie: 'Reality has been deprived of its value, its meaning, its veracity to the same degree as an ideal world has been *fabricated*. . . . The *lie* of the ideal has hitherto been the curse of reality; through it mankind itself has become mendacious and false down to its deepest instincts—to the point of worshipping the *inverse* values to those which alone could guarantee it prosperity and a future, the exalted *right* to a future.' What can the lie of the ideal be if not the truth of the masters? When theft needs legal justification, when authority waves the banner of the general interest in order to pursue private ends with impunity, is it any wonder that the lie captures minds, so distorting people by shaping them to its 'laws' that their very deformity comes to resemble a natural human attitude? It is true that human beings lie because in a world governed by lies they cannot do otherwise: they are themselves false, and shackled by their falsehood. As for common sense, it supports nothing except the decree against the truth promulgated in everyone's name. Common sense is the lie codified and vulgarized.

All the same, nobody lies groaning under the yoke of inauthenticity twenty-four hours a day. In the case of the most radical thinkers, the mendacity of words may secrete revelatory flashes of truth; similarly, there are very few everyday alienations that are not dispelled at least for an instant, for an hour, for the duration of a dream, by subjective rebuttal. Just as no one is ever completely hoodwinked by what is destroying them, words are never utterly in thrall to Power. Merely prolonging transient moments of truth, the tip of the iceberg of subjectivity, will suffice to sink the *Titanic* of the lie.

//////

After shattering myth, the tide of material reality has washed the fragments out to sea. Once the driving force of this tide, the bourgeoisie will end up as so much foam drifting out along with all the other flotsam. When he describes the backlash effect whereby the King's hired assassin returns in due time to carry out his orders upon the one who gave them, Shakespeare seems to give us a curiously prophetic account of the fate reserved for the class that killed God. Once the hired killers of the established order lose their faith in the myth, or, if you will, in the God who legalizes their crimes, the machinery of death no longer recognizes its master. In this sense revolution was the bourgeoisie's finest invention. It is also the running noose which will help it take its leap into oblivion. It is easy to see why bourgeois thought, strung up as it is on a rope of radicalism of its own making, clings with the energy of desperation to every reformist solution, to anything that can lengthen its reign, even though its own weight must inevitably drag it down to its doom. Fascism is in a way the herald of this ineluctable fall. It resembles the aesthete dreaming of dragging the whole world down with him into the abyss, lucid as to the death of his class but a sophist when he announces the inevitability of universal annihilation. Today this *mise en scène* of death chosen and refused lies at the core of the spectacle of incoherence.

The organization of appearances aspires to the immobility of the shadow of a bird in flight. But this aspiration, bound up with the ruling class's efforts to solidify its power, amounts to no more than a vain hope of escaping from the course of history. There is, however, an important difference between myth and its fragmented, deconsecrated avatar, the spectacle, with respect to the way each resists reality's critique. The varying importance assumed in unitary systems by artisans, merchants and bankers explains the continual oscillation in these societies between the *coherence of myth* and the *myth of coherence*. With the triumph of the bourgeoisie something very different happens: by introducing history into the arsenal of appearances, the bourgeois revolution historicizes appearances and thus makes the shift from the *incoherence of the spectacle* to the *spectacle of incoherence* an irreversible one.

In unitary societies, whenever the merchant class, with its disrespect for tradition, threatened to deconsecrate values, the coherence of myth would give way to the myth of coherence. What does this mean? What had hitherto been taken for granted had suddenly to be vigorously reasserted. Spontaneous faith gave way to loudly professed faith and respect for the great of this world had to be preserved by resort to the principle of absolute monarchy. I hope closer study will be given to those paradoxical interregnums of myth during which the bourgeoisie may be seen striving to sanctify its rise by means of a new religion and by self-ennoblement, while the nobility embraces the directly opposite strategy of wagering on an impossible transcendence (I am thinking of the Fronde here, and also of Heraclitean dialectic and Gilles de Rais). The aristocracy had the elegance to turn its last words into a witticism; the bourgeoisie's disappearance from the scene will be accompanied only by the solemnity of bourgeois thought. As for the forces of revolutionary supersession, surely they have more to win from light-hearted death than from the dead weight of survival.

Undermined by the critical effect of the fascism of the facts, the myth of coherence has proved unable to establish a new mythic coherence. Appearances—the mirror in which human beings hide their own choices from themselves—shatter into a thousand pieces and fall into the public realm of individual supply and demand. The demise of appearances means the end of hierarchical power—a façade 'with nothing behind it'. There can be no doubt as to this final outcome. The French Revolution was barely over before God-substitutes turned up at deep-discount prices. First came the Supreme Being and the Bonapartist *concordat,* and then, hard on their heels, nationalism, individualism, socialism, national socialism, and a host of neo-isms—not to mention the individualized dregs of every imaginable hand-me-down *Weltanschauung* and the thousands of portable ideologies offered as free gifts every time you buy a TV, a cultural artefact or a box of detergent. In due course the disintegration of the spectacle entails the resort to the spectacle of disintegration. It is in the logic of *things* that the last actor should film his own death. As it happens, the logic of things is the logic of what can be consumed, and sold as it is consumed. Pataphysics, sub-Dada, and the *mise-en-scène* of impoverished everyday life line the road that leads us with many a twist and turn to the last graveyards.

2

The development of the drama as a literary genre repeatedly illuminates the question of the organization of appearances. After all, a play is the simplest form of that organization, and, in a sense, a set of instructions for it. The earliest theatrical productions were indeed nothing else, intended as they were to reveal the mystery of transcendence to mankind. The gradual desanctification of theatre produced the template for later, spectacular stage management. Aside from the machinery of war, all ancient machines were responses to the needs of the theatre. The crane, the pulley and other hydraulic devices started out as theatrical paraphernalia; only much later did they revolutionize production relations. It is a striking fact that, no matter how far we go back in time, the domination of the earth and of human beings seems to depend on techniques which serve the purposes not only of work but also of illusion.

The birth of tragedy was already a narrowing of the arena in which early humans and their gods faced off in a cosmic dialogue. It meant a distancing, a putting in parentheses, of magical participation, which was now organized according to a refracted version of the principles of initiation, and no longer according to the rites themselves. What emerged was a *spectaculum*, a thing seen, while the gradual relegation of the gods to the role of mere props seemed to presage their eventual eviction from the social scene as a whole. Once mythic relationships had been dissolved by secularizing tendencies, tragedy was superseded by drama. Comedy is a good indicator of this transition: with all the vigour of a completely new force, its corrosive humour devastated tragedy in its dotage. Molière's *Don Juan* and the parody of Handel in John Gay's *Beggar's Opera* bear eloquent testimony to this.

With the rise of the drama, human society replaced the gods on the stage. And while it is true that nineteenth-century theatre was merely one form of entertainment among others, we must not let this obscure the fact that during this period theatre left the theatre, so to speak, and *colonized the entire social arena.* The cliché which likens life to a play seems to evoke a fact so obvious as to need no examination. The carefully maintained conflation of life and play-acting brooks no discussion. Yet what is natural about the fact that I stop being myself a hundred times a day and slip into the skin of people whose concerns and significance I have really not the slightest desire to assume? Not that I might not choose to be an actor on occasion—to play a role for diversion or pleasure. But this is not the type of role-playing I have in mind. The actor supposed to play a condemned man in a realist play is quite free to remain himself: herein lies, in fact, the paradox of fine acting. The freedom he enjoys obviously stems from the fact his physical being is not threatened by any sneering executioner; the threat is directed solely at the stereotypical image that he creates by means of his dramatic technique and flair. The roles played in everyday life, by contrast, permeate individuals, distancing them from what they are and what they really want to be; they are nuclei of alienation embedded in the flesh of lived experience. At this point the game is over: there is no more 'playing'. The function of stereotypes is to dictate to each person on an individual (even an 'intimate') level the same things that ideology imposes collectively.

//////

Piecemeal conditioning has replaced the ubiquitous conditioning of divinity, for Power must now call upon a host of minor forms of brainwashing in its attempt to attain the *quality* of the law and order of old. This means that prohibitions and lies have been personalized, and bear down hard on each individual to force them into an abstract mould. It also means that from one point of view—that of the government of human beings—progress in human knowledge improves the mechanisms of alienation: the more we see ourselves through official eyes, the greater our alienation. Science is a rationale for the police. It teaches how much torture people can endure before they die, and above all to what degree a person may be turned into a *heautontimoroumenos*, a dutiful self-torturer. It teaches how to become a thing while still retaining a human appearance, and this in the name of a certain appearance of humanity.

The greatest victories of cinema and its personalized version, television, are not won on the battlefield of ideas. They have little effect on public opinion. Their influence works in a quite different way. An actor on the stage impresses the audience by the general thrust of his gestures and by the conviction with which he delivers his lines; on the big or little screen, the same character is broken down into a sequence of exact details each of which affects the spectator in a separate and subtle way. This is a school of perception, a lesson in dramatic art in which a particular facial expression or motion of the hand supplies thousands of viewers with a supposedly adequate way of expressing particular feelings, wishes, and so on. Through the still rudimentary technology of the image, individuals thus learn to model their existential attitudes on identikit portraits cobbled together by psycho-sociologists. Their most personal tics and idiosyncrasies become the means whereby Power integrates them into its schemata. The poverty of everyday life reaches its nadir when choreographed in this way. Just as the passivity of consumers is an active one, so the passivity of spectators lies in the ability to assimilate roles and fill them according to official norms. The repetition of images and stereotypes offers a set of models from which everyone is urged to fashion a role. The spectacle is a museum of images, a showroom of stick figures. It is also an experimental theatre. The human being as consumer lets himself be conditioned by the stereotypes (passive aspect) upon which he then models his behaviour (active aspect). The task of dissimulating passivity by inventing new variants of spectacular participation and enlarging the range of available stereotypes falls to our happeners, Pop Art practitioners and sociodramatists. The machines of production-based society are increasingly pressed into the service of the spectacle: the computer as art object. We are returning in this way to the original conception of theatre, to a general participation in the mystery of divinity. But thanks to technology this now occurs on a higher level, and by the same token embodies possibilities of supersession that could not exist in high antiquity.

Stereotypes are simply debased forms of the old ethical categories: knight, saint, sinner, hero, felon, faithful servant, *honnête homme*, etc. The images which drew their effectiveness within the mythic system of appearances from their qualitative force work in the context of spectacular appearances solely by virtue of the frequency of their iteration as conditioning factors (slogans, photos, stars, catchwords and so on). As we have seen, the technical reproduction of magical relationships such as faith or identification eventually dissipated magic. Coupled

with the demise of the great ideologies, this development precipitated
the chaos of stereotypes and roles. Hence the new demands placed upon
the spectacle.

Real events reach us only as empty scripts. We get their form, never
their substance. And even their form is more or less clear according to
how often it is repeated and according to its position in the structure
of appearances. For as an organized system appearances are a vast filing
cabinet in which events are broken up, isolated from one another, labelled
and arbitrarily classified: lonely hearts columns, political affairs, wining
and dining, etc. Suppose a stroller on the Boulevard Saint-Germain is
killed by a young hoodlum. What are we told by the press? We are given
a preestablished scenario designed to arouse pity, indignation, disgust or
envy. The event is broken down into abstract components that are really
just clichés: youth, delinquency, crime in the streets, law and order, etc.
Images, photographs and styles are prefabricated and systematically
combined so as to constitute a sort of automatic dispenser of ready-made
explanations and emotions. Real people reduced to roles serve as bait: the
Strangler, the Prince of Wales, Louison Bobet, Brigitte Bardot, François
Mauriac—they all make love, get divorced, think thoughts and pick
their noses for thousands of people. The dissemination of prosaic details
invested with significance by the spectacle makes for strange bedfellows
among roles. The husband who murders his wife's lover competes for
attention with the Pope on his deathbed, and Johnny Hallyday's jacket
is on a par with Khrushchev's shoe. It's all one: everything is equivalent
to everything else in the perpetual spectacle of incoherence. The fact is
that the structures of the spectacle are in crisis, because so many balls
have to be kept in the air at the same time. The spectacle has to be everywhere, so it is watered down and inconsistent. The old, ever-serviceable
Manichaeanism is tending to disappear. The spectacle is not beyond
good and evil: it falls short of them. The Surrealists were quite mistaken
when, in 1930, they hailed the act of the exhibitionist as subversive. They
were merely adding the sort of spice to the spectacle of morality that it
needed to recover its vigour. Behaving in effect exactly like the gutter
press. Scandal is the bread and butter of news, along with black humour
and cynicism. The real scandal consists in the rejection and sabotage of
the spectacle—something which Power can hope to postpone only by
revamping and rejuvenating the structures of appearance. Perhaps this
will turn out in the end to have been the structuralists' chief function.

The fact remains that poverty cannot be offset by widening its sphere. The spectacle's degeneration is in the nature of things, and the dead weight that enforces passivity is bound to lighten; the resistance put up by lived experience and spontaneity must eventually lance the boil of inauthenticity and pseudo-activity.

XV Roles

Stereotypes are the dominant images of the era, the images of the dominant spectacle. The stereotype is the model of the role; the role is a model form of behaviour. The repetition of an attitude creates a role; the repetition of a role creates a stereotype. The stereotype is an objective form into which it is the role's task to induct people. Skill in playing and handling roles determines rank in the spectacular hierarchy. The disintegration of the spectacle multiplies stereotypes and roles, which by the same token become risible, and converge perilously upon their own negation, namely spontaneous action [1, 2]. Access to roles is ensured by identification. The need to identify is more important to Power's stability than the models identified with. Identification is a pathological state, but only bungled identifications are officially classed as mental illness. The function of roles is to suck the blood of the will to live [3]. They represent lived experience but reify it, offering consolation for this impoverishment of life by supplying a surrogate, neurotic gratification. We must break free of roles by restoring them to the realm of play [4]. A role successfully adopted guarantees promotion in the spectacular hierarchy, the rise from a given rank to a higher one. This is the process of initiation, as manifested notably in the cult of names and the use of photography. Specialists are those initiates who supervise initiation. Their cumulated inconsistencies constitute the consistency of Power, at once destructive and self-destructive [5]. The crumbling of the spectacle makes roles interchangeable. The proliferation of spurious variations creates the preconditions for a unique and real change, a truly radical change. The weight of inauthenticity eventually elicits a violent and quasi-biological reaction from the will to live [6].

1

Our efforts, our troubles, our failures, the absurdity of our actions—all stem largely from the imperious necessity in our present situation of playing hybrid parts, parts which appear to answer our desires but which are really antagonistic to them. 'We would live,' says Pascal, 'according to the ideas of others; we would live an imaginary life, and to this end we cultivate appearances. By striving to beautify and preserve this imaginary being we neglect our real being.' This was an original thought in the seventeenth century: at a time when the system of appearances was still hale, its coming crisis was apprehended only in the intuitive flashes of the most lucid. Today, amid the disintegration of all values, Pascal's observation is a banality, obvious to all. By what magic do we attribute the vivacity of human passions to lifeless forms? Why do we succumb to the seduction of borrowed attitudes? What are roles?

Is what drives people to seek power not the very weakness to which Power reduces them? The tyrant is irked by the duties the very subjection of his people imposes on him. The price he pays for the divine consecration of his authority over human beings is perpetual mythic sacrifice, a permanent humiliation before God. The moment he quits God's service, he no longer 'serves' his people—and his people are immediately released from their obligation to serve him. What vox populi, vox dei really means is: 'What God wants, the people want.' Slaves are not willing slaves for long if they are not compensated for their submission with a shred of authority: all subjection entails the right to a measure of power, and there is no power without submission. This is why some agree so readily to be governed. Wherever it is exercised, on every rung of the ladder, power is partial, not absolute. It is ubiquitous, thus ever open to challenge.

The role is a consumption of power. It locates one in the representational hierarchy, and hence in the spectacle: at the top, at the bottom, in the middle—but never outside the hierarchy, whether short of it or beyond it. It falls to roles to integrate individuals into the mechanisms of culture; this is a form of initiation. It is also the medium of exchange of individual sacrifice, and in this capacity performs a compensatory function. And lastly, as a precipitate of separation, roles strive to construct a behavioural unity; in this endeavour they rely on identification.

2

The original, restricted meaning of the expression 'to play a role in society' clearly indicates that roles were at first a distinction reserved for a chosen few. Roman slaves, mediaeval serfs, agricultural day-labourers or oletarians brutalized by a thirteen-hour day do not have roles—or such rudimentary roles that refined people treat them as animals rather than human beings. There is of course such a thing as a poverty from which it is impossible to rise to the level of the spectacle's poverty. By the nineteenth century the distinction between good worker and bad worker had begun to gain ground as a popular notion, just as the master-slave idea had spread, under the mythic system, with the coming of Christ. True, the currency of this new idea was achieved with less effort, and it never acquired the importance of the master-slave scheme (although Marx deemed it worthy of his derision). Like mythic sacrifice, roles have been democratized. Inauthenticity for everyone: the triumph of socialism.

Consider a thirty-five-year-old man. Each morning he starts his car, drives to the office, pushes papers, has lunch in town, plays poker, pushes more papers, leaves work, has a couple of drinks, goes home, greets his wife, kisses his children, eats a steak in front of the TV, goes to bed, makes love and falls asleep. Who reduces a man's life to this pathetic sequence of clichés? A journalist? A cop? A market researcher? A populist author? Not at all. He does it himself, breaking his day down into a series of poses chosen more or less unconsciously from the range of prevalent stereotypes. Taken over body and consciousness by the blandishments of a succession of images, he turns away from authentic pleasure and makes an emotionally arid asceticism the basis of a satisfaction so attenuated yet so ostentatious that it can only be a façade. The assumption of one role after another, provided he mimics stereotypes successfully, is titillating to him. The satisfaction of a well-played role is fuelled by his eagerness to remain at a distance from himself, to deny and sacrifice himself.

What omnipotence masochism can boast! Just as others were Count of Sandomir, Palatine of Smirnoff, Margrave of Thorn, Duke of Courlande, our Everyman can bestow a quite personal majesty upon his gestures as motorist, employee, superior, subordinate, colleague, customer, seducer, friend, philatelist, husband, paterfamilias, television viewer, or citizen. And yet such a man is not just the idiot machine, the lethargic stooge that all this suggests. For brief moments his everyday life generates an energy which, of only it were not co-opted, dispersed and squandered in roles, would suffice to overthrow the universe of survival. Who can gauge the striking-power of an impassioned daydream, of pleasure taken in love, of a nascent desire, of a rush of sympathy? Everyone seeks spontaneously to prolong such brief instants of genuine life; at bottom, everyone wants to extend them to the whole of their everyday experience. But conditioning succeeds in making most of us pursue these moments in exactly the wrong way—by way of the inhuman—and lose them forever the very instant we reach them.

//////

Stereotypes have a life and death of their own. An image whose allure makes it a model for thousands of individual roles will eventually crumble and disappear in accordance with the laws of consumption, the laws of novelty and obsolescence. So how does spectacular society develop new stereotypes? It does so thanks to injections of real creativity that prevent some roles from conforming to aging stereotypes (rather as language gets a new lease on life by assimilating popular forms). Thanks, in other words, to that element of play which transforms roles.

To the extent that it conforms to a stereotype, a role tends to congeal, to take on the static nature of its model. Such a role has neither present, nor past, nor future, because its time is that of the *pose*, and is, so to speak, a pause in time: time compressed into the dissociated space-time which is the space-time of Power (once again according to the principle that Power's strength resides in its ability to effect both real separation and false union). The role might well be compared to the cinematic image, or rather to a feature of cinema, namely one of the predetermined attitudes which, repeated over and over in quick succession, and with minimal variation, make up a sequence. In the case of roles, reproduction is ensured by the rhythms of the advertising and news media, whose capacity to stimulate word of mouth is prerequisite to a role's promotion to the status of a stereotype (Brigitte Bardot, Françoise Sagan, Bernard Buffet, James Dean, etc.). But no matter how much or how little weight roles attain on the scales of the conventional wisdom, their main purpose is always adaptation to social norms—the integration of people into the well-policed universe of things. Which is why the hidden cameras of celebrity are always ready to catapult the most pedestrian of lives into the spotlight of instant fame. Broken hearts fill columns and stray hairs become an aesthetic issue. By disguising a jilted lover as a discount Tristan, marketing a tattered derelict as a piece of nostalgia, or turning a drudging housewife into a good fairy of the kitchen, the spectacle, battening on everyday life, has long been way ahead of Pop Art. It was to be expected that people would model themselves on collages (always profitable) of smiling spouses, crippled children or do-it-yourself geniuses. The fact remains that by stooping to such ploys the spectacle is manifestly approaching a critical stage—the last stage before the eruption of everyday reality itself. Roles have drawn perilously close to their own negation: already failures are hard put to it to play their role properly, while the maladjusted shun theirs altogether. As the spectacular system falls apart, it scrapes the barrel: trawling the most deprived areas of society, it is reduced to feeding on its own refuse. Thus tone-deaf singers, talent-free artists, reluctant laureates and pallid stars of all kinds periodically cross the firmament of the media, their rank in the hierarchy reflected in the frequency with which they achieve this feat.

Which leaves the hopeless cases—those who reject all roles and those who theorize and practise that rejection. It is undoubtedly from such maladjustment to spectacular society that a new poetry of real experience and a reinvention of life will spring. The deflation of roles precipitates the decompression of spectacular time in favour of lived space-time. What is living intensely if not the redirection of the current of time, so long lost in appearances? Are not the happiest moments of our lives glimpses of an expanded present that rejects Power's accelerated time, which flows away year after empty year for as long as it takes to grow old?

3. *Identification*

The principle of Szondi's test is well known. The patient is asked to choose, from forty-eight photographs of people in various types of paroxysmal crisis, those facial expressions which evoke sympathy in him and those which evoke aversion. Subjects invariably prefer expressions suggesting instinctual feelings which they accept in themselves, while rejecting those suggesting feelings that they repress. They define themselves, in other words, by means of positive and negative identifications. The results enable the psychiatrist to draw up an instinctual profile of a patient which can help determine whether they should be discharged or sent to the air-conditioned crematorium known as a mental hospital.

Consider now the needs of consumer society, where the essence of the human being is to consume—to consume Coca-Cola, literature, ideas, emotions, architecture, TV, power, etc. Consumer goods, ideologies, stereotypes—all resemble photos in a gigantic version of Szondi's test in which each of us is supposed to take part, not only by making a choice, but also by making a commitment, and by engaging in practical activity. This society's need to market objects, ideas and model forms of behaviour calls for a decoding centre where an instinctual profile of the consumer can be developed to help in product design and improvement, and in the creation of new needs better suited to the consumer goods on offer. Market research, motivation techniques, opinion polls, sociological surveys and structuralism all contribute to this project, no matter how anarchic or feeble their efforts may be as yet. If we give them free rein, our cyberneticians can be counted on to remedy the lack of coordination and rationalization.

At first glance the main thing would seem to be the choice of the 'consumable image'. The housewife-who-uses-Fairy-Snow is different (and the difference is measured in profits) to the housewife-who-uses-Tide. The Labour voter differs from the Conservative voter, and the Communist from the Christian Democrat, in much the same way. But such differences are increasingly hard to discern. The spectacle of incoherence ends up putting a value on the zero point of values. Eventually identification with anything at all, like the need to consume anything at all, becomes more important than brand loyalty to a particular type of car, idol, or politician. The essential thing, surely, is to alienate people from their desires and pen them in the spectacle, in the policed zone. Good or bad, honest or criminal, left-wing or right-wing—what does the *mould* matter, so long as we are engulfed by it? Let those who cannot identify with Khrushchev identify with Yevtushenko—and the hooligans will be kept well under control. And indeed it is only the third force that has nothing to identify with—no opposition leader, no pseudo-revolutionary leader. The third force is the force of *identity*—in the sense of the identity in which each individual can recognize and discover him- or herself. A sphere where nobody decides for me, or in my name; where my freedom is the freedom of all.

//////

There is no such thing as mental illness. It is merely a convenient label for grouping and banishing cases where identification has not worked properly. Those whom Power can neither govern nor kill, it taxes with madness. The category includes extremists and megalomaniacs of the role, as well as those who deride roles or refuse them. It is the isolation of such individuals that singles them out. Let a general identify with France, with the support of millions of voters, and an opposition immediately springs up which takes his pretensions seriously enough to contest them.

Was not Hanns Hörbiger promoting a 'Nazi physics' hailed far and wide? As were General Edwin Walker and Barry Goldwater for contrasting superior, white, divine and capitalist man on the one hand to black, diabolical, Communist man on the other? And Franco for communing with God and begging him for guidance in tyrannizing Spain? And tyrants the world over for arguing from their ice-cold delusions that human beings are machines in need of regulation? Identification, not isolation, is what makes for madness.

The role is a self-caricature that we carry about with us everywhere, and which brings us everywhere face to face with an absence. An absence, though, which is structured, dressed up, prettified. The roles of paranoiac, schizophrenic, or sadistic killer do not carry the seal of social utility; in other words, they are not distributed under the label of Power, as are the roles of cop, boss, or army officer. But they are useful in specific places, notably in asylums and prisons, which are museums of a sort, serving the double purpose, from Power's point of view, of confining dangerous opponents while supplying the spectacle with negative stereotypes. Bad examples and their exemplary punishment add spice to the spectacle and protect it. If identification were somehow encouraged and isolation increased, the false distinction between mental and social alienation would quickly dissolve.

At the opposite extreme from absolute identification is a particular way of putting a distance between the role and one's self, of establishing a zone of free play, a breeding ground for attitudes disruptive of the spectacular order. Nobody is ever completely swallowed up by a role. Even turned upside-down, the will to live retains a potential for violence liable to divert individuals from the paths laid down for them. The faithful lackey who has always identified utterly with his master may slit his throat at an opportune moment. A time comes when his right to bite like a dog arouses his desire to strike back like a human being. Diderot has described this well in *Rameau's Nephew*—and the case of the Papin sisters is even more eloquent in this regard. The fact is that identification, like all manifestations of inhumanity, has its roots in the human. Inauthentic life feeds on authentically felt desires. And identification through roles is doubly successful in this respect. In the first place, it co-opts the play of metamorphoses, the pleasure of putting on masks and being everywhere in every guise. Secondly, it appropriates mankind's ancient love of mazes, of getting lost solely in order to find one's way again: the pleasure in simply wandering and changing. Roles also lay under contribution the reflexive search for identity—the desire to find the richest and truest part of ourselves in others. Play then ceases to be a game, and is reified because the players can no longer make up the rules. The quest for identity degenerates into identification.

Let us reverse the perspective for a moment. A psychiatrist tells us that 'Recognition by society leads the individual to discharge his sexual impulses in pursuit of cultural goals, and this is the best way for him to defend himself against those impulses'. Read: the aim of roles is to absorb vital forces, to exhaust erotic energy by means of permanent sublimation. The less erotic reality there is, the more abundant sexualized forms in the spectacle become. Roles—Reich would say 'armouring'—ensure orgastic impotence. Conversely, true pleasure, *joie de vivre* and orgastic potency shatter body armour and roles. If individuals could only stop seeing the world through the eyes of the powers-that-be, and look at it from their own point of view, they would have no trouble discerning which actions are really liberating, which moments are lived the most authentically—lightning flashes in the dark night of roles. Real experience can illuminate roles—can x-ray them, so to speak—in such a way as to redirect the energy invested in them, to extricate the truth from the lies. This task is at once individual and collective. Though all roles alienate equally, some are more vulnerable than others. It is easier to escape the role of a libertine than the role of a cop, executive, or priest. A fact to which everyone should give a little thought.

4. Compensation

How is it that people may come to place a higher value on roles than on their own life? The answer is that their lives have no value in the sense, the ambiguous sense, that life is beyond price, meaning that it cannot be given a price tag or offered for sale in any way; and that by the lights of the spectacle such riches can only be described as intolerable poverty. For consumer society poverty is whatever cannot be consumed. The reduction of people to consumers is thus an enrichment: the more things we have, the more roles we play, the more we *are*. So decrees the organization of appearances. But from the point of view of lived reality every increase in power so acquired is paid for by a corresponding sacrifice of the will to authentic self-fulfilment. What is gained on the level of appearances is lost on the levels of being and of what-ought-to-be.

Lived experience is always the raw material of the social contract, the coin in which the entry fee is paid. Life is sacrificed, and the loss compensated through the dazzling manipulation of appearances. The poorer everyday life becomes, the greater the appeal of inauthenticity; the greater the sway of illusion, the greater the impoverishment of everyday life. Ousted from its essential place by the bombardment of prohibitions, constraints and lies, lived reality seems so trivial that appearances get all our attention. We live our roles better than our own lives. Given the prevailing *state of things*, compensation alone confers weight. The role compensates for a lack: the inadequacy of life—or the inadequacy of another role. A worker covers up his prostration by assuming the role of Secret Agent OSS 117, and the poverty of that role itself beneath the incomparably superior image of a Peugeot 403 owner. But all roles are paid for by injury (overwork, the forgoing of life's comforts, survival, etc.). The role serves as an unreliable stopgap after the expulsion of the self and of real life. Its brutal removal exposes a gaping wound. It is at once a threat and a protective shield. Its threatening aspect is felt only negatively, however, and does not exist officially. Officially, the only danger lies in the loss or devaluation of the role: in loss of honour, loss of dignity, or (happy phrase!) loss of *face*. This ambiguity accounts to my mind for people's addiction to roles. It explains why roles stick to our skin, why we wager our lives on them: they impoverish lived experience but they also protect it against any awareness of that intolerable impoverishment. An isolated individual may well fail to withstand such a brutal revelation. Roles contribute to organized isolation, to separation and false union; compensation, like alcohol, is the drug that ensures the realization of all the potential of inauthentic being. Identification can be highly intoxicating.

Survival and its protective illusions form an inseparable whole. Roles perish, of course, when survival comes to an end (even if the *names* of the dead may sometimes be linked to stereotypes). To survive without roles is to be officially dead. Just as we are condemned to survival, so we are condemned to 'cutting a fine figure' in the realm of the inauthentic. Armouring inhibits freedom of gesture but simultaneously deadens blows. Beneath this carapace we are completely vulnerable. We still have one recourse, however: we can always play 'let's pretend'—and be cunning with roles.

Rozanov's approach is not a bad one: 'Externally, I decline. Subjectively, I am quite indeclinable. I don't agree. I am a kind of adverb.'

In the end, of course, it is the world that should be modelled on subjectivity, the world that should concur with me so that I can then concur with it. But, right now, throwing out all roles like a bag of old clothes would amount to denying the fact of separation and plunging into mysticism or solipsism. I am in enemy territory, and the enemy is within me. I do not want that enemy to kill me, which is why I let the armour of roles protect me. I work, I consume, I know how to be polite, and never make a scandal. All the same, this world of pretence has to be destroyed, which is why intelligent people let roles play among themselves. Seeming to have no responsibility is the best way of behaving responsibly towards oneself. All jobs are dirty—so do them dirtily! All roles are lies, so let them contradict one another! I love the arrogance of Jacques Vaché when he writes: 'I wander from ruins to village with my crystal monocle and an unsettling theory of painting. Turn by turn I have been a lionized author, a famous drawer of pornography and a scandalous Cubist painter. Now I am going to stay at home and let others explain and debate my character in the light of the above particulars.'

I feel it suffices to be absolutely honest with those who are on my side, those who genuinely defend authentic life. The more detached one is from a role, the easier it is to turn it against an adversary. The more effectively one avoids the weight of things, the easier it is to achieve lightness of movement. Real friends care little for forms. They argue openly, confident in the knowledge that they can inflict no wounds. Where communication is genuinely sought, misunderstandings are no crime. But if you accost me armed to the teeth, understanding agreement only in terms of a victory for you, then you will get nothing out of me but an evasive pose, and an eloquent silence signalling that discussion is ended. Duels between roles deprive dialogue of any interest from the outset. Only the enemy would want to enter the lists of the spectacle and joust on the ground of roles. It is hard enough keeping one's own demons at bay without so-called friendships adding fuel to the fire. If only biting and barking could wake people up to the dog's life roles force them into—wake them up to the importance of their own selves!

As luck would have it, the spectacle of incoherence is obliged to introduce an element of play into the world of roles. By preaching that 'black is white and white is black', it dispels all seriousness. Such a facetious attitude to roles plunges them into a sea of sameness. Hence the distinctly unhappy efforts of our reorganizers of appearances to boost the

play element by means of television game shows and the like, to press
a carefree attitude into the service of consumption. Distantiation from
roles is only reinforced by the crumbling of appearances. Some roles,
being dubious or ambiguous, embody their own self-criticism. Nothing,
in the long run, can prevent the spectacle from being repurposed as a
collective game, and everyday life, seizing whatever means are to hand,
will inevitably lay the groundwork for that game's endless expansion.

5. *Initiation*

As it seeks to safeguard the poverty of survival while loudly protesting
against it, the compensatory tendency bestows upon each individual a
certain number of formal possibilities of participating in the spectacle—
a sort of permit for the scenic representation of one or more slices of
life—private or public, no matter. Just as God used to bestow grace on all
human beings, leaving each free to choose salvation or damnation, so
modern social organization grants everyone the right to gain entrance—
or fail to do so—into the social world. But whereas God alienated human
subjectivity in one fell swoop, the bourgeoisie breaks it down into a host
of partial alienations. In a sense, then, subjectivity, which was nothing,
becomes something: it attains its own truth, its mystery, its passions, its
rationality, its rights. This official recognition requires its subdivision
into components graded and pigeonholed according to Power's norms.
The subjective is integrated into the objective forms known as stereotypes
by means of identification. It makes its entry in pieces, in would-be-
absolute fragments, and ridiculously denuded (think of the Romantics'
grotesque view of the self—and its antidote, humour).

I possess badges of power, therefore I am. In order to be someone
the individual must, so to speak, pay things their due. He must keep his
roles in order, polish them up, put them back on the stocks repeatedly,
initiating himself little by little until he qualifies for promotion in the
spectacle. The conveyor belts called schools, the advertising industry, the
conditioning mechanisms essential to any Order—all conspire to lead
the child, the adolescent and the adult as painlessly as possible into the
great family of consumers.

There are stages of initiation. Established social groups do not all
enjoy the same measure of power, nor is that measure equally distributed within each group. From president to party workers, from star to
fans, or from representative to voters, the ladder of promotion is long.

Some groups are rigidly structured, while others are very loose, but all are founded on the illusion of participation shared by group members whatever their standing. The illusion is fostered through meetings, insignia, the assignment of minor tasks and responsibilities, etc. The resulting cohesiveness is spurious—and often friable. Yet this appalling boy-scout mentality generates its own stereotypes at each level: each field has its own martyrs, heroes, models, geniuses, thinkers, faithful servants, great successes and so on. For example: Danielle Casanova, Cienfuegos, Brigitte Bardot, Mathieu, Kostas Axelos, a veteran *boules* champion, President Wilson, and so on. (Readers are invited to assign these figures to their proper categories.)

Can the collectivization of roles successfully replace the lapsed power of the grand ideologies of an earlier time? Let us remember that Power stands or falls with its organization of appearances. The fission of myth into particles of ideology has produced roles as fallout. The poverty of Power now has no other means of self-concealment than its shattered lie. The prestige of a film star, a head of household, or a chief executive is no longer worth a Bronx cheer. Nothing can obviate the effects of this nihilistic process of disintegration except its supersession. The triumph of technocracy, by blocking such a supersession, dooms people to meaningless activity, rites of initiation into nothing, pure sacrifice, the assumption of vacuous roles, and systematic specialization.

The specialist indeed prefigures the ghostly being, cog, or mechanical *thing* embedded in the rationality of a perfected social order of zombies. Specialists are everywhere—among politicians, among hijackers. Specialization is in a sense the science of roles, the science of endowing appearances with the *éclat* formerly bestowed by nobility, wit, extravagance, or a large bank account. The specialist does more than this, however, by assuming the role of role-assigner. He is the vital link between the techniques of production and consumption and the technique of spectacular representation. Yet he is, so to speak, an isolated link—a monad. Knowing everything about a fragment, he enlists others to produce and consume within the confines of this area so that he himself may receive a surplus-value of power and enlarge the footprint of his hierarchical image. He knows, if need be, how to give up a multitude of roles for one only, how to concentrate his power instead of spreading it around, how to make his life unilinear. In so doing he becomes a manager. His misfortune is that the sphere he controls is always too restricted, too partial. He is in the position of a gastroenterologist who cures a gut but destroys the rest of the body in the process. Certainly, the comparative significance of the group he lords it over may allow him the illusion of power, but the anarchy is such, the partial interests so contradictory and contentious, that he is bound to realize eventually how powerless he really is. Rather like heads of state with the power to unleash thermonuclear war who succeed only in paralysing one other, so specialists, working at cross-purposes, end up building and operating a gigantic machine—Power, social organization—which dominates them all and crushes them with varying degrees of consideration, gently or not so gently, according to their place in the apparatus. They build and operate the machine blindly, because it is simply an aggregate of their crossed purposes. It is to be expected, therefore, that most specialists, when they suddenly become aware of their own disastrous passivity, and consider how hard and long they have fought in its name, will be all the more eager to embrace an authentic will to live. It is likely too that others, those who have been longer or more intensely exposed to the radiation of authoritarian passivity, will be obliged to follow the example of the officer in Kafka's 'In the Penal Colony' and perish along with the machine, tormented to the end by its last spasms. Every day the crossed purposes of those with power, the specialists, make and unmake the tottering majesty of Power. We have seen with what results. Let us now try to imagine the glacial nightmare into which we would be plunged were the cyberneticians able so effectively to pool their efforts as to achieve a rational organization of society, eliminating or at least controlling the effects of crossed purposes. They would have no rivals for the Nobel Prize, save perhaps the proponents of thermonuclear suicide.

//////

The commonest use of name and photograph, as in what are oddly referred to as 'identification' papers, is rather obviously tied to the police function in modern societies. But the connection is not merely with the vulgar police work of search and seizure, surveillance, harassment, the third degree, or methodical killing. It also involves much more occult forces of law and order. The frequency with which an individual's name or image passes through the printed and audio channels of communication is an index of that individual's rank and category. It goes without saying that the name most often uttered in a neighbourhood, town, country, or in the world has a powerful fascination. Charted statistically for any given time and place, this information would supply a perfect relief map of Power.

Historically, however, the deterioration of roles goes hand in hand with the increasing meaninglessness of names. The aristocrat's name crystallizes the mystery of birth and pedigree. In consumer society the spectacular exposure of the name of a Bernard Buffet can serve to transform a very ordinary talent into a famous painter. The manipulation of names fabricates leaders in exactly the same manner as it sells hair tonic. But this also means that a famous name is no longer the attribute of the one who bears it. The label 'Buffet' does not designate anything (to paraphrase Napoleon) but a *thing* in a silk stocking. A fragment of power.

The humanists make me laugh when I hear them whining about the reduction of people to numbers, to ciphers. As if the destruction of people complete with tricked-up names were somehow less inhuman than their destruction as a string of figures. I have already said that the confused conflict between so-called progressives and reactionaries comes down to the issue of whether people should be broken by the carrot or the stick. As for the carrot of a famous name, thank you for nothing!

But so many *things* get names these days that *beings* get fewer and fewer of them. To reverse the perspective, though, I like reminding myself that no name can ever exhaust or subsume what I am. My pleasure is nameless: those all too rare moments when I create myself afford no purchase to external manipulation. Only by virtue of self-dispossession do I risk petrification amid the names of the things that oppress us. This is the sense too in which I would wish Albert Libertad's burning of his identification papers to be understood. His act—echoed much later by the black workers of Johannesburg—was more than just a rejection of police control: he was also giving up one name so as to have the pick of a thousand. Such is the admirable dialectic of the change in perspective: since prevailing conditions forbid me to bear a name which is—as it was for the feudal lord—a true emanation of my own strength, I refuse to be called by any name, and suddenly, beneath the unnameable, I discover the wealth of lived experience, inexpressible poetry, the preconditions of supersession. I enter the nameless forest where Lewis Carroll's Gnat explains to Alice: 'If the governess wanted to call you for your lessons, she would call out "Come here—", and there she would have to leave off, because there wouldn't be any name for her to call, and of course you wouldn't have to go, you know.' How blissful is the forest of radical subjectivity!

To my mind, Giorgio de Chirico, displaying a fine consistency, found
his own pathway to Alice's forest. What holds for names holds too for
the representation of the face. The photograph is the expression *par excellence* of the role, of the pose. It imprisons the soul and offers it up for
interpretation—which is why a photograph is always sad. We examine
it as we examine an object. Is it not obvious that to identify oneself with
a range of facial expressions, no matter how varied a range, is to make
oneself into an object? The God of the mystics at least had the good sense
to avoid this trap. But let me come back to Chirico—a near contemporary
of Libertad's. (Were it a human being, Power would have every reason
to congratulate itself on the host of rich encounters it has managed to
prevent.) The blank faces of Chirico's figures are a perfect charge-sheet
against inhumanity. His deserted squares and lithified décor are the backdrop to personages dehumanized by the things they have made—things
which, frozen in an urban space that distils the oppressiveness of ideologies, rob them of their substance and suck their blood. (I forget who
described a painting as a vampiric landscape—André Breton perhaps.)
More than this, the very absence of facial features seems to conjure up
new faces, to materialize a presence capable of investing the very stones
with humanity. For me this ghostly presence is that of collective creation:
because they have no one's face, Chirico's figures have *everyone's* face.

In striking contrast to the fundamental tendency of modern culture,
which goes to great lengths to express its own nothingness and concocts
a semiology from its nullity, Chirico gives us paintings where absence
opens the door wide to what lies beyond it, namely the poetry of reality
and the realization of art, of philosophy, of mankind. As the sign of a
reified world, the blank space is incorporated into the canvas at the
crucial spot, and implies that the countenance is no longer part of the
representational universe, but is about to become part of everyday praxis.

Some day the peerless richness of the decade between 1910 and 1920
will become apparent. The immense genius and chaos of those years
sought for the first time to bridge the gulf between art and life. I think we
may safely say that, the Surrealist adventure aside, nothing was achieved
in the period between the demise of this vanguard of supersession and
the inception of the current Situationist project. The disenchantment of
an older generation, which has been marking time for the last forty years
with respect to art and revolution alike, merely reinforces this view. The
Dadaist movement, Malevich's *White on White*, Joyce's *Ulysses*, Chirico's

canvasses—all of them ushered the presence of the whole human being into the void of human beings reduced to the status of things. Today the whole human being is simply the project on which the majority of human beings are working for the sake of a forbidden creativity.

6

In the unitary world, under the serene gaze of the gods, adventure and pilgrimage were paradigms of change in an unchanging universe. Inasmuch as this world was given for all time there was really nothing to be discovered, but revelation awaited the pilgrim or knight-errant at the crossroads. The truth was that revelation lay within each individual: one would travel the world seeking it in oneself, seeking it in far lands, until suddenly it would surge forth, a magical spring released by the purity of a gesture at the very place where an ill-starred seeker would have found nothing. The *spring* and the *castle* dominate the creative imagination of the Middle Ages. The symbolism here is plain: beneath movement lies immutability, and beneath immutability, movement.

The greatness of a Heliogabalus, a Tamerlane, a Gilles de Rais, a Tristan, or a Perceval lies in this: defeated, they withdraw into a living God; they identify with the demiurge, relinquishing their unfulfilled humanity in order to reign and die under the mask of Christ's divine terror. This death of human beings in an unchanging God allowed life to bloom beneath the shadow of its scythe. Our dead God weighs more heavily than that living God of old; the fact is that the bourgeoisie did not really rid us of God, but managed only to air-condition his corpse. Romanticism was the stench of that putrefying God, a disgusted wrinkling of the nostrils at the conditions of survival.

The bourgeoisie is a class, rent by contradictions, that founds its dominion on world-transformation yet refuses to transform itself. It is thus movement wishing to avoid movement. In unitary societies the image of changelessness subsumed movement; in fragmented societies change strives to reproduce the absence of change: wars (or the poor, or slaves), it claims, will always be with us. The bourgeoisie in power can tolerate change only if it is empty, abstract, cut off from the totality: partial change, or changes of parts. Now although the habit of change is intrinsically subversive, it is also the main prerequisite to the functioning of consumer society. People have to change cars, fashions, ideas, etc., all the time. If they did not, a more radical change would occur, putting an end to a form of authority which has no other choice, if it is to endure, than to put itself up for sale—to consume itself and consume each of us to boot. Sad to say, in this headlong rush towards death, this desperate and would-be endless race there is no real future: ahead lies only the past, hastily reoutfitted and thrust ahead into the future. For almost a quarter of a century now, the self-same 'novelties' have been turning up in the marketplace of fad and fancy with but the barest attempt to conceal their decrepitude. The same goes for the marketing of roles. How could a range of roles be offered that was varied enough to compensate for the loss of the qualitative force of the role as conceived in feudal times? The task is hopeless for two reasons. In the first place, the quantitative character of roles is a limitation by definition, and calls inevitably for a conversion into quality; secondly, the poverty of the spectacle gives the lie to all claims of renewal. Serial role-changing uses up costumes. And the proliferation of trivial changes titillates the desire for real change but can never satisfy it. By precipitating changes of illusion, Power inevitably exposes itself to the reality of radical change.

It is not just that the multiplication of roles tends to make them indistinguishable: it also fragments them and makes them ludicrous. The quantification of subjectivity has created spectacular categories for the most prosaic acts and the most ordinary attributes: a certain smile, a chest measurement, a hairstyle. Great roles are scarcer and scarcer; walk-ons are two a penny. Even the Ubus—the Stalins or Hitlers or Mussolinis—have but the palest of progeny. Most people are well acquainted with the malaise that accompanies any attempt to join a group and make contact with others. This feeling amounts to stage fright, the fear of not playing one's part properly. Only with the crumbling of officially controllable attitudes and poses will the true source of this anxiety become clear to us. For it arises not from our clumsiness in handling roles but from the loss of self in the spectacle, in the reigning order of things. In his book *Médecine et homme total*, Doctor Pierre Solié has this to say about the alarming spread of neurotic disorders: 'There is no such thing as disease *per se*, no such thing, even, as a sick person *per se*; there is only authentic or inauthentic being-in-the-world.' The rechanneling of the energy siphoned off by appearances back towards the will to live authentically is a function of the dialectic of appearances itself. The refusal of inauthenticity triggers a near-biological defensive reaction which because of its violence has every prospect of destroying those who have been orchestrating spectacular alienation for so long. This fact should give pause to all who pride themselves on being idols, artists, sociologists, thinkers, or specialists of every kind of stage-management. Explosions of popular anger are never accidental in the sense that the eruption of Krakatoa is accidental.

//////

According to a Chinese philosopher, 'Confluence is the approach to the void. In total confluence presence stirs'. Alienation extends to all human activities and separates them to the maximum. But in the process it is itself divided and becomes everywhere more vulnerable. In the disintegration of the spectacle we may discern what Marx called 'the new life which becomes conscious of itself, destroys what is already destroyed, and rejects what is already rejected'. Beneath dissociation lies unity; beneath fatigue, concentrated energy; beneath the fragmentation of the self, radical subjectivity. In short, the qualitative. But wanting to remake the world as you might make love to your sweetheart does not suffice.

As the factors responsible for the desiccation of everyday life become exhausted, the life forces tend to get the upper hand over the power of roles. This is the beginning of the reversal of perspective. The new revolutionary theory should concentrate its efforts here so as to open the breach that will lead to supersession. The era of calculation and the era of suspicion, as ushered in by capitalism and Stalinism respectively, are already being challenged by a clandestine tactical phase of the construction of an *era of play*.

The degenerate state of the spectacle, individual experience, and collective acts of refusal need to combine and generate practical tactics for dealing with roles. Collectively, it is quite possible to abolish roles. The spontaneous creativity and festive atmosphere unleashed in revolutionary moments afford ample evidence of this. Once the spirit of the people is filled with joy, no leader, no *mise-en-scène* can recapture it. Only by starving the revolutionary masses of joy can they be subdued and their advance and the extension of their gains brought to a halt. Even now it is possible for a group dedicated to theoretical and practical actions, such as the Situationists, to infiltrate the political and cultural spectacle as a subversive force.

Individually, however—and thus in a strictly temporary way—we must learn how to sustain roles without nourishing them to the point where they harm us. How to use them as a protective shield while at the same time protecting ourselves against them. How to retrieve the energy they absorb and actualize the illusory power they dispense. How to play the game of a Jacques Vaché.

If your role imposes roles on others, assume a power that is not you, then set this phantom loose. Nobody wins contests for status, so eschew them. Down with pointless quarrels, vain discussions, forums, conferences and Weeks for Marxist Thought! When the time comes to strike for your real liberation, strike to kill. Words don't kill.

Do people come up and want to *discuss* things with you? Do they admire you? Spit in their faces. Do they make fun of you? Help them recognize themselves in their mockery. Roles are inherently ridiculous. Do you see nothing but roles around you? Treat them to your nonchalance, your humour, your distance. Play cat and mouse with them, and there is a good chance that one or two people about you will wake up to themselves and discover the prerequisites for real dialogue. Remember: all roles alienate equally, but some are less despicable than others. The range of stereotyped behaviour includes alienating forms that only barely conceal lived experience and its requirements. To my mind, temporary alliances are permissible with certain attitudes, with certain revolutionary images, just so long as a glimmer of radicalism shines through the ideological screen which they presuppose. A good example is the cult of Lumumba among young Congolese revolutionaries. In any case, so long as one bears in mind that the only proper treatment for others, as for oneself, is a higher dose of radicalism, it is impossible to go wrong or come to grief.

XVI The Fascination of Time

By virtue of a monstrous *bewitchment*, people believe that time slips away, and this belief is the basis of time actually slipping away. Time is the work of attrition of that adaptation to which human beings must resign themselves so long as they fail to change the world. Age is a role, an acceleration of 'lived' time on the plane of appearances, an attachment to *things*.

The worsening of civilization's discontents is pushing therapeutic measures towards a new demonology. At one time invocation, sorcery, possession, exorcism, black sabbaths, metamorphoses and talismans enjoyed the ambiguous power to heal and hurt; now, similarly (and more effectively), the consolations of the oppressed—medicine, ideology, compensatory roles, modern conveniences and world-transforming technology—all serve to buttress oppression itself. That the *order of things* is sick is what our leaders would conceal at all costs. In a fine passage in *The Function of the Orgasm*, Wilhelm Reich relates how after long months of psychoanalytic treatment he managed to cure a young Viennese working woman. She was suffering from depression brought on by the conditions of her life and work. Once she was well Reich sent her back home. A fortnight later she killed herself. Reich's intransigent honesty, as we know, would doom him to exclusion from the psychoanalytic establishment, to isolation, delusion, and death in prison: the duplicity of our demonologists cannot be exposed with impunity.

Those who organize the world organize both suffering and the painkillers for dealing with it; this much is common knowledge. Most people live like sleepwalkers, torn between the wish to awake and the fear of doing so, trapped between their neurotic state and the traumatic prospect of a return to real life. Things are now reaching the point, however, where maintaining survival calls for doses of anaesthetics so high that the organism is saturated and what magic-workers call a backlash occurs. The imminence of such an upheaval and its nature are what make it possible to speak of the present conditioning of human beings as a monstrous bewitchment.

Bewitching of this kind presupposes a spatial network linking up the most distant objects sympathetically, according to specific laws: formal analogy, organic coexistence, functional symmetry, symbolic affiliation, and so on. Such correspondences are established through the endlessly repeated association of given forms of behaviour with related signals. This constitutes a generalized system of conditioning. The current vogue for loudly condemning the role of conditioning, propaganda, advertising and the mass media in modern society must surely be understood as a sort of partial exorcism designed to maintain and to deflect suspicion from a vaster and more essential bewitchment. Outrage at the tabloid *France-Soir* goes hand in hand with subservience to the more elegant lies of *Le Monde*. Media, language, time—such are the giant claws with which Power manipulates humanity and forces it into its perspective. These claws are not very adept, admittedly, but their effectiveness is enormously increased by the fact that people are unaware that they can resist them, and often do not even know the extent to which they are already spontaneously doing so.

Stalin's show trials proved that it only takes a little patience and perseverance to get a man to accuse himself of every imaginable crime and appear in public begging to be executed. Now that we are aware of such techniques, and on our guard against them, how can we fail to see that the set of mechanisms controlling us uses the very same insidious persuasiveness—though with more powerful means at its disposal, and with greater persistence—when it lays down the law: 'You are weak, you must grow old, you must die.' Consciousness acquiesces, and the body follows suit. I like to take a remark of Artaud's in a materialist sense: 'We do not die because we have to die,' he says. 'We die because one day, and not so long ago, our consciousness was forced to deem it necessary.'

In an unfavourable soil, plants die. Animals adapt to their environment. Human beings transform theirs. Thus death is not the same thing for plants, animals and humans. In favourable soil, the plant lives like an animal: it can adapt. Where humans fail to change their surroundings, they are likewise in the situation of an animal. Adaptation is the law of the animal world.

For Hans Selye, the theorist of stress, the general adaptation system has three stages: the alarm reaction, the stage of resistance and the stage of exhaustion. On the level of appearances, human beings have been able to fight for eternal life, but in terms of real life they have not surpassed animal adaptation: spontaneous reactions in childhood, consolidation in maturity, exhaustion in old age. And today, the harder people try to find salvation in appearances, the more emphatically does the spectacle's ephemeral and inconsistent nature remind them that they live like dogs and die like tufts of dry grass. Can the day really be far off when human beings face the fact that the social organization they have constructed to bend the world to their wishes no longer serves this purpose—that it is nothing more, in practice, than a system for blocking the deployment, in accordance with the requirements of a superior, yet to be created form of organization, of the techniques of liberation and individual self-fulfilment they have developed during the history of privative appropriation, of exploitation of man by man, of hierarchical authority?

We now live in a closed, suffocating system. Whatever we gain in one sphere we lose in another. Mortality, for instance, though quantitatively defeated by the progress of sanitation, has reemerged qualitatively in the form of survival. Adaptation has been democratized, made easier for everyone, but only by abandoning the essential—namely the adaptation of the world to human needs.

A struggle against death exists, of course, but it takes place *within* the adaptation system—thus making death part of the remedy for death. Significantly, therapeutic efforts concentrate on the exhaustion phase, as though the main aim were to extend the stage of resistance as far as possible, even into old age. Thus shock treatment is tried only once weakness and impotence have done their work, for, as Reich understood well, any all-out attack that really targeted the attrition wreaked by adaptation would imply a direct onslaught on social organization—which is what bars any supersession of the adaptation system. Partial cures are preferred because they leave the overall social pathology untouched. But what will happen when the proliferation of such partial cures ends up spreading the malaise of inauthenticity to every last corner of everyday life? And when the essential role of exorcism and bewitchment in the maintenance of a sick society becomes plain for all to see?

//////

The question 'How old are you?' is never asked without an immediate reference to power. Dates themselves serve to pigeonhole and constrain

us. Is not the passage of time always marked off from the establishment
of some authority or other—from the year of the instatement of a god,
messiah, leader or conquering city? To the aristocratic mind, moreover,
such accumulated time was a guarantor of authority: the prepotency
of the lord was increased both by his own age and by the length of his
lineage. At his death the noble bequeathed a vigour to his descendants
that was underpinned by the past. The bourgeoisie, for its part, has no
past—or at any rate recognizes none, for its fragmented power does not
depend on heredity. It retraces the steps of the nobility in a parodic
manner, seeking identification with forebears in nostalgic fashion by way
of photos in the family album; and its identification with cyclical time,
with the time of the eternal return, is nothing but a blind identification
with scraps, with a succession of rapid passages of linear time.

The link between age and the starting-post of measurable time is
not the only telling sign of age's kinship with power. I maintain that
people's measured age is nothing but a role, a speeding-up of lived time
in the mode of nonlife—on the plane, therefore, of appearances, and in
accordance with the dictates of adaptation. To acquire power is to acquire
age. In earlier times power was exercised only by the old, whether old in
nobility or old in experience. Today the young are granted the dubious
privilege of aging. Indeed consumer society fosters premature senility;
after all, it invented teenagers as a new target group for conversion into
consumers. To consume is to be consumed by inauthenticity, nurturing
appearances to the benefit of the spectacle and the detriment of real life.
Consumers die with the things they attach themselves to, because those
things—commodities, roles—are dead.

Whatever you possess possesses you in return. Everything that makes
you into an owner adapts you to the order of things—and makes you old.
Time-which-slips-away is what fills the void left by the absent self. The harder
you run after time, the faster time goes: this is the law of the consumable.
Try to stop it, and it will wear you out and age you all the more easily.
Time must be caught on the wing, in the present—but the present has
yet to be constructed.

We were born never to grow old, never to die. But all we can hope
for is the awareness of having come too soon—and a certain contempt for
the future that can already grant us a generous helping of life.

Survival and Its Pseudo-Negation

Survival is life reduced to economic imperatives. In the present period, therefore, survival is life reduced to what can be consumed (XVII). Reality addresses the problem of supersession before our so-called revolutionaries have even formulated it. Whatever is not superseded rots, and whatever is rotten cries out to be superseded. Unbuttressed refusal, oblivious to both these tendencies, speeds up the process of disintegration and becomes an integral part of it. It thus makes the task of supersession easier—but only in the sense in which we sometimes say of a murdered man that he made his murderer's task easier. Survival is nonsupersession become unlivable. The mere refusal of survival dooms us to impotence. It is imperative to retrieve the core of radical demands abandoned by initially revolutionary movements of the past (XVIII).

XVII Survival Sickness

> Capitalism has demystified survival. It has made the poverty of
> everyday life intolerable in view of the growing abundance of
> technical possibilities. Survival has become an economizing on
> life. The civilization of collective survival increases dead time in
> individual lives to the point where the forces of death threaten to
> overwhelm collective survival itself. Unless, that is, the passion for
> destruction is replaced by the passion for life.

Until now human beings have merely adapted to a *system* of world-transformation. The task now is to adapt that system to the transformation
of the world.

The organization of human societies has changed the world, and the
world in changing has brought upheaval to the organization of human
societies. But while hierarchical organization struggles to control nature,
and is itself transformed by that struggle, the share of freedom and creativity falling to the individual is drained away by the necessity of adapting to various kinds of social norms. This is true, at any rate, so long as
no generalized revolutionary moment occurs.

The time belonging to the individual in history is for the most part
dead time. Only a rather recent awakening of consciousness has made
this fact intolerable to us. For with its revolution the bourgeoisie does
two things. On the one hand, it proves that mankind *can* accelerate
world transformation, and that it *can* improve individual lives (where
improvement means accession to the ruling class, to wealth, to capitalist
success). But at the same time the bourgeois order nullifies the individual freedom by interference: it increases the dead time in everyday life
(imposing the need to produce, consume, calculate); and it capitulates
before the haphazard laws of the market, before the inevitable cyclical
crises with their burden of wars and impoverishment, and before the
strictures of common sense ('You can't change human nature', 'The
poor will always be with us', etc.). The politics of the bourgeoisie, as of

the bourgeoisie's socialist successors, resembles the action of a driver pumping the brake with the accelerator jammed fast to the floor: the more his speed increases, the more frenetic, perilous and useless become his attempts to slow down. The helter-skelter pace of consumption is set at once by the rate of the disintegration of Power and by the imminence of the construction of a new order, a new dimension, a parallel universe born of the collapse of the Old World.

The changeover from the aristocratic system of adaptation to the 'democratic' one brutally widened the gap between the individual's submissiveness and the social dynamism that transforms nature—the gap, in other words, between individual powerlessness and the power of new technology. The contemplative attitude was perfectly suited to the feudal myth, to a virtually motionless world circumscribed by its eternal Gods. But how could the spirit of submission possibly adjust to the energetic vision of merchants, manufacturers, bankers and discoverers of riches—men acquainted not with the revelation of the changeless, but rather with the ever-shifting economic world, its insatiable hunger for profit and its need for continual innovation. Yet wherever the bourgeoisie's action succeeded in popularizing and placing value on the temporary, the transient, and the sense of hope, it simultaneously sought, qua Power, to imprison real human beings within them. The bourgeoisie replaced the old theology of stasis with a metaphysics of motion. Although both these pictures of the world hinder the forward march of reality, the first does so more effectively and more harmoniously than the second, for it is more consistent, more unified. To press an ideology of change into the service of what does not change creates a paradox which nothing can now either conceal from consciousness or justify to consciousness. In our universe of expanding technology and modern conveniences we see people turning in upon themselves, shrivelling up, living trivial lives and dying for details. It is a nightmare where we are promised absolute freedom but granted a miserable square inch of individual autonomy—a square inch, moreover, that is strictly policed by our neighbours. A space-time of mean-spiritedness and low thoughts.

Under the *Ancien Régime*, the prospect of death in a living God lent everyday life an illusory dimension which achieved the fullness of a multifaceted reality. It is arguable that mankind has never come closer to fulfilment while still shackled to inauthenticity. But what is one to say of a life lived out in the shadow of a God that is dead—the decomposing

God of fragmented power? The bourgeoisie has dispensed with God by economizing on human lives. It has turned economics into a sacred imperative and life into an economic system. This is the model that our future programmers are preparing to rationalize, to submit to proper planning—in a word, to humanize. And, never fear, cybernetic programming will be no less irresponsible than the corpse of God.

Kierkegaard describes survival sickness well: 'Let others bemoan the maliciousness of their age. What irks me is its pettiness, for ours is an age without passion. . . . My life comes out all one colour.' Survival is life reduced to bare essentials, to life's abstract form, to the level of activity required for the individual's participation in production and consumption. The entitlement of a Roman slave was rest and sustenance. As beneficiaries of the Rights of Man we receive the wherewithal to nourish and cultivate ourselves, enough consciousness to play a role, enough initiative to acquire power, and enough passivity to flaunt its insignia. Our freedom is the freedom to adapt after the fashion of *higher animals.*

Survival is life in slow motion. (Just think of the energy needed to keep up appearances!) The media gives wide currency to a whole personal hygiene of survival: avoid strong emotions, watch your blood pressure, eat less, drink in moderation, survive in good health so that you can continue playing your role. 'OVERWORK: THE EXECUTIVE'S DISEASE', ran a recent headline in *Le Monde.* We must handle survival cautiously, for it wears us down; live it as little as possible, for it belongs to death. In former times one died a death quickened by the presence of God. Today our respect for life prohibits us from touching it, reviving it, or snapping it out of its lethargy. We die of inertia, whenever the quota of death that we carry within us reaches saturation point. What scientific institute could measure the intensity of the deadly radiation that kills our everyday actions? In the end, by dint of identifying ourselves with what we are not, of switching from one role to another, from one fragment of power to another, and from one age to another, how can we avoid ourselves becoming part of that endless transition which is the process of disintegration?

The presence within life itself of a mysterious yet tangible death so misled Freud that he postulated an ontological curse in the shape of a death instinct. First pointed out by Reich, this mistake of Freud's has now been glaringly exposed by the phenomenon of consumption. The three aspects of the death instinct—Nirvana, the repetition compulsion and masochism—turn out to be simply three tools for the exercise of Power: constraint passively accepted, the seduction of conformity, and mediation perceived as an ineluctable law.

As we know, the consumption of goods—which comes down always, in the present state of things, to the consumption of power—carries within itself the seeds of its own destruction, the conditions of its own supersession. The consumer cannot and must not ever attain satisfaction: the logic of the consumable object demands the creation of fresh, false needs, yet the accumulation of such needs aggravates the malaise of people strictly confined (albeit with increasing difficulty) to the sole status of consumers. What is more, wealth in consumer goods impoverishes authentic life, and this in two ways. First, it replaces authentic life with *things*. Secondly, it makes it impossible, with the best will in the world, to become attached to these things, precisely because they have to be *consumed*, which is to say destroyed. Whence an ever more oppressive absence of life, a self-devouring dissatisfaction. Which said, the need to live remains ambivalent, and this is a site where the perspective can be reversed.

In the consumer's manipulated view of things—the view produced by conditioning—the absence of life appears as a shortfall in the consumption of power and a failure to let oneself be consumed for the sake of power. As a palliative to the absence of real life we are offered death on the instalment plan. A world that condemns us to a bloodless death is naturally obliged to propagate the taste for blood. Where survival sickness reigns, the desire to live lays hold spontaneously of the weapons of death: senseless murder and sadism flourish. When the passion for life is destroyed, it is reborn as the passion for destruction. If these conditions persist, no one will survive the era of survival. Already the despair is so great that many people would concur with Antonin Artaud: 'I bear the stigma of an insistent death that strips real death of all terror for me.'

Human beings under the conditions of survival are creatures of Reich's pleasure anxiety, incomplete, mutilated. How could they find themselves in the endless self-loss into which everything draws them? They are wanderers in a labyrinth with no centre, a maze of mazes. They drag themselves through a world of equivalents. Does suicide beckon? Killing oneself, though, implies some feeling of resistance: one must be endowed with a value that can be destroyed. Where there is nothing, destructive acts themselves crumble to nothing. You cannot hurl a void into a void. 'If only a rock would fall and kill me,' wrote Kierkegaard, 'at least that would be a way out.' I doubt if there is anyone today who has not been touched by the horror of a thought of that kind. Inertia is the surest killer, the inertia of those who settle for senility at eighteen, plunging eight hours a day into degrading work and feeding upon ideologies. Beneath the miserable tinsel of the spectacle there are only gaunt figures yearning for, yet dreading Kierkegaard's 'way out', so that they might never again have to desire what they dread and dread what they desire.

At the same time, the passion for life emerges as a biological need, the reverse side of the passion for destroying and letting oneself be destroyed. 'So long as we have not managed to abolish any of the causes of human despair we have no right to try and abolish the means whereby men attempt to get rid of despair.' The fact is that human beings possess both the means to eliminate the causes of despair and strength enough to deploy those means. No one has the right to ignore the fact that the sway of conditioning accustoms them to survive on one hundredth of their potential for life. So general is survival sickness that any greater concentration of lived experience cannot fail to unite most of humanity in a common will to live; that the refusal of despair must initiate the construction of a new life; and that economizing on life will perforce lead to the death of the economy and carry us beyond the realm of survival.

XVIII Unbuttressed Refusal

A moment of supersession must come, historically determined at once by the strength and weakness of Power, by the fragmentation of the individual into mere atoms of subjectivity, and by the intimacy of everyday life with what destroys it. This supersession will be general, undivided, and constructed by subjectivity [1]. Once they abandon their initial radicalism, revolutionary elements are doomed to reformism. A well-nigh general abandonment of the revolutionary spirit today subtends the reforms of the regime of survival. It behoves any new revolutionary organization to identify the kernels of supersession in the great movements of the past. In particular, it must rediscover and carry through the project of individual freedom, perverted by liberalism; the project of collective freedom, perverted by socialism; the project of the rediscovery of nature, perverted by fascism; and the project of the total human being, perverted by Marxist ideologies. This last project, though expressed in the theological terms of the time, also informed the great mediaeval heresies, with their anticlerical rage, whose recent exhumation is so apt in our own century with its new priestly caste of 'specialists' [2]. The man of *ressentiment* is the perfect survivor the man devoid of the consciousness of possible supersession, the man of the age of disintegration [3]. By becoming aware of spectacular disintegration, the man of *ressentiment* becomes a nihilist. Active nihilism is prerevolutionary. There is no consciousness of the necessity of supersession without consciousness of disintegration. Juvenile delinquents are the legitimate heirs to Dada [4].

1. *The Question of Supersession*

Refusal is multiform; supersession is one. Faced by modern dissatisfaction and called by it to testify, human history stands quite simply as the history of a radical refusal that always foreshadows supersession and always tends towards its own self-negation. The multifaceted nature of this refusal fails to obscure the basic identity of the dictatorships of a God, a monarch, a leader, a class or a social organization. What fool was it who spoke of revolt having its own ontology? The movement of history, by transforming natural alienation into social alienation, teaches human beings freedom in slavery; it teaches revolt and submission alike. Revolt needs metaphysics less than metaphysicians need revolt. Hierarchical power, which has been with us for millennia, provides a perfectly adequate explanation both for the permanence of rebellion and for the repression that breaks that rebellion.

The overthrow of feudalism and the creation of masters without slaves are one and the same project. The partial failure of this project in the French Revolution has continued to render it more familiar and more attractive, even as later revolutions, each in its own way abortive (the Paris Commune, the Bolshevik Revolution), have at once clarified its contours and deferred its realization.

All *philosophies* of history without exception collude with this failure, which is why *consciousness* of history can no longer be divorced from consciousness of the necessity of its supersession.

How is it that the moment of supersession is increasingly easy to discern on the social horizon? The question of supersession is a tactical one. In broad outline, it may be characterized as follows:

1. (a) Anything that does not kill Power strengthens it; anything that Power does not kill weakens it.

(b) As the requirements of consumption subsume the requirements of production, so government by constraint gives way to government by seduction.

(c) With the democratic extension of the right to consume comes a corresponding extension to the largest number of the right to exercise authority (in varying degrees, of course).

(d) Once seduced by Authority, people are weakened and their capacity for refusal withers. Power is reinforced thereby, certainly, but it has meanwhile been reduced to the level of the consumable, and is indeed consumed, dissipated and, *inevitably*, made vulnerable.

The point of supersession is one moment in this dialectic of strength and weakness. While it is undoubtedly the task of a radical critique to locate this point and work tactically to fortify it, we must not forget that it is the *facts* all around us that provoke such a radical critique. Supersession straddles a contradiction that haunts the modern world, fills the headlines and shapes most of our behaviour. This is the contradiction between *ineffectual refusal*, or reformism, and *extreme refusal*, or nihilism (two types of which, the active and the passive, should be distinguished).

2. As it crumbles, hierarchical power extends its reach but loses its fascination. Fewer people live on the margins of society, as tramps for instance, and fewer respect an employer, a prince, a leader, or a role; more survive within society, yet more hold the system in contempt. Everyone is at the centre of this conflict *in their everyday life*. This has two consequences:

(a) The individual is the victim not only of social atomization but also of fragmented power. Now that subjectivity is conspicuous, and under fire, it has itself become the most crucial revolutionary demand. Henceforward the construction of a harmonious society will require a revolutionary theory founded not on communitarianism but rather on subjectivity—founded, in other words, on specific cases, on the direct experience of *individuals*.

(b) Paradoxically, an extremely fragmented refusal lays the groundwork for a global one. The new revolutionary society will emerge by virtue of a chain reaction from one subjectivity to the next. The construction of a community composed of complete individuals will inaugurate the reversal of perspective without which no supersession is possible.

3. Lastly, the very notion of a reversal of perspective is gaining wide currency. People are too close for comfort to what negates them. The life forces rebel. The allure of distant objects fades as the eye gets closer, and the same goes for the perspective. By imprisoning human beings in its décor of things, and by clumsily insinuating itself into individuals, Power spreads only anxiety and malaise. Vision and thought get muddled, values blur, forms become vague, and anamorphic distortions confuse us as though we were looking at a painting with a nose pressed against the canvas. Incidentally, the change in pictorial perspective exemplified by an Uccello or a Kandinsky paralleled the shift in social perspective. The rhythms of consumption thrust the mind into that interregnum where far and near coincide. The facts themselves will soon come to the aid of the mass of human beings in the longstanding struggle to experience the state of freedom aspired to (though they lacked the means to attain it) by the Swabian heretics of 1270 mentioned by Norman Cohn in his *Pursuit of the Millennium*, who 'said that they had mounted up above God and,

reaching the very pinnacle of Divinity, abandoned God. Often the adept would affirm that he or she had no longer any need of God'.

2. The Renunciation of Poverty and the Poverty of Renunciation

Almost every revolutionary movement embodies the desire for total change, yet up to now almost every one has settled for changing only details and proclaiming victory. As soon as the armed mass of the people renounces its own will and kowtows to the will of its advisors, it abdicates its freedom and enthrones its so-called revolutionary leaders as its oppressors-to-be. Such is the cunning, as it were, of fragmentary power: it gives rise to fragmentary revolutions, revolutions dissociated from any reversal of perspective, cut off from the totality, paradoxically detached from the proletariat which makes them. How could a totalitarian regime *not* be the price immediately paid when the demand for total freedom is renounced once a handful of partial freedoms has been won? People talk in this connection of a curse: the revolution devours its children. As if Makhno's defeat, the crushing of the Kronstadt revolt, or Durruti's assassination were not already latent in the structure of the original Bolshevik cells, perhaps even in Marx's authoritarian positions in the First International. Historical necessity and reasons of state are simply the needs and reasons of leaders who must justify their renunciation of the revolutionary project and of their own radicalism.

Renunciation equals nonsupersession. Issue-politics, partial refusal and piecemeal demands are precisely what block supersession. The worst inhumanity is never anything but a wish for emancipation that has compromised and fossilized beneath strata of successive renunciations. Liberalism, socialism and Bolshevism have all built new prisons under the sign of liberty. As it fights for a better-upholstered alienation, the Left resorts to the cheap ruse of invoking the barricades, the Red Flag and the finest revolutionary moments of the past. Ossified, then resurrected and used as lures, sometime radical impulses are thus doubly betrayed, twice renounced. Amid worker-priests, biker-preachers, Communist generals, red princes, and 'revolutionary' bosses, radical chic harmonizes perfectly with a society able to sell lipstick under the slogan 'Red Revolution! Revolution with Redflex!' Not that all this is without risk for the system. Who is to say that advertising's endless caricaturing of the most authentic revolutionary desires may not produce a backlash, a resurgence of such feelings in a newly purified form? There is no such thing as lost allusions.

The new wave of insurrection rallies young people who have remained outside specialized politics, whether right- or left-wing, or who have passed but briefly through these spheres because of excusable errors of judgement or ignorance. All currents merge in the tide-race of nihilism. The important thing is what lies beyond this confusion. The revolution of everyday life will be made by those who, with varying degrees of facility, discern the seeds of total fulfilment preserved, countered and concealed in ideologies of every kind—those who, in consequence, cease to be either mystified or mystifiers.

//////

Even though a spirit of revolt once informed Christianity, I deny anyone still got up as a Christian the right to claim that spirit or the capacity to understand it. There are no more heretics. The theological language that gave voice to so many magnificent uprisings was the mark of a particular period; it was simply the only language then available. Translation is now necessary—not that it presents any difficulty. Allowing for the times in which I live, and the objective assistance they give me, what can I say in the twentieth century that improves on what the Brethren of the Free Spirit said in the thirteenth: 'A man may be so at one with God that whatever he does he cannot sin. I am part of the freedom of Nature and I satisfy all my natural desires. The free man is perfectly right to do whatever gives him pleasure. Better that the whole world be destroyed and perish utterly than that a free man should abstain from a single act to which his nature moves him.' One cannot but admire Johann Hartmann's words: 'The truly free man is lord and master of all creatures. All things belong to him, and he is entitled to make use of whichever pleases him. If someone tries to stop him doing so, the free man has the right to kill him and take his possessions.' The same goes for John of Brünn, who justified his practice of fraud, plunder and armed robbery by asserting that 'All things created by God are common property. Whatever the eye sees and covets, let the hand grasp it'. Or again, consider the followers of Arnold of Brescia—the *Pifles* or Poplecans—who held themselves to be so pure as to be incapable of sinning no matter what they did (1157). Such jewels of the Christian spirit always sparkled a little too brightly for the rheumy eyes of the Christians. The great heretical tradition may still be discerned—dimly perhaps, but with its dignity still intact—in the acts of the anarchist Jean Pauwels leaving a bomb in the Church of La Madeleine on 15 March 1894 or of the young Robert Burger slitting a priest's throat on 11 August 1963. To my mind, the last full-fledged exemplars of priests genuinely loyal to the revolutionary origins of their religion were Jean Meslier and Jacques Roux fomenting *jacquerie* and riot. Such attitudes are of course beyond the ken of the modern ecumenicism that emanates from Moscow and Rome alike, its sectaries ranging from cybernetician riffraff to the creatures of Opus Dei. This being the new clergy, it is not hard to divine what the supersession of heresy is going to look like.

///////

No one would wish to deny liberalism the glory of having spread the seeds of freedom to every corner of the world. Freedom of the press, freedom of thought, freedom of expression—there is a sense in which, if nothing else, all these 'freedoms' bear witness to the sham of liberalism. The most eloquent of epitaphs, in fact. After all, it is no mean feat to imprison liberty in the name of liberty. Under the liberal system, the freedom of individuals is destroyed by reciprocal interference: one person's liberty begins where the other's ends. Those who reject this basic principle are destroyed by the sword; those who accept it are destroyed by justice. Nobody gets their hands dirty: a button is pressed and the axe of police and State intervention falls. A very unfortunate business, to be sure. The State is the bad conscience of liberals, the instrument of a necessary repression for which deep in their hearts they disavow. As for day-to-day business, it is left to the freedom of the capitalists to keep the freedom of the worker within proper bounds. Which is where the upstanding socialist comes onstage to denounce this hypocrisy.

What is socialism if not a way of getting liberalism out of its basic contradiction, namely the fact that it simultaneously safeguards and destroys individual freedom. Socialism proposes (and there could be no more worthy goal) to prevent individuals from negating each other through interference. The solution it actually produces, however, is very different, for it removes interference without liberating individuals; worse, it dissolves individual will in collective mediocrity. True, only the economic sphere is affected by socialist reforms, and opportunism—that is, liberalism in the sphere of everyday life—is hardly incompatible with bureaucratic planning of all activities from above, with promotions for militants, with power struggles among leaders and so on. But by abolishing economic competition and free enterprise, socialism puts an end to interference on one level, but retains the race for the consumption of power as the only authorized form of freedom. So it is a laughably trivial difference that divides the partisans of two kinds of self-limiting freedom: those in favour of liberalism in production and those in favour of liberalism in consumption.

The contradiction in socialism between the struggle for radical change and its renunciation is well exemplified by two statements from the minutes of the debates of the First International. In 1867, Chémalé reminded his listeners that 'A product is *exchanged* for another product of equal value; anything less amounts to trickery, to fraud, to robbery'. According to Chémalé, therefore, the problem was how to rationalize exchange, how to make it fair. The task of socialism was to correct capitalism, to humanize it, to plan it, and to empty it of its substance (profit)— for who profits from the end of capitalism? But there was already another view of socialism, coexistent with this one, as voiced by Varlin, Communard-to-be, at the Geneva Congress of this same International Association of Workingmen in 1866: 'So long as anything stands in the way of the *employment of oneself* freedom will not exist.' There is thus a freedom locked up in socialism, but today nothing would be more fool-hardy than to try and release this freedom without declaring total war on socialism itself.

Is any further comment needed on why every variety of latter-day Marxism has abandoned the Marxist project? The Soviet Union, China, Cuba: what is left here of the construction of the whole human being? The material poverty which fed the revolutionary desire for supersession and radical change has been attenuated, but a new poverty has emerged, a poverty rooted in renunciation and compromise. The renunciation of poverty has led to the poverty of renunciation. Was it not the feeling that he had allowed his initial project to be fragmented and carried through piecemeal that occasioned Marx's disillusioned witticism 'I am not a Marxist'?

Even the obscenity of fascism springs from a will to live, but a will to live denied, turned against itself like an ingrown toenail: a will to live become a will to power, a will to power become a will to passive obedience, a will to passive obedience become a death wish. For when it comes to the qualitative, to give an inch is to give up everything.

By all means let us destroy fascism—but let the same destructive flame consume all ideologies without exception, and their lackeys to boot.

//////

Everywhere, things being what they are, poetic energy is abandoned or left to lie fallow. To break out of their isolation, people abandon their individual will, their subjectivity. Their recompense is the illusion of community and a sharpened leaning towards death. Renunciation is the first step towards the individual's co-optation by the mechanisms of Power.

There is no practice, no thinking that does not spring initially from a will to live; but there is no officially approved practice or thinking that does not urge us on towards death. The traces of renunciation are clues to a history still little known to us. The very study of such traces helps forge the weapons of total supersession. Where is the radical core—the qualitative dimension? This question has the power to shatter habits of mind—and habits of life; asking it furthers the development of the strategy of supersession and the building of new networks of radical resistance. It may be put to philosophy, where ontology attests to the renunciation of being-as-becoming. It may be put to psychoanalysis, a technique of liberation which 'liberates' us in the main from the need to attack the organization of society. It may be put to all the dreams and desires stolen, violated and travestied by social conditioning. It may be put to the radicalism of an individual's spontaneous acts, so often denied by that individual's own perception of himself and of the world. It may be put to play, whose present imprisonment in the categories of permitted games—from roulette to war, by way of the lynch party—leaves no place for the authentic game of playing with each moment of everyday life. And it may be put to love, so inseparable from revolution yet so pitifully detached at the moment from the pleasure of giving.

Take away the qualitative and all that is left is despair—despair in every form available to a system designed to kill human beings, namely hierarchical Power: reformism, fascism, philistine apoliticism, mediocracy, activism/passivity, boy-scoutism, ideological masturbation, etc. A friend of Joyce's noted: 'I don't remember Joyce ever saying a word during all those years about Poincaré, Roosevelt, de Valera, Stalin; never a mention of Geneva or Locarno, Abyssinia, Spain, China, Japan, the Prince affair, Violette Nozière . . .'. What, indeed, could Joyce have added to *Ulysses* and *Finnegans Wake*? With the *Capital* of individual creativity written, the main thing was that the Leopold Blooms of the world should unite, cast off their miserable state of survival and actualize the richness and diversity of their 'interior monologues' in the lived reality of their existence. Joyce was never a comrade-in-arms to Durruti; he fought shoulder to shoulder with neither the Asturians nor the Viennese workers. At least he had the decency to pass no comment on the news of the day, to the anonymity of which he abandoned *Ulysses* (that 'monument of culture', in the words of one critic), while abandoning himself, Joyce, man of total subjectivity. To the spinelessness of the man of letters, *Ulysses* is testimony. As for the spinelessness of renunciation, its witness is always the 'forgotten' radical moment. Revolution and counterrevolution follow hard upon one another's heels, sometimes within a twenty-four-hour period, even on the least eventful of days. And consciousness of the radical act and of its renunciation is ever more widespread and ever more discriminating. How could it be otherwise? Survival today is nonsupersession become unlivable.

3. *The Man of* Ressentiment

The more widely Power is dispensed in consumer-sized packs, the narrower the sphere of survival; eventually we enter that reptilian world where pleasure, the struggle for freedom, and death agony are all expressed in a single spasm. Base thought and short sight have long signalled the fact that the bourgeoisie belongs to a civilization of troglodytes in the making, a civilization of survival now discovering its apotheosis in the modern conveniences of the fallout shelter. The grandeur of the bourgeoisie was borrowed, acquired less by conquering an enemy than simply through contact with that enemy: a mere shadow, therefore, of feudal virtue, of God, of Nature, and so on. Once these barriers slipped from its direct control, the bourgeoisie found itself reduced to squabbling over details, inflicting wounds on itself so long as they did not threaten its existence. Thus the same Flaubert who skewered the bourgeois with his mockery issued a call to arms when it came to putting the Paris Commune down.

The nobility made the bourgeoisie aggressive; the proletariat puts it on the defensive. What does the proletariat represent for the bourgeoisie? Not even a true adversary—at most a guilty conscience, one that it strives to conceal. Withdrawn, seeking a posture of minimum exposure to attack, proclaiming that reform is the only legitimate form of change, the bourgeoisie has made calculating envy and *ressentiment* the usual stuff of its half-way revolutions.

I have already said that in my view no insurrection is ever fragmented in its initial impulses, that it splinters only when the poetry of agitators and animators gives way to authoritarian leaders. What Max Scheler called the man of *ressentiment* is the official version of a revolutionary: someone bereft of awareness of the possibility of supersession, and unable to grasp the necessity for a reversal of perspective, who, eaten up by jealousy, spite and despair, tries to turn these feelings into weapons against a world perfectly designed to oppress him. A man isolated. A reformist trapped between total rejection and absolute acceptance of Power. The man of *ressentiment* rejects hierarchy out of umbrage at not having a place therein, and this makes him, as a rebel, an ideal slave to the designs of his masters of the moment. Power has no firmer support than thwarted ambition, which is why it makes every effort to console losers in its rat race by tossing them the privileged as a target for their hate.

Short of a reversal in perspective, therefore, hatred of Power is merely a form of obeisance to Power's ascendancy. Someone who walks under a ladder to prove their freedom from superstition in fact proves just the opposite. Obsessive hatred for Power and an insatiable thirst for positions of authority wear down and impoverish people to the same degree—though perhaps not in the same way: after all, there is more humanity in fighting against Power than in prostituting oneself to it. A world of difference separates struggling to live from struggling not to die. Revolts within the realm of survival are measured by the yardstick of death, which explains why they always demand self-abnegation on the part of militants, along with an *a priori* renunciation of that will to live for which everyone is struggling *in actuality*.

The rebel with no horizon save a wall of constraints is fated either to bang his head against this wall or end up defending it with dogged stupidity. And whether one rejects Power or embraces it, to view oneself in terms of constraints is to see things the way Power wants. This is man at zero point—swarming with vermin, as Rozanov put it. Hemmed in on all sides, he resists any kind of intrusion and mounts a jealous guard over himself, never realizing that he has become sterile, and is keeping watch over a grave. He has internalized his own lack of existence. Zealously applying the principle of fair play, he assumes Power's impotence in order to fight Power. At this price, it costs him little to be pure—to play at being pure. How the most compromised people love to give themselves credit for integrity out of all proportion to the odd minor points over which they have preserved any! They get on their high horses because they refused a promotion in the army, gave out a few leaflets at a factory gate or got in a brawl with the cops. And all their bragging goes hand in hand with the most obtuse militantism in the Communist Party or one of its offshoots.

Once in a while, too, a man at zero point finds that he has a world to conquer, that he needs more *Lebensraum,* a vaster ruin to swallow him up. The rejection of Power can so easily extend to things that Power has appropriated—as for example the rebel's own self. Defining oneself in opposition to Power's constraints and lies can result in those constraints and lies entering the mind as so many caricatures of revolt—and generally without a trace of irony to offer a breath of air. No chain is harder to break than the one which the individual attaches to himself when he abandons his refusal in this way. When he places his freedom in the service of unfreedom, the resulting increase in unfreedom's strength enslaves him. While it may well be that nothing more resembles unfreedom as the striving for freedom, unfreedom has this distinguishing feature: once bought, it loses all its value, even though its price is every bit as high as that of freedom.

The walls close in and we can't breathe. The more people struggle for breath, the worse it gets. The ambiguity of the signs of life and freedom, which oscillate between their positive and negative forms according to the ineluctable determinants of global oppression, tends to generalize a confusion in which one hand is forever undoing the work of the other. Inability to apprehend ourselves encourages us to apprehend others on the basis of their negative representations, on the basis of their roles—and thus to treat them as objects. Old maids, bureaucrats—all, in fact, who thrive on survival—have no emotional acquaintanceship with any other reason for existing. Needless to say, Power's best hopes of co-optation rely precisely on this shared malaise. The greater the mental confusion, the easier Power's task.

Myopia and voyeurism are the twin prerequisites of human adaptation to the social meanness of the age. Look at the world through a keyhole! That is what all the specialists urge us to do. And what the man of *ressentiment* delights in doing. Unable to play a leading part, he demands the best seats in the theatre. He is hungry for minute platitudes to chew on: all politicians are crooks, de Gaulle is a great man, China is a workers' paradise, etc. He longs for a live adversary to tear to pieces, or else for the hand of some dignitary to kiss—but he never loves or hates a *system*. How easy it is to understand the success of such crass images as the dirty Jew, the thieving Black, or the Two Hundred Families! Give the enemy a face and the face of the masses instantly assumes the traits—the admirable traits—of the Defender of the Fatherland, the Chief, or the Führer.

The man of *ressentiment* is available, but for that availability to come into play, and thereby end, passage through a sort of chrysalis stage of consciousness is required: that stage is nihilism. If he does not kill the organizers of his angst, or at least those who appear as such in the fore-front of his vision (managers, specialists, ideologues, etc.), the man of *ressentiment* will end up killing on behalf of some authority, on behalf of some reason of state, or on behalf of consumption of ideology. And if the state of things fails to spark a brutal explosion of violence, he will continue, locked in the tight grip of his bitterness, to flounder in a sea of roles and spread his saw-toothed conformism everywhere, applauding revolt and repression alike, and feeling nothing but irremediable confusion.

4. The Nihilist

What is nihilism? Rozanov's definition is perfect: 'The show is over. The audience get up to leave their seats. Time to collect their coats and go home. They turn round. No more coats and no more home.'

As soon as a mythical system enters into contradiction with economic and social reality, a chasm opens between the way people live and the prevailing explanation of the world, which is suddenly inadequate, completely surpassed. A whirlwind gets up, sucking up and smashing all traditional values. Deprived of its alibis and justifications, stripped of the illusions that had concealed it, the weakness of human beings is left naked and defenceless. Yet, inasmuch as myth was not only the shield and disguise of that weakness but also its cause, myth's break-up opens the door to new possibilities. Its disappearance frees up an energy and creativity too long siphoned off from authentic experience into religious transcendence and abstraction. The interregnum between the collapse of classical philosophy and the construction of the Christian myth witnessed an unprecedented flowering of thoughts and actions each richer than the next. Then came the dead hand of Rome, co-opting whatever it could not destroy. Later, in the sixteenth century, the Christian myth itself disintegrated, and another period of frenetic experimentation and research burst upon the world. But this time there was an important difference, for after 1789 any reconstitution of myth was strictly impossible.

Whereas Christianity defused the explosive nihilism of certain Gnostic sects and improvised a protective covering for itself from the remains, the nihilism born of the bourgeois revolution was a concrete one, a nihilism quite impossible to co-opt. As I have shown, the reality of exchange stymies dissimulation, defies all artifice. Until the spectacle is abolished, it can never be anything but the spectacle of nihilism. The vanity of the world, which the Pascal of the *Pensées* wanted to make people conscious of, this to the greater glory of God, is now propagated by historical reality itself, in the absence of God, himself a casualty of the shattering of myth. Nihilism has swept everything before it, God included.

For the last century and a half, the most lucid contributions to art and life have been the fruit of free experimentation in the field of destroyed values. Sade's passionate rationalism, Kierkegaard's sarcasm, Nietzsche's havering irony, the violence of Maldoror, Mallarmé's icy dispassion, Jarry's *Umour*, Dada's negativism—these are some of the impulses that have spread far and wide, investing human consciousness with a little of the darkness of decaying values; yet also, along with the darkness, the hope of a total supersession—a true reversal of perspective.

There is a paradox here. On the one hand, the great proponents of nihilism lacked an essential weapon: the sense of historical reality, the sense of the reality of decay, erosion and fragmentation. On the other hand, the greatest *makers* of history have been tragically lacking in a sharp awareness of history's immense destructive power in the bourgeois era: Marx failed to analyse Romanticism and the general issue of art; Lenin was almost wilfully blind to the importance of everyday life, of the Futurists, of Mayakovsky, or of the Dadaists.

Consciousness of the rise of nihilism and consciousness of the movement of history seem curiously far apart. Through the breach between them surge hordes of passive liquidators, crushing the very values they claim to be defending under the weight of their stupidity. They include Communist bureaucrats, Fascist brutes, ideologues, shady politicians, sub-Joycean writers, neo-Dadaist thinkers, and priests of the piecemeal—all working assiduously for the Big Nothing in the name of one order or another: family, administration, morality, culture, revolutionary cybernetics (!), etc. Had history not advanced so far, perhaps nihilism would not yet seem like a general truth, a basic banality. But advanced it has. Nihilism is a self-destruct mechanism: today a flame, tomorrow ashes. Reification has imbued everyday reality with nothingness. The values of the past, now in ruins, fuel the intensive production of consumable and 'futurized' values marketed under the quaint label of 'modern', but they also thrust us inevitably towards a future yet to be constructed, or in other words towards the supersession of nihilism. In the desperate consciousness of the new generation a slow reconciliation is occurring between *history as dissolution and history as construction*. An alliance between nihilism and the forces of supersession means that supersession will be total. Herein without doubt lies the only wealth to be found in the affluent society.

When the man of *ressentiment* becomes aware that survival is a losing proposition, he turns into a nihilist. So tightly does he embrace the impossibility of living that even survival is fatally challenged. But nihilist angst is unlivable: an absolute void cannot hold. The whirlwind of past and future reduces the present to zero point. And from that still point there are two ways out, namely the two varieties of nihilism that I describe as *active* and *passive*.

//////

Grounded in compromise and indifference, nihilist *passivity* combines an awareness of the collapse of all values with a deliberate, often self-interested choice to defend one or other such discredited value come hell or high water, 'gratuitously', for Art's sake. Nothing is true, so a few gestures have virtue. Delusional followers of the Fascist Charles Maurras, pataphysicians, jingoists, aesthetes of the *acte gratuit*, informers, O.A.S. bombers, Pop Artists—an endless parade of charmers, all working out their own particular version of the *credo quia absurdum est*: you don't believe in it, but you do it anyway; you get used to it and even get to like it. Passive nihilism is a plunge into conformism.

Which said, nihilism can never be more than a transition, a shifting, ambiguous sphere, a period of wavering between two extremes, one leading to submission and subservience, the other to permanent revolt. Between these two poles lies a no-man's-land, the wasteland of the suicide and the solitary killer, of that criminal described so aptly by Bettina as the crime of the State. Jack the Ripper is forever inaccessible—beyond the reach of either hierarchical Power or revolutionary will. An *in-itself*, so to speak! He gravitates around that zero point where destruction is no longer the continuation of the destruction wrought by Power but instead runs ahead of it, leaving it behind and so accelerating things that the machine of 'In the Penal Colony' shatters into pieces and flies apart. In the figure of Maldoror the dissolution wrought by modern social organization reaches its climax, namely self-destruction. The individual's absolute rejection of society echoes society's absolute rejection of the individual. Is this not the still point of the reversal of perspective, the moment of equilibrium where neither movement, nor dialectics, nor time exist? Noon and eternity of the great refusal. Before it, the pogroms; beyond it, the new innocence. The blood of Jews or the blood of cops.

//////

Active nihilism combines consciousness of disintegration with a desire to expose its causes by speeding up the process. The disorder thus fomented is merely a reflection of the chaos ruling the world. Active nihilism is prerevolutionary; passive nihilism is counterrevolutionary. And many ordinary people, torn this way and that, dance a tragicomical hesitation waltz between the two—rather like the Red Army soldier described by some Soviet author (Viktor Shklovsky perhaps) who never charged without shouting, 'Long Live the Tsar!' But sooner or later circumstances are bound to draw the line, and people suddenly find themselves, once and for all, on one side or the other.

//////

Dancing for oneself always means learning to disregard the beat of the official world. One's demands, furthermore, must be carried to their logical conclusion, and one's radicalism never abandoned at the first turn. As it approaches the point of exhaustion in its search for new motivations, the race for consumable items is ingenious enough to enlist the way-out, the bizarre and the shocking. Black humour and atrocity are readily incorporated into the advertising mix. There are ways, too, of flirting with nonconformity that conform to the prevailing value system. Awareness of the decay of values has its place in sales strategy. Disintegration is itself a commodity, and the vacuity of both ideas and objects, if loudly enough proclaimed, sells well. The figurine salt-shaker of Kennedy now in supermarkets, complete with 'bullet-holes' through which to pour the salt, should be enough to convince anybody if need be how easily the sort of gag that would once have delighted Émile Pouget and his Père Peinard is now a source of profit.

Consciousness of decay reached its highest expression with Dadaism. Dada really did contain the seeds of nihilism's supersession, but the movement left them to rot along with everything else. As for Surrealism, its whole failing lay in the fact that it was an accurate critique made at the wrong moment. What this means is that while their critique of Dada's aborting of supersession was perfectly justified, the Surrealists' own attempt to surpass Dada did not go back to Dada's initial nihilism, did not build on Dada-anti-Dada, and did not view Dada historically. History was the nightmare from which the Surrealists never awoke: they were defenceless before the Communist Party; they were caught short by the Spanish Civil War. For all their yapping they slunk after the official Left like faithful dogs.

Certain features of Romanticism had already shown, without awakening the slightest interest on the part of Marx or Engels, that art—the pulse of culture and society—was the first indicator of the disintegration of values. A century later, while Lenin deemed the issue frivolous, the Dadaists saw in an abscessed art the symptom of a generalized cancer, a sickness of society as a whole. The unpleasant in art is just a reflection of the art of unpleasure practised everywhere under the rule of Power. That is what the Dadaists of 1916 so clearly demonstrated. The only way forward from their analysis was armed struggle. The neo-Dadaist maggots of Pop Art swarming in the dung heap of present-day consumerism have naturally found better things to do!

The Dadaists, working to cure themselves and their contemporaries of the dissatisfaction of their lives—working, in the last reckoning, more consistently than Freud—set up the first laboratory for the rehabilitation of everyday life. In this respect their action went well beyond their thinking. 'The point was to work completely in the dark,' the painter Georg Grosz recalled later. 'We didn't know what we were doing.' The Dada group was a sausage-machine taking in all the banalities and empty self-importance in the world; from the other end everything came out transformed, original, brand new. People and things were the same, but they had acquired new meanings and signs. The reversal of perspective began with this magical recovery of direct experience. In this way, repurposing—the tactics of the reversal of perspective—shattered the changeless framework of the old world. Lautréamont's 'poetry made by everyone' found its full meaning in this achievement—a far cry indeed from the literary mentality to which the Surrealists eventually, and so pitifully, surrendered.

The initial weakness of Dada lay in its extraordinary humility. Think of Tzara, who, it is said, used every morning to repeat Descartes's statement, 'I do not even want to know that there were men before me'. This Tzara, a buffoon taking himself as seriously as a pope, may easily be recognized as the same individual who later disregarded the likes of Ravachol, Bonnot, or Makhno and his companions and joined Stalin's herds. If Dada broke up when faced with the impossibility of supersession, it was because the Dadaists lacked the wit to look to history for those occasions when supersession was in fact possible—those moments when the masses arise and take their destiny into their own hands.

The first act of renunciation is always terrible. From Surrealism to neo-Dadaism, Dada's original error has had ever-broadening repercussions. The Surrealists for their part did look to the past, but consider the results. Their attempt to correct the Dadaists' mistake only made thing worse, for in lionizing such genuinely admirable figures as a Sade, a Fourier or a Lautréamont, they wrote so much (and so well) about them that these protégés of theirs won the dubious honour of mention in school curricula—a literary celebrity akin to that which the neo-Dadaists were to win for their forebears in today's spectacle of disintegration.

//////

For an international phenomenon today that in any way resembles Dada, one would have to consider the finest exploits of juvenile delinquents. The same contempt for art and bourgeois values. The same refusal of ideology. The same will to live. The same ignorance of history. The same primitive revolt. The same lack of tactics.

What the nihilist fails to realize is that other people are nihilists too, yet the nihilism of other people is now an active historical factor. The nihilist has no consciousness of the possibility of supersession. Remember, however, that the present reign of survival, in which all the talk about progress expresses nothing so much as despair of its possibility, is itself a product of history, itself the outcome of all the renunciations of the human over the centuries. I venture to say that the history of survival is the historical movement that will undo history itself. For clear awareness of survival and of its intolerable conditions is on the point of fusing with a consciousness of the successive renunciations of the past, and thus too with the real desire to pick up the movement of supersession *everywhere in space and time* where it has been prematurely interrupted. Supersession—which is to say the revolution of everyday life—will consist in retrieving all such abandoned radical seeds and injecting them with the unmatched violence of *ressentiment*. The resulting chain reaction of underground creativity cannot fail to demolish Power's perspective. *In the last reckoning, the nihilists are our only allies.* Although they now suffer the despair of nonsupersession, a coherent theory may be expected, by demonstrating the mistakenness of their viewpoint, to place all the potential energy of their accumulated rancour at the service of their will to live. Once armed with two basic notions—the understanding of what it means to renounce radical demands and the historical consciousness of disintegration—anyone can fight for the radical transformation of everyday life and of the world. *Nihilists,* as Sade would have said, *one more effort if you would be revolutionaries!*

PART TWO
REVERSAL OF PERSPECTIVE

XIX Reversal of Perspective

> The light of Power obscures. The eyes of the illusion of community are holes in a mask, holes to which the eyes of individual subjectivity cannot adapt. The individual point of view must prevail over the point of view of false collective participation. Taking the totality as our reference point, we must confront the social realm with the weapons of subjectivity and rebuild everything on the basis of the self. The reversal of perspective is the positive aspect of the negative—the swelling fruit about to shatter the husk of the old world.

1

One day Herr Keuner was asked just what he meant by 'reversal of perspective', and he told the following story. Two brothers, deeply attached to each another, had a strange habit. They would use pebbles to record the nature of each day's events, a white stone for each moment of happiness, a black one for any misfortune or distress. They soon discovered, on comparing the contents of their jars of pebbles at the end of each day, that one brother collected only white pebbles, the other only black. Intrigued by the remarkable consistency with which they each experienced similar circumstances in a quite different way, they resolved to seek the opinion of an old man famed for his wisdom. 'You don't talk about it enough', said the wise man. 'Each of you should seek the causes of your choices and explain them to the other.' The two brothers followed this advice, and soon found that while the first remained faithful to his white pebbles, and the second to his black ones, in neither of the jars were there now so many pebbles as formerly. Where there had usually been thirty or so, each brother would now collect scarcely more than seven or eight. Before long the wise man had another visit from the two brothers, both looking very downcast. 'Not long ago,' began the first brother, 'my jar would fill up with pebbles as black as night. I lived in unrelieved despair. I confess that I only went on living out of force of habit. Now, I rarely collect more than eight pebbles in a day. But what these eight symbols of misery represent has become so intolerable that I simply cannot go on living like this.' The other brother told the wise man: 'Every day I used to pile up my white pebbles. These days I only get seven or eight, but these exercise such a fascination over me that I cannot recall these moments of happiness without immediately wanting to live them over again, even more intensely than before. In fact I long to keep on experiencing them forever, and this desire is a torment to me.' The wise man smiled as he listened. 'Excellent, excellent', he said. 'Things are shaping up well. You must persevere. One other thing. From time to time, ask yourselves why this game with the jar and the pebbles excites you so much.' The next time the two brothers visited the wise man, they had this to say: 'Well, we asked ourselves the question, as you suggested, but we have no answer. So we asked everyone in the village. You should see how much it has aroused them. Whole families sit outside their houses in the evenings arguing about white pebbles and black pebbles. Only the elders and notables refuse to take part in these discussions. They laugh at us, and say that a pebble is a pebble, black or white.' The old man could not conceal his delight at this. 'Everything is going as I had foreseen. Don't worry. Soon the question will no longer arise; it has already lost its importance, and I daresay that one day soon you will have forgotten that you ever concerned yourselves with it.' Not long thereafter the old man's predictions were confirmed in the following manner. A great joy seized the people of the village. And as dawn broke after a night full of comings and goings, the first rays of sunlight fell upon the heads of the elders and notables, freshly struck from their bodies and impaled upon the sharp-pointed stakes of a palisade.

2

The world has always been a geometry. The angle and perspective from which people were supposed to see each other, speak to each other, and represent each other were once subject to the sovereign decision of the gods of the unitary system. Then human beings—specifically, the bourgeoisie—played a dirty trick on those gods: they put them in perspective, situating them within a historical process in which they were born, developed, and died. History has been the twilight of the gods.

Once historicized, God became inextricable from the dialectic of his material nature, from the dialectic of master and slave, and from the history of the class struggle and of hierarchical social power. Thus in a sense the bourgeoisie instigated a reversal of perspective, but only to restrict it immediately to the plane of appearances: God has been abolished but the pillars which supported him still rise towards an empty sky. The explosion that demolished the cathedral of sacred values must have produced very slow shock waves, for only now, two centuries after the deicide, are the last chunks of the masonry of myth being ground to powder as the spectacle crumbles. The bourgeoisie presides over one phase only of the dynamiting of a God whose absolute disappearance is now in the offing; so completely will God vanish, indeed, that every trace of his material origins—which is to say man's domination by man—will disappear along with him.

The mechanisms of the economy, the control and force of which the bourgeoisie in part mastered, exposed Power's material basis while enabling it to dispense with the divine phantom. But at what price? God, that grand negation of humanity, once offered the faithful a sort of refuge where, paradoxically, they found a justification for rising up, as the mystics so often did, against temporal authorities, invoking God's absolute power against the 'usurped' power of priests and rulers. Today, however, Power comes down to humans, makes advances to them, and makes itself consumable. It weighs more and more heavily upon them, reduces the sphere of life to mere survival, and shrinks time to the transience of roles. Somewhat schematically speaking, Power might be compared to an angle—an acute angle, to begin with, its point lost in the heavens, then gradually widening as its tip descends and emerges from the clouds, eventually becoming so wide that it disappears altogether and we are left with a straight line that is no more than a series of equivalent, weak points. Beyond this line, which represents the moment of nihilism, a new perspective opens which is neither a reflection nor an inversion of the earlier one. Rather, it is an ensemble of harmonized individual perspectives which never clash but which successfully construct a coherent and collective world. All these angles, though different, open in the same direction, as individual will and collective will gradually become one.

The function of conditioning is to assign and adjust people's positions on the hierarchical ladder. The reversal of perspective entails a kind of anticonditioning. Not a new form of conditioning, but a playful tactic, namely *détournement*, or repurposing.

The reversal of perspective replaces knowledge by praxis, hope by freedom, and mediation by the will to immediacy. It enshrines the victory of a system of human relationships founded on three inseparable principles: participation, communication and fulfilment.

To reverse perspective is to stop seeing things through the eyes of the community, of ideology, of the family, of other people. To grasp hold of oneself as something solid, to take oneself as starting-point and centre. To base everything on subjectivity and to follow one's subjective will to be everything. In the sights of my insatiable desire to live, the totality of Power is merely one target on a wider horizon. Nor can Power spoil my aim by deploying its forces: on the contrary, I can track their movements, gauge the threat they pose, and study their responses. My creativity, as insignificant as it may be, is a far better guide for me than all the knowledge with which my head has been crammed. In the night of Power, its glimmer keeps the enemy forces at bay. Those forces are cultural conditioning, specialization of every kind, and *Weltanschauungen* that are inevitably totalitarian. In creativity everyone possesses the ultimate weapon. But this weapon, like some talismans, must be used wittingly. Where creativity is mobilized against the grain, in the service of lies and oppression, it turns into a sad farce, and is duly consecrated as art. Acts that destroy Power and acts that construct individual free will have the same form but their range is different; as any good strategist knows, you prepare in different ways for defence and attack.

We have not chosen the reversal of perspective out of some kind of voluntarism. It has chosen us. Caught up as we are in the historical stage of NOTHING, the next step can only be a change in EVERYTHING. Consciousness of total revolution—or rather, of the necessity for it—is the only way we have left of being historical, our last chance to undo history under specific conditions. The game we are about to join is the game of our creativity. Its rules are radically opposed to the rules and laws of our society. It is a game of loser wins: what is left unsaid is more important than what is said, what is actually lived more important than what is represented by appearances. And the game must be played out to the end. How can anyone who has suffered oppression till their very bones rebel turn down the life-raft of the will to *live without reservations?* Woe betide those who abandon their violence and their radical demands along the way. As Nietzsche noted, murdered truths become poisonous. If we do not reverse perspective, Power's perspective will succeed in turning us against ourselves once and for all. German Fascism was spawned in the blood of Spartakus. Our everyday renunciations—no matter how trivial— lend fuel to our foe, who seeks nothing short of our complete destruction.

XX Creativity, Spontaneity and Poetry

Human beings live in a state of creativity twenty-four hours a day. The manipulation of the notion of freedom by the mechanisms of domination, once it is exposed to view, sheds a positive light on its opposite, namely the exercise of a genuine freedom inseparable from individual creativity. Thereafter, the injunctions of production, consumption and organization can no longer co-opt the passion to create, which dissolves the consciousness of constraint [1]. Spontaneity is the mode of existence of creativity: not an isolated state, but the unmediated experience of subjectivity. Spontaneity concretizes the passion for creation and initiates its practical realization: it is the precondition of poetry, of the impulse to change the world in accordance with the demands of radical subjectivity [2]. The qualitative is the manifest presence of creative spontaneity, a direct communication of the essential, and poetry's opportunity. It crystallizes possibilities, increases knowledge and effectiveness, and provides the proper *modus operandi* for intelligence. Its criteria are of its own making. The qualitative leap sparks a chain reaction, as may be seen in all revolutionary moments. Such a reaction must be kindled by the positive scandal of free and total creativity [3]. Poetry organizes creative spontaneity inasmuch as it projects it into the world. Poetry is the agency that engenders new realities: the fulfilment of radical theory, the revolutionary act *par excellence* [4].

1

In a fractionary world whose common denominator throughout history has been hierarchical social power, only one freedom has ever been tolerated: the freedom to change the numerator, the unchanging freedom to change masters. Freedom so understood has finally lost its appeal, the more so since even the worst totalitarianisms, East and West, are incessantly invoking it. The present generalization of the refusal to simply change bosses coincides with a reorganization of the State. All the governments of the industrialized or semi-industrialized world now tend to model themselves—to a greater or lesser extent, depending on the level of development—on a single prototype: the common aim is to rational-ize—to automate, as it were—the old mechanisms of domination. And herein lies freedom's first opportunity. The bourgeois democracies have clearly shown that individual freedoms can be tolerated only insofar as they limit and destroy one another. Now that this is clear, it has become impossible for any government, no matter how sophisticated, to wave the *muleta* of liberty without everyone discerning the sword concealed behind it; without the incessant evocation of freedom producing a back-lash, as freedom, rediscovering its true roots in individual creativity, violently refuses to be no more than the permitted, the licit, the toler-able—the smile on the face of authority.

Freedom's second opportunity comes once it has retrieved its crea-tive authenticity, and it relates to the mechanisms of Power themselves. Abstract systems of exploitation and domination are obviously human creations, brought into being and refined through the redirection or co-optation of creativity. The only forms of creativity that authority can deal with, or wishes to deal with, are those which the spectacle can co-opt. But what people do officially is nothing compared with what they do in secret. Creativity is usually evoked apropos of works of art, but what are works of art alongside the creative energy displayed by each individual a thousand times a day? Alongside seething unsatisfied desires, daydreams in search of a foothold in reality, feelings at once confused and lumi-nously clear, ideas and actions presaging nameless upheavals? All this energy, of course, is relegated to anonymity and deprived of adequate means of expression, imprisoned by survival and obliged to find outlets by sacrificing its qualitative riches and conforming to the spectacle's categories. Think of Cheval's palace, Fourier's inspired system, or the pictorial universe of Douanier Rousseau. Even closer to home, consider the incredible diversity of *our own* dreams—landscapes the brilliance of whose colours qualitatively surpass the finest canvases of a Van Gogh. We are all forever at work on an ideal world within ourselves, even as our outward motions comply with soulless routines.

No one, no matter how alienated, is without (or unaware of) an irreducible core of creativity, a *camera obscura* safe from intrusion by lies and constraints. If ever social organization extends its control to this stronghold of humanity, its dominion will no longer be exercised over anything save robots, or corpses. And, in a sense, that is why conscious-ness of creative energy increases, paradoxically enough, as a function of consumer society's efforts to co-opt it.

Argus is blind to the danger right in front of him. Where quan-tity reigns, quality has no recognized legal existence; but this is the very thing that safeguards and nourishes it. I have already noted that the dissatisfaction bred by the manic pursuit of quantity calls forth a radical desire for the qualitative. The more oppression is justified in terms of the freedom to consume, the more the malaise arising from this contradiction exacerbates the thirst for total freedom. The crisis of production-based capitalism pointed up the element of repressed crea-tivity in the energy expended by the worker. The alienation of creativity through forced labour, thanks to the exploitation of the producers, was denounced once and for all by Marx. Whatever the capitalist system and its successors (even antagonistic ones) have lost on the production front they try to make up for in the sphere of consumption. The plan is that, as they gradually free themselves from their duties as producers, human beings should be trapped by newer obligations as consumers. By opening up the empty lot of leisure time to a creativity liberated at long last by shorter working hours, the well-intentioned apostles of humanism have merely mustered an army fit for drilling on the training-grounds of the consumer economy. Now that the alienation of the consumer is being laid bare by consumption's own internal dialectic, one may wonder what kind of prison awaits the highly subversive forces of individual creativity. As I pointed out earlier, the rulers' last chance here is to turn us all into organizers of our own passivity.

With touching candour, Dewitt Peters suggests that handing out paints, brushes and canvas to everyone who requested them would produce very interesting results. It is true that if this policy were applied in a variety of well-defined and well-policed spheres, such as the theatre, the plastic arts, music, writing, etc., and in a general way to any such sphere susceptible of total isolation from all others, then the system might have a hope of endowing people with the consciousness of the artist, which is to say the consciousness of someone who professes to exhibit their creativity in the museums and shop windows of culture. The popularity of such a culture would be a clear sign of Power's success. Fortunately, the chances of people being successfully 'culturized' in this way are now slight. Do the cyberneticians and their ilk really imagine that people can be talked into 'free experimentation' within bounds laid down by authoritarian decree? Or that prisoners at last aware of their creative capacity might daub their cells with 'original graffiti' and leave it at that? What would prevent them from extending their new-found penchant for experiment to weapons, desires, dreams, and all manner of means of self-fulfilment? The crowd, after all, is already full of agitators. No: the last possible way of co-opting creativity—the organization of artistic passivity—is, happily, doomed to failure.

'What I am trying to reach,' wrote Paul Klee, 'is a far-off point, at the source of creation, where I suspect a single explanatory principle applies for man, animals, plants, fire, water, air and all the forces that surround us.' As a matter of fact, this point is far off only in Power's deceiving perspective: the source of all creation lies in individual creativity; it is from here that everything, being or thing, is ordered in accordance with poetry's grand freedom. This is the starting-point of the new perspective, the perspective that everyone is striving with all their might and at every moment of their existence to reach. 'Subjectivity is the only truth', says Kierkegaard.

Power cannot co-opt true creativity. In 1869 the Brussels police thought they had found the famous gold of the International, about which the capitalists were losing so much sleep. They seized a huge strongbox hidden in some dark corner, but when they opened it they found only coal. Little did the police know that the pure gold of the International would turn into coal if touched by enemy hands.

A revolutionary alchemy transmutes the basest metals of daily life into gold in the laboratories of individual creativity. The most important thing is to dissolve the consciousness of constraint, the sense of impotence, by means of creativity's magnetic power; to melt such feelings away in a surge of creative energy serene in the affirmation of genius. As sterile as it may be in the race for prestige in the spectacle, megalomania is a vital feature of the struggle of the self against the massed forces of conditioning. The creative spark, which is the spark of true life, shines all the more brightly in the night of nihilism triumphant. But as the project of a new and improved survival aborts, such sparks will proliferate and gradually coalesce into a single light, the promise of a form of organization based on the harmonizing of individual wills. History is leading us to the crossroads where radical subjectivity meets the real prospect of changing the world: that privileged moment when the perspective is reversed.

2. *Spontaneity*

Spontaneity is the mode of being of individual creativity, its original, immaculate form, neither polluted at the source nor threatened by co-optation. Whereas creativity is the most equitably distributed thing imaginable, spontaneity seems to be the privileged possession of those whom long resistance to Power has endowed with a consciousness of their own value as individuals. In revolutionary moments this means the majority; at other times, when the revolution must be prepared day by day, it means more people than one might suppose. Wherever the light of creativity continues to shine, spontaneity has a chance.

'The new artist protests', wrote Tzara in 1919. 'He no longer paints: he creates directly.' Immediacy is certainly the most succinct, but also the most radical demand that must characterize the new artists of today, who are destined to be constructors of situations to be lived directly. I say 'succinct' because it is important after all not to be misled by the word 'spontaneity'. The spontaneous can never spring from internalized constraints, even subconscious ones, nor can it abide alienating abstraction or spectacular co-optation: clearly it is a conquest, not a given. The reconstruction of the individual presupposes the reconstruction of the unconscious (consider the construction of dreams).

What spontaneous creativity has lacked up to now is the clear consciousness of its own poetry. Common sense has always treated spontaneity as a primary state, an initial stage in need of theoretical adjustment, of transposition into abstract terms. This view isolates spontaneity, treats it as a thing-in-itself—and thus recognizes it only in the travestied forms which it acquires within the spectacle (e.g., action painting). In point of fact spontaneous creativity carries the seeds of its effective development within itself. It is possessed of its own poetry.

For me spontaneity is immediate, the consciousness of a lived experience which, though hemmed in on all sides and threatened by prohibitions, is not yet alienated, not yet reduced to inauthenticity. The centre of lived experience is where we all get closest to ourselves. Within this unique space-time, I am quite convinced, being real exempts me from necessity. It is always the feeling of necessity that alienates me. I was taught to look upon myself as in default (in the legal sense); but all it takes is an instant of awareness of authentic life to sweep away all evasions, consigning the absence of a future to the same void as the absence of a past. Consciousness of the present harmonizes with lived experience by virtue of a kind of improvisation. I cannot help thinking that the pleasure this brings us—poor, because it is still isolated, yet rich in that it already reaches out towards an identical pleasure in others—bears a striking resemblance to the pleasure of jazz. At its best moments, the improvisational style in everyday life has much in common with jazz as described by Alfons Dauer: 'The African conception of rhythm differs from the Western in that it is perceived through bodily movement rather than aurally. The technique consists essentially in the introduction of discontinuity into the static equilibrium imposed on the passage of time by rhythm and metre. This discontinuity, which results from the presence of ecstatic centres of gravity out of time with the musical rhythm and metre proper, creates continual tensions between the static beat and the ecstatic beat superimposed on it.'

The instant of creative spontaneity is the minutest possible manifestation of the reversal of perspective. It is a unitary moment, that is to say one and many. The eruption of lived pleasure is such that in losing myself I find myself; forgetting that I exist, I am fulfilled. Consciousness of immediate experience is simply this oscillation, this jazz, this balancing act. By contrast, thought directed towards lived experience with analytic intent is bound to remain detached from that experience. This applies to all reflections on everyday life, including, to be sure, the present one. That is why I am continually at pains to introduce an element of self-criticism in hopes of staving off the kind of co-optation that so often prevails. The traveller who is always thinking about the length of the road ahead tires more easily than his companion who lets his imagination wander as they go along. Similarly, anxious attention paid to lived experience can only impede it, abstract it, and make it into nothing more than a series of memories-to-be.

If thought is really to find a basis in lived experience, it has to be free. The way to ensure this is to think *other* in the register of *the same*. As you construct yourself, imagine another yourself that will one day construct you in its turn. Such is my conception of spontaneity: the highest possible level of self-consciousness that is still inseparable from the self and from the world.

All the same, we have to find the path back to a spontaneity that industrial civilizations have allowed to become overgrown. And getting the right grip on life is no easy matter. Individual experience is also an easy target, a golden opportunity, for madness. Kierkegaard describes this state of affairs as follows: 'It is true that I have a lifebelt, but I cannot see the pole which is supposed to pull me out of the water. This is a hideous way to experience things.' The pole is there, of course, and no doubt everyone could grab on to it, though many would be so slow about it that they would die of anxiety before realizing its existence. But exist it does, and its name is radical subjectivity: the consciousness that all people have the same will to authentic self-fulfilment, and that their subjectivity is strengthened by the perception of this same subjective will in others. This way of getting out of oneself and radiating outwards, not so much towards others as towards that part of oneself that is to be found in others, is what gives creative spontaneity the strategic importance of a gun emplacement. The concepts and abstractions which rule us have to be returned to their source, to lived experience, not in order to validate them, but on the contrary to correct them, to turn them on their heads, to restore them to that sphere whence they derive and which they should never have left. This is a necessary precondition of people's imminent realization that their individual creativity is indistinguishable from universal creativity. The sole authority is one's own lived experience—and this it is up to everyone to prove to everyone else.

3. *The Qualitative*

I have already said that creativity, though equitably distributed to all, finds direct, *spontaneous* expression only on specific occasions. These are pre-revolutionary moments, the source of the poetry that changes life and transforms the world. They must surely be placed under the sign of the qualitative—that modern equivalent of grace. The presence of the divine abomination was intimated by a cloying spirituality suddenly conferred upon anyone, from the most rustic to the most refined, on an idiot like Paul Claudel as readily as on a Saint John of the Cross; similarly, a gesture, an attitude, perhaps merely a word, may suffice to signal that poetry's chance is at hand, that the total construction of everyday life, a global reversal of perspective—in short, the revolution—are within reach. The qualitative encapsulates and crystallizes these possibilities; it is a direct communication of the essential.

One day Kagame heard an old woman of Rwanda, who could neither read nor write, complaining: 'Really, these whites are incurably naïve. They have no brains at all.' 'How can you be so stupid?' he answered her. 'I would like to see you invent so many unimaginably marvellous things as the whites have done.' With a condescending smile, the old woman replied, 'Listen, my child. They may have learned a lot of things, but they have no brains. They don't understand anything'. And she was right, for the curse of technological civilization, of quantified exchange and scientific knowledge, is that they have created no means of freeing people's spontaneous creativity *directly;* indeed, they do not even allow people to *understand* the world in any unmediated fashion. The sentiment expressed by the Rwandan woman—whom the Belgian administrator doubtless looked upon, from the heights of his superior intelligence, as a wild animal—may also be found, though laden with guilt and bad faith, and hence marred by crass stupidity, in the old saw according to which 'I have studied a great deal and therefore know that I know nothing.' For it is false, in a sense, to say that studying something can teach us nothing, so long as our study does not abandon the point of view of the totality. What is really meant by 'nothing' here is the various stages of the qualitative—whatever, at whatever level, advances the qualitative. By way of an analogy, imagine a number of apartments located immediately above one another, communicating directly by means of a central lift and also indirectly linked by an outside spiral staircase. People on any floor have one-stop access by elevator to any higher one, but cannot communicate with those in the process of climbing the stairs outside. Between those capable of such qualitative leaps and those obliged to ascend step by step, no dialogue is possible. Most of the revolutionary workers of 1848 were no doubt incapable of reading the *Communist Manifesto,* yet they possessed within themselves the essential lessons of Marx and Engels's text. In fact this is what made the Marxist theory truly radical. It was the objective conditions of working-class life and its corollaries, explained in theoretical terms on a higher floor, as it were, that made it possible for the most illiterate proletarian to understand Marx *immediately* when the moment came. Cultivated individuals who use their culture like a flame-thrower are bound to connect with the less cultivated, who experience in the lived reality of their everyday lives what the former express in scholarly terms. The arms of criticism do indeed have to join forces with criticism by force of arms.

Only the qualitative permits a higher floor to be reached in one bound. This is the lesson that any endangered group must learn, the pedagogy of the barricades. The graduated world of hierarchical power, however, can only envisage knowledge as being likewise graduated: those people on the outside stairs, experts on the type and number of steps, meet, pass, bump into one another and trade insults. What difference does it make? At the bottom we have the autodidact gorged on platitudes, at the top the intellectual collecting ideas like butterflies: mirror images of foolishness. The distinction between Miguel de Unamuno and the repulsive Millan Astray, between the paid thinker and his reviler, is an empty one: where the qualitative is not in evidence, intelligence is a fool's cap and bells.

The alchemists called those elements needed for the Great Work the *materia prima*. Paracelsus describes it in terms that apply perfectly to the qualitative: 'It is obvious that the poor possess it in greater abundance than the rich. People squander the good portion of it and keep only the bad. It is visible and invisible, and children play with it in the street, but the ignorant crush it underfoot every day.' The consciousness of this qualitative *materia prima* will surely become more and more acute in most minds as the bastions of specialized thought and graduated knowledge collapse. Those who make a profession of creating, and those whose profession prevents them from creating, both artists and workers, are being pushed into the same nihilism by the process of proletarianization. This process, which is accompanied by resistance to it—resistance, that is, to co-opted forms of creativity—occurs amid such a plethora of cultural goods—records, films, paperback books—that once these commodities have been freed from the laws of consumption they will pass immediately into the service of true creativity. The sabotage of the mechanisms of economic and cultural consumption is epitomized by young people who steal the books in which they expect to find confirmation of their radicalism.

Once reconquered by the qualitative, the most varied kinds of knowledge combine and form a magnetic network powerful enough to overthrow the most oppressive traditions. The force of simple spontaneous creativity increases knowledge at an exponential rate. Using makeshift equipment and negligible funds, a German engineer recently built an apparatus able to perform all the functions of the cyclotron accelerator. If individual creativity can achieve such results with such meagre prompting, what marvels of energy may be anticipated from the qualitative shock waves and chain reactions that will occur when the spirit of freedom still alive in the individual emerges once more in collective form to celebrate the great social fête, with its joyous breaking of all taboos.

The task of a coherent revolutionary group, far from being the creation of a new type of conditioning, is to establish protected areas where the intensity of conditioning tends towards zero. Making everyone aware of their creative potential will be a hapless task if no recourse is had to qualitative shock tactics. Nothing more can be expected from mass parties and other groupings based on the principle of quantitative recruitment. Something *can* be expected, on the other hand, from micro-societies whose members recognize their peers by their radical action or thinking, groups maintained in a permanent state of practical readiness by strict attention to theoretical consistency. Cells established along such lines have every chance of one day wielding sufficient influence to free the creativity of the greatest number of people. The despair of the anarchist bomb-throwers must be changed into hope; their tactics, worthy of medieval warriors, must be transformed into a modern strategy.

4. Poetry

What is poetry? It is the organization of creative spontaneity, the deployment of the qualitative in accordance with its coherent inner logic. Poetry is what the Greeks call *poiein*, or 'making', but making restored to the purity of its original impulse—restored, in a word, to the totality.

Without the qualitative, no poetry is possible. The void left by poetry is filled by poetry's opposites: information, transitional programmes, specialization, reformism—all the motley guises of the fragmentary. But the presence of the qualitative does not of itself ensure the progression of poetry. The richest complex of signs and possibilities may well lapse into confusion, fall apart for lack of consistency or crumble by reason of crossed purposes. The yardstick of effectiveness must always remain supreme. Poetry is thus also radical theory completely integrated into action, the mortar binding tactics and revolutionary strategy, and the high point of the great game of everyday life.

What is poetry? In 1895, during an ill-advised and seemingly doomed French rail strike, a militant of the National Railwaymen's Union stood up and suggested an ingenious and cheap way of advancing the strikers' cause: 'It takes two pennyworth of a particular substance used in the right way to immobilize a locomotive.' It was not very long before the government and the bosses caved in. Poetry in this case was clearly the act that brought a new reality into being, that reversed the perspective. The *materia prima* is within everyone's reach. Poets are those who know how to use it to best effect. Furthermore, two pennyworth of some chemical is as nothing compared with the abundance of peerless ready energy afforded by everyday life itself: the energy of the will to live, the power of desire unleashed, the passion of love, the love of passion, the force of fear and anxiety, the rising tide of hate and the repercussions of wild destructiveness. Who knows what poetic upheavals may confidently be expected to stem from such universally experienced feelings as those associated with death, old age and sickness? This still marginal consciousness will surely be the starting-point of the long revolution of everyday life, the only true poetry made by all and not by one alone.

'What is poetry?' ask the aesthetes. So, for their benefit, let us state the obvious: rarely does poetry today involve poems. Most works of art are betrayals of poetry. How could it be otherwise, when poetry and Power cannot be reconciled? At best the artist's creativity builds a prison for itself, cloistering itself, awaiting its moment, within an *oeuvre* that has not yet said its last word; but, however high its author's hopes, that last word—supposed to herald perfect communication—can never be pronounced so long as the revolt of creativity has not yet brought art to its fulfilment.

The African work of art—poem, music, sculpture or mask—is not considered complete until it has become creative speech, an active word: it must *function*. This holds true well beyond African art. There is no art in the world which does not seek to *function*; and to function—later co-optation notwithstanding—in accordance with the will that generated it, the will to live continually in the euphoria of the moment of creation. Why is it that the greatest works never seem to be finished? The answer is that great art cries out in every possible way for fulfilment, for the right to enter the world of lived experience. The degeneration of present-day art is a bow perfectly readied for such an arrow.

Nothing can save past culture from the cult of the past except those pictures, writings, musical or built architecture, and so on, whose qualitative dimension reaches us independently of their forms (contaminated by the decay now affecting all artistic forms). The works of Sade and Lautréamont are good examples, of course, but so are those of Villon, Lucretius, Rabelais, Pascal, Fourier, Bosch, Dante, Bach, Swift, Shakespeare, Uccello, etc. All are liable to shed their cultural chrysalis, emerge from the museums to which history has relegated them and become so much lethal shrapnel for the infernal devices of those who are going to fulfil art. Old works of art should thus be appraised by measuring the sum of radical theory embodied in them, the hard core of creative spontaneity awaiting release by the creators of the future for the purposes of—and by means of—an unprecedented kind of poetry.

Radical theory excels at deferring actions initiated by creative spontaneity without mitigating or sidelining them. Similarly, the artistic approach seeks in its finest moments to stamp the world with the mark of a mobile subjectivity always tentacular in nature and always hungry to create—and to create itself. But whereas radical theory hews fast to poetic reality, to reality under construction, to the world as it is being transformed, art takes an identical tack but at much greater risk of going astray or being corrupted. Only an art armed against itself—against its own weakest, most aesthetic self—can resist co-optation.

As we know, consumer society reduces art to a range of consumable products. This vulgarizing tendency accelerates degeneration but by the same token improves the prospects of supersession. That communication so urgently sought by the artist is jammed and banned even in the simplest relationships of everyday life. So true is this that the search for new forms of communication, far from being the preserve of painters and poets, is now part of a collective effort. This is the end of the old specialization of art. There are no more artists because everyone is an artist. The work of art of the future will be the construction of a passionate life.

The object created is less important than the process that engenders it, the act of creating. What makes artists artists is their creativity, not art galleries. Unfortunately, artists rarely recognize themselves as creators: for the most part they play to the public, showing off. The contemplative attitude towards art was the first stone thrown at the creators. They encouraged this attitude in the first place, but today it is their undoing, for it amounts to no more than an obligation to consume, reflecting the crassest of economic imperatives. Which is why there is no longer any such thing as a work of art in the classical sense of the word. Nor can there be such a thing—and so much the better. Poetry resides elsewhere: in deeds, in the events we bring about. The poetry of deeds, formerly always treated as marginal, now stands at the centre of everyone's concerns, at the centre of everyday life—a sphere which in fact it never left.

True poetry cares nothing for poems. In his quest for the Book, Mallarmé wanted nothing so much as to abolish the poem. And what better way to abolish the poem than to fulfil it? Indeed a few of Mallarmé's contemporaries proved themselves rather brilliant exponents of just such a new poetry. Did the author of *Hérodiade* have an inkling, perhaps, when he described them as 'angels of purity', that the anarchists with their bombs offered the poet a key which, walled up in his words, he could never use?

Poetry is always somewhere. If it leaves the realm of the arts, it is all the easier to see that it belongs first and foremost in action, in a way of living and in the search for a way of living. Everywhere repressed, this poetry springs up everywhere. Brutally put down, it is reborn in violence. It consecrates riots, embraces rebellions and animates all great revolutionary carnivals until the bureaucrats place it under house arrest in their hagiographical culture.

Lived poetry has effectively shown throughout history, even in partial revolts, even in crime—which Coeurderoy so aptly dubbed the 'revolt of one'—that it is the protector *par excellence* of everything irreducible in mankind, meaning creative spontaneity. The will to unite the individual and the social, not on the basis of illusory community but on that of subjectivity, is what makes the new poetry into a weapon that everyone must learn to handle *by themselves*. Poetic experience is now at a premium. The organization of spontaneity will be the work of spontaneity itself.

XXI Masters Without Slaves

Power is that social organization whereby masters maintain the
conditions of servitude. God, State, Organization: these three words
adequately sum up the relative significance of autonomy and
historical determinism for Power. Three principles have held sway in
succession: the principle of domination (feudal power), the principle
of exploitation (bourgeois power), and the principle of organization
(cybernetic power) (2). Secularization and mechanization have
both helped perfect hierarchical social organization, but at the
same time the contradictions of that organization have become
more acute. It has been humanized precisely to the extent that
it has stripped human beings of their human substance. It has
gained in autonomy at the expense of the masters (those in charge
are themselves governed by the levers of Power). Those who
enforce Power's directives today are the modern descendants of
the race of those submissive slaves who, Theognis tells us, were
born with head bowed. They cannot even enjoy the unhealthy
pleasure of domination. Confronting these master-slaves are those
who refuse—the new proletariat, rich in revolutionary traditions.
Out of this confrontation will come the future masters without
slaves, and a higher form of society destined to realize both the
lived project of childhood and the historical project of the great
aristocrats (1 and 3).

1

'Everyone would like if possible to be master of all men, or better still God
himself.' Thus Plato in the *Theages*. A feeble enough ambition in view
of the weakness of masters and gods. After all, slaves are puny in that
they are in thrall to those who govern them; masters—and God himself—
are puny because of the shortcomings of those whom they govern. The
master experiences the positive pole of alienation, the slave its negative
one, but both are denied full mastery.

How does the feudal lord behave in this dialectic of master and slave? As slave of God and master of men—and master of men *because* he is a slave of God, according to the rules of the myth—he finds himself condemned, in his dealings with God, to mingle execration with self-interested genuflection, for it is to God that he owes obedience and from God that he derives his power over men. In short, he reproduces the same relationship between himself and God that obtains between nobles and monarch. What is a king? An elect of the elect: the struggle for succession to the throne usually resembles a contest between equals. Feudal lords serve the monarch, but they serve him as potential equals. By the same token, if they submit to God they do so qua rivals, qua competitors.

The dissatisfaction of the masters of old is not hard to understand. Through God, they inhabit the negative pole of alienation; through those whom they oppress, they inhabit its positive pole. How could they truly wish to be God, familiar as they are with the trials of positive alienation? And at the same time how could they fail to want to destroy God, who tyrannizes them? The 'to be or not to be' of the high and mighty always came down to the question, insoluble in the feudal world, of how to negate yet preserve God—in other words how to supersede and realize Him.

History records two practical attempts to achieve such a supersession: that of the mystics and that of the great negators. Meister Eckhart: 'I pray to God to deliver me from God.' Similarly, the Swabian heretics claimed in 1270 that they had risen above God, and that since they had themselves attained the highest possible degree of divinity, they had abandoned God. Following another path, the negative path, such towering figures as Heliogabalus, Gilles de Rais or Elizabeth Báthory were clearly trying to attain complete mastery over the world by eliminating the intermediaries, those who alienated them positively, namely their slaves. Perversely, they sought to arrive at the total human being via total inhumanity. What this shows is that the passion for ruling without restrictions and the slave's absolute rejection of constraints follow one and the same path: that up-hill-and-down-dale road on which Caligula and Spartacus, Gilles de Rais and György Dosza all travel, together yet apart. But it is not enough simply to note that the thoroughgoing revolt of slaves (and I say thoroughgoing because I am not talking about inadequate revolts like the Christian, bourgeois or socialist ones) is akin to extreme revolts by feudal lords. The fact is that the will to abolish slaves and their descendants (proletarians, administrators, abject and passive individuals) opens up a unique opportunity for the will to reign over the world with no restrictions save those imposed by a finally reinvented nature and by the resistance of things to being transformed.

This opportunity is part of a historical process. History exists because the oppressed exist. The struggle against nature, and against the various forms of social organization devised in that struggle, has always been the struggle for human emancipation, for the whole human being. The refusal to be a slave is the only thing that really changes the world.

What then is the goal of history? Made 'under specific conditions' (Marx) by slaves and against slavery, history can have but one end: the destruction of the masters. For his part, the master strives incessantly to escape from history, rejecting it by massacring those who make it—and who make it against *him*.

Let me review the paradoxes here:

(a) The most human aspect of the masters of old lay in their aspiration to absolute dominion. Such a project implied the complete arrest of history, and hence a radical rejection of its emancipatory tendencies. In short, total inhumanity.

(b) The desire to escape history only makes one more vulnerable to it: to flee it is to break cover and expose oneself to its blows. Diehard conservatism is every bit as susceptible to the repeated assaults of real life as it is to the dialectic of the forces of production. The masters fall victim to history. History crushes them in accordance with what, from atop the pyramid of the present, with three thousand years' worth of hindsight, gives every appearance of a *plan*, a systematic programme, a line of force which tempts us to speak of history as having a goal (the end of the world of slavery, the end of the feudal world, the end of the bourgeois world).

It is because they seek to escape history that the masters are in due course filed in history's pigeonholes; they enter linear temporal development however much they resist. By contrast, those who make history—revolutionaries, slaves drunk with total freedom—seem to act *sub specie aeternitatis*, under the sign of the timeless; they are drawn by an insatiable thirst for life intensely lived, and they remain faithful to this goal regardless of changing historical conditions. Perhaps the philosophical concept of eternity is tied up with the historical quest for emancipation, and destined to be realized one day—along with philosophy—by those who embody total freedom and the end of traditional history.

(c) The superiority of alienation's negative pole to its positive one lies in the fact that it is only from the negative starting-point that thoroughgoing revolt can make the project of absolute mastery feasible. It is slaves, struggling to throw off their chains, who unleash the movement whereby history abolishes masters, and who can already glimpse, beyond history, the possibility of a new kind of power over things—a power which no longer has to appropriate beings in order to appropriate objects. Given the slow workings of history, however, it was inevitable that the masters would not vanish in an instant; instead, they degenerated slowly, until today we have no more masters, just slaves-who-consume-power, distinguishable from one another only by reference to the relative degree and quantity of power they consume.

That the forces of production could but slowly create the material preconditions of total emancipation, that they had first to pass through the bourgeois stage, was unavoidable. Now that automation and cybernetics, if applied in a truly human way, permit the fulfilment of the dreams of the masters of old, and the dreams of slaves of every age, all we have left of the old system is a socially shapeless magma in which each individual is in some confused and partial way both master and slave. This reign of *equivalent values* is nevertheless destined to spawn the masters of the future: masters without slaves.

I should like *en passant* to pay homage to Sade. His appearance at a great turning-point in history and his astonishing lucidity together qualify him as the last insurgent *grand seigneur*. His *120 Days of Sodom* shows us the lords of the Château of Selling making their bid for absolute mastery and eternal delight by massacring all their servants. Marquis and sansculotte, Donatien Alphonse François de Sade couples in his person the perfectly logical hedonism of Sganarelle's 'wicked nobleman' and the revolutionary will to revel endlessly in a subjectivity freed at last from the shackles of hierarchy. His desperate efforts to abolish alienation both positive and negative place him in the highest rank among theorists of the whole human being. It is high time revolutionaries read him as carefully as they read Marx. (Admittedly, the knowledge of Marx of specialists in the study of revolution tends to be limited to what Marx wrote under the pseudonym of 'Stalin'—or at best as 'Lenin' and 'Trotsky'.) At all events, no genuine quest to change everyday life in radical fashion can afford to ignore either the great negators of Power or any of those masters of an earlier day who had the capacity to feel straitjacketed by the authority with which God had invested them.

2

Bourgeois power draws sustenance from the crumbs of feudal power. It is simply bits and pieces of feudal power. Gnawed by revolutionary criticism, then trampled and shattered—but without this destruction ever being carried to its logical conclusion, namely the abolition of hierarchical power—aristocratic authority outlived the demise of the aristocracy in a parodic form, like the fixed grin of a dead man. The leaders of the bourgeoisie, tightly confined within their fragmented power, striving to pass pieces off as the totality (this is, surely, the essence of totalitarianism), were destined to see their prestige, infected by the disintegration of the spectacle, fall into tatters. With the gravitas of myth and the belief in authority gone, the only forms of government left were burlesque terror and idiot democracy. What lovely children Bonaparte had! Louis-Philippe, Napoleon III, Thiers, Alfonso XIII, Hitler, Mussolini, Stalin, Franco, Salazar, Nasser, Mao, de Gaulle—so many fertile Ubus spawning ever more cretinous offspring in every corner of the world. Only yesterday these travesties of the truly powerful could still strike sparks of authority and threaten Jupiter's wrath; today their weedy successors are lucky if they can achieve a miserable *succès d'estime* on the social stage. There are no leading roles for them any more. Of course, as grotesque as he might be, a Franco still kills. But mark my words: the stupidity of Power is about to become a far deadlier killer than stupidity in power.

The brainwashing machine of our penal colony is the spectacle. Our master-slaves are the spectacle's faithful servants, its actors and stage-managers. Who would care to judge them? We may be sure that they will plead not guilty. And indeed they are not guilty. What they depend on is less cynical compliance than spontaneous allegiance, less terror than willing victims, less brute force than herds of masochists. The ruler's justification lies in the spinelessness of the ruled. But everyone is ruled now, manipulated like a thing by an abstract Power, by an ontologically autonomous organization whose rules apply as readily to the would-be rulers as to anyone else. And you cannot judge *things;* you can only prevent them from doing harm.

In October 1963, the sociologist Jean Fourastié reached the following conclusions with regard to the leader of the future: 'The leader has lost

his former *magical* power; he is now, and will continue to be, someone
capable *of provoking action*. Ultimately decision-making will become the
responsibility of work groups. The leader will be a committee chairman,
albeit one able to *come to conclusions and make decisions.*' (Emphasis mine.)
Discernible in this definition are three principles governing three phases in
the historical development of the master: (a) the principle of domination,
characteristic of feudal society; (b) the principle of exploitation, characteristic of bourgeois society; and (c) the principle of organization, characteristic of cybernetic society. In actuality, all three principles are in play at all
times. There is no domination without exploitation and organization. But
the relative importance of each varies with the era under consideration.
As one stage gives way to the next, the independence and the sway of the
masters decline. In proportion as their humanity tends towards zero, the
inhumanity of disembodied Power tends towards infinity.

Under the *principle of domination*, the master denies his slaves an
existence which would limit his own. Under the *principle of exploitation*, the boss grants his workers the degree of existence which fattens
and develops his own. The *principle of organization* breaks individual
existences down into fractions, classifying them according to degrees in
each's leadership and executive abilities. A foreman might be described,
for example, after careful examination of his productivity, representativ-
ity, etc., as 56 percent leader, 40 percent executive and (as Fourier might
have put it) 4 percent ambiguous.

Domination is a right, exploitation a contract, and organization
an order of *things*. The tyrant dominates according to his will to power;
the capitalist exploits according to the laws of profit; the organizer
programmes and is programmed. The first aspires to the arbitrary, the
second to justice, the third to rationality and objectivity. The inhumanity of the feudal lord is a humanity in search of itself. The inhumanity
of the exploiter seeks to buy its way out by bribing humanity with technological progress, amenities and the banishing of hunger and disease.
The inhumanity of the cybernetician is an inhumanity perfectly at peace
with itself. Thus the inhumanity of masters has become progressively less
human. A camp for systematic extermination is more atrocious than the
murderous frenzy of feudal barons engaged in a pointless war. Yet the
massacres of Auschwitz have a well-nigh lyrical quality when compared
with the icy grasp of the generalized conditioning that the programmers
of technocratic organization have in mind for society in a frighteningly

near future. I am not saying that there is more 'humanity' in a *lettre de cachet* than in brainwashing techniques. That is like choosing between the hangman's rope and the guillotine. No, it is simply that the dubious pleasure derived from dominating and crushing people is tending to disappear. It was capitalism that brought in the need to exploit people without getting any gratification out of it. No sadism, none of the negative pleasure in existing to be had from the infliction of pain, not even a *perverted* humanity: the reign of things in its perfected form. When they gave up the principle of hedonism the masters gave up mastery itself. It will fall to the masters without slaves to correct this error.

What production-centred capitalism set in motion is now being completed by the dictatorship of consumption. The principle of organization is putting the finishing touches to the total mastery of dead things over people. Whatever power remained to those who possessed the means of production is lost as soon as control of the machines passes from the hands of their owners to the hands of technicians who organize their use. Even these organizers are doomed to be ingurgitated by their own plans and systems. The simple machine will then be seen to have been the last justification for the existence of bosses, the last prop for their vestigial humanity. The cybernetic organization of production and consumption calls ineluctably for the control, planning and rationalization of everyday life.

Specialists are those truncated masters, those masters-as-slaves, who proliferate in the sphere of everyday life. Their prospects, we may be sure, are nil. As early as 1867, at the Basel Congress of the First International, Francau had this to say: 'We have been in tow for far too long to the dukes of the diploma and the potentates of science. Let us take care of our own affairs; no matter how inept we are, we will never make such a poor job of it as these people do, in our name.' Fine words of wisdom, these—and all the more apt today, as swarms of experts insinuate themselves into every aspect of individual life. A clear polarization is occurring between those who succumb to the magnetism of the great Kafkaesque machine of cybernetics and those who follow their deepest impulses and seek to escape this machine at all costs. These last are the sole trustees of all that is human, because there is no one left in the camp of the former masters who can make any claim to humanity. On the one hand, there is nothing left but things, all falling at the same speed into the void; on the other, nothing but the age-old project of slaves drunk with the prospect of total freedom.

3. *The Master Without Slaves, or the Aristocratic Supersession of Aristocracy.*

The master exits through the same door as God. He topples like a golem as soon as he ceases to love human beings, that is to say, as soon as he ceases to love the pleasure he takes in oppressing them, as soon as he renounces the principle of hedonism. There is scant pleasure to be drawn from the ordering of things, from the manipulation of beings as passive and inert as bricks. With his refined tastes, God needs living creatures; appetizing, throbbing flesh; souls trembling in terror and humility. To get the feeling of his own grandeur he must sense the presence of subjects who are fervent in prayer, in rebellion, in subterfuge—even in blasphemy. The Catholic God is quite willing to dispense true freedom, but he extends it, like a pawnbroker, only against collateral. He plays cat and mouse with humans until the Day of Judgement, then he gobbles them up. With the arrival of the bourgeoisie on the scene towards the end of the Middle Ages, this God is slowly humanized, but humanized in a paradoxical way, for at the same time he becomes an object, and so do human beings. Calvin's God, by dooming people to predestination, abdicates his pleasure in arbitrary judgement: he is no longer free to crush whomever he wishes as the mood takes him. This is the God of the business transaction, bereft of divine whim, quantifiable, cold as a discount rate. And he hides his head in shame: *Deus absconditus*. The connection is broken. Hence Pascal's despair, and Descartes's muddled attempt to find an anchorage for a soul suddenly adrift. Later—too late—Kierkegaard tried to revive a subjective God by reviving human subjectivity. But there was no reanimating a God who was by now the 'Great External Object' in the minds of men—dead as the dodo, lithified, his bones of coral made. Caught, now, in the *rigor mortis* of God's dying embrace (i.e., Power's hierarchical *form*), people seem doomed to reification, and everything human to annihilation. From Power's perspective there is nothing to be seen but things—chips of the divine fossil. And is this not indeed the lens through which the so-called human sciences of sociology, psychology and economics pursue their 'objective' researches?

What obliges the master to relinquish his hedonism? What prevents him achieving complete gratification, if not the very fact of his being a master, his commitment to the principle of hierarchical superiority? The scope of this renunciation of his can only widen as hierarchy is comminuted, as masters—but reduced masters—become legion, as history parcels out power in democratic doses. The imperfect gratification of the masters turns into the gratification of imperfect masters. We have witnessed the bourgeois leaders—Ubuesque plebeians—consummating their beer-hall revolt in the funeral feast of fascism. But soon there will be no feasting at all for the master-slaves—last avatars of hierarchical man. The only thing left to them will be the melancholy of things, a morose serenity, the malaise of roles, and the awareness of *being nothing*.

What is to become of the *things* that govern us? Must they be destroyed? If so, the best-equipped to liquidate slaves-in-power are those who have been fighting slavery all along. The creativity of the people, which neither lords nor capitalists have managed to crush, will never kowtow to programmed needs and technocratic planning. It will be objected that there is less passion and enthusiasm for the liquidation of an abstract form, a system, than for the killing of hated masters. But this is to see the problem from the wrong angle—from the point of view of Power. For, in contrast to the bourgeoisie, the proletariat is not defined in terms of its class opponent, but heralds the end of class distinctions and of hierarchy per se. The bourgeoisie's role was strictly negative, as Saint-Just reminds us with fine arrogance when he observes that 'What constitutes a republic is the total destruction of everything that stands opposed to it.'

Whereas the bourgeoisie was content to forge arms against the feudal system—arms that will one day be turned against the bourgeoisie itself—the proletariat carries within itself the possibility of its own supersession. The proletariat is poetry, momentarily alienated by the ruling class or by technocratic organization, but ever apt to burst out of its bondage. As the sole depository of the will to live—for it alone has experienced in its full force the intolerable pressure of mere survival—the proletariat is destined to demolish the walls of constraint in the whirlwind of its pleasure and the spontaneous violence of its creative energy. All the joy and laughter that this will release the proletariat already possesses, for its strength and passion are drawn from within. What it is preparing to build will, in addition, destroy whatever stands in its way, like a fresh tape-recording automatically erasing the previous one. The power of things will be abolished by a proletariat in the act of abolishing itself, by virtue of a luxurious, nonchalant afterthought, by virtue of the sort of grace displayed by someone calmly manifesting their superiority. From the new proletariat will emerge, not the robotic humanists dreamt of by the onanists of the supposedly revolutionary Left, but masters without slaves. The insurrectional violence of the masses is but one aspect of the proletariat's creativity: this class is just as impatient to abolish itself as it is to carry out survival's self-imposed death sentence.

I find it helpful, if artificial, to distinguish three dominant passions active in the overthrow of the reified order:

(a) *The passion for absolute power,* a passion for placing objects directly in the service of human beings without the mediation of human beings themselves; and the consequent destruction of those who cleave to the order of things, slaves who possess crumbs of power. 'Because we cannot stand the sight of them, we shall abolish slaves,' says Nietzsche.

(b) *The passion for smashing constraints,* for breaking chains. In Sade's words, 'How can lawful pleasures be compared to those which embody not only much more piquant delights but also the priceless joy of breaking all social restraints and overturning all laws?'

(c) *The passion for rectifying an unhappy past,* for revisiting and fulfilling dashed hopes, this in the individual's life as in the history of defeated revolutions. Just as it was right to punish Louis XVI for the crimes of his predecessors, passion gives us every reason—there being no way of visiting vengeance on things—to cleanse the memory, so offensive to any free human being, of executed Communards, tortured peasants in 1525, workers massacred, revolutionaries hunted down and murdered, civilizations demolished by colonialism, and all past oppression which the present has yet to rectify. Righting that past has become a passionate pursuit because it has at last become historically possible to wash away the blood of Babeuf, Lacenaire, Ravachol and Bonnot with the blood of the obscure descendants of all those who, though themselves enslaved to an order based on profit and financial mechanisms, have contrived to put cruel checks on human emancipation.

The pleasure to be had from overturning Power, becoming a master without slaves, and righting the past gives pride of place to the subjectivity of each individual. In revolutionary moments everyone has a chance to make their own history. *Naturally, the cause of the freedom to fulfil oneself mobilizes subjectivity* (and thereby ceases to be a cause). This is the only perspective that opens up those dizzying heights of possibility where every kind of pleasure comes within the grasp of all.

//////

The destroyers of the old order of things must beware lest they bring it down upon their own heads. Unless collective shelters of some kind can be devised against conditioning, against the spectacle and hierarchical organization, there is a real danger that a consumerist avalanche will sweep us all down with it into oblivion. From such shelters future offensives can be launched. Microsocieties already in gestation will realize the project of the masters of old, duly divested of its hierarchical canker. The supersession of the 'wicked nobleman' will amount to a strict application of Keats's admirable principle according to which everything that can be abolished must be abolished if the children are to be saved from slavery. This supersession must occur in three spheres simultaneously: (a) the supersession of patriarchal social organization; (b) the supersession of hierarchical power; (c) the supersession of subjective arbitrariness, of authoritarian caprice.

(a) The magical power of the aristocracy resides in lineage, in the authority passed on in this way from generation to generation. The bourgeoisie undermines feudal authority, but by the same token it involuntarily undermines the family, along with the organization of society in general. This negativity of the bourgeoisie is undoubtedly its greatest virtue, its most 'positive' side. But what the bourgeoisie lacks is the possibility of supersession. What would constitute a real supersession of the family in its aristocratic form? The answer can only be the establishment of coherent groups in which individual creativity is totally invested in collective creativity and strengthened by it; in which an unmediated, lived *present* becomes the source of the energy potential which under feudalism was derived from the *past*. The relative powerlessness of the lord imprisoned by his hierarchical system is strikingly reminiscent of the weakness of the child held fast in the setting of the bourgeois family.

Children enjoy a subjective experience of freedom unknown to any animal species, but at the same time they remain objectively dependent on their parents, whose care and love they need. What distinguishes young humans from young animals is a boundless sense of the transformability of the world, that is to say, a sense of *poetry*. But at the same time they have no access to the techniques which adults direct for the most part, precisely, against poetry, including ways of conditioning children themselves. And by the time children *are* old enough to handle such techniques, they have been so broken, so constrained, that in their 'maturity' they lose whatever made their childhood a privileged state. The universe of the masters of old is cursed in the same way as the universe of children: the means of liberation are out of reach in both cases. Feudal lords could only dream of the *transformation* of the world while remaining bound by the laws of *adaptation* to it. Once the bourgeoisie brings world-transforming technology to a high degree of sophistication, hierarchical organization—arguably the best way of focusing social energy in a world where that energy lacks the invaluable support of machines—becomes an anachronism, a brake on the development of human control of the world. Hierarchy, the power of man over man, obscures the true enemy; it prohibits the transformation of the milieu and imposes the need for adaptation to that environment as it is, the need for enrolment as a thing in an order of things.

(b) The destruction of the social screen which alienates our view of the world requires the absolute rejection of all hierarchy within the social group. In this connection the notion of the dictatorship of the proletariat calls for scrutiny. Historically, the dictatorship of the proletariat has largely turned into dictatorship *over* the proletariat; in other words, it has been institutionalized. In Lenin's words, 'The dictatorship of the proletariat is a stubborn struggle, bloody and bloodless, violent and peaceful, military and economic, educational and administrative, against the forces and traditions of the old society.' The proletariat cannot institute an enduring despotism, nor head a willingly accepted dictatorship. The imperative need to crush the enemy nevertheless obliges it to concentrate a highly consistent repressive power in its own hands. It is a matter, therefore, of passing through a dictatorship that is self-negating, and for the proletarian party, as for the proletariat itself, 'Victory must also mean annihilation'. The proletariat must use its dictatorship to place its own negation on the immediate order of the day. It has no choice but to liquidate in short order—as bloodily or as bloodlessly as the circumstances decree—all those who stand in the way of its project of total liberation, all those who oppose the end of the proletariat as such. These enemies must be completely exterminated, like swarming vermin. Furthermore, within each individual, the proletariat must erase even the most vestigial concern with status, stirring up against such hierarchical tendencies (i.e., against roles) a tranquil energy directed towards authentic life.

(c) The end of roles means the triumph of subjectivity. Once acknowledged and given pride of place, this subjectivity will give rise, paradoxically, to a new objectivity. A new world of objects—a new 'nature', as it were—will be constituted on the basis of the requirements of individual subjectivity. Here again there is a parallel between the child's point of view and the feudal lord's. In both instances—though in different modes—the possible is obscured by the screen of social alienation.

How can anyone forget those spaces of primitive immensity which open before the solitary child? When we were children every stick was a magic wand. Then we had to adapt, to become social and sociable. The life went out of our solitude, the child chose to grow old despite himself, and the immensity was suddenly closed up like a storybook. In this world nobody manages to leave the murky waters of puberty completely behind. Now childhood itself is being gradually colonized by consumer society. The 'preteens' are already a category on a par with teenagers in the big happy family of consumers; will they grow up faster if they consume their childhood instead of living it? It is quite impossible not to be startled by the resemblance between the historical decadence of the old masters and the growing decadence of the realm of childhood. The corruption of the human has surely reached its nadir. Never have we been so near to, yet so far from the whole human being.

The capriciousness of the lord and master of earlier times is inferior to the child's in that, odiously, it calls for the oppression of other people. The subjectivity embodied in feudal arbitrariness 'I give you riches or I give you death, as I see fit'—is tainted and hobbled by its poverty of expression. In fact the lord's subjectivity is fulfilled only through the denial of the subjectivity of others; in this way it chains itself up, for by shackling others it shackles itself.

Children do not have the advantage of this imperfection: they lose their right to pure subjectivity in one fell swoop. They are forever being taxed with childishness and urged to behave like grown-ups. And grow up they must, repressing their childhood all life long, until dotage and agony let them imagine that they have lived adult lives.

Child's play—just like the play of the *grand seigneur*—needs to be liberated and restored to its former glory. The present moment is historically propitious. Let us save childhood by fulfilling the project of the masters of old: childhood complete with its sovereign subjectivity; with its laughter, that first murmur of spontaneity; and with its way of reaching deep into itself to illuminate the world and bathe objects in a strangely familiar light.

We have lost the beauty of things; we have lost touch with things' way of being by leaving them to die in the clutches of Power and the gods.

The splendid daydream that was Surrealism sought in vain to revive them by means of poetic radiation, but the power of imagination alone is not enough to burst the husk of social alienation in which things are imprisoned, and, try as it might, cannot restore them to the free play of subjectivity. From Power's point of view, a stone, a tree, a mixer, a cyclotron are all dead objects—so many gravestones over the will to see them otherwise, and to change them. Yet I know, aside from what they are made to mean, that these things could thrill me to the core. I know what passionate enthusiasm machines can arouse once pressed into the service of play, fantasy and freedom. A world in which everything is alive—even stones and trees—can have no place for passively contemplated signs. Everything in such a world would bespeak joy. The triumph of subjectivity will give life back to things; and does not the present intolerable domination of subjectivity by dead things itself constitute at bottom our best historical chance of one day attaining a higher state of life?

How so? By actualizing in today's language—in the language of praxis—what a heretic once said to John of Ruysbroeck: 'God cannot know anything, will anything or do anything without me. With God I created myself, I created all things, and my hand holds up heaven, earth and all the creatures of the earth. Without me there is nothing.'

//////

New limits have to be discovered. The restrictions imposed by social alienation continue, if not to imprison us, then at least to abuse us. People have been standing for centuries before a worm-eaten door, making pinholes in it with growing ease. At this point a good kick would break it down, for only on the far side does everything begin. The proletariat's problem is no longer how to seize power but how to abolish Power forever. Beyond the world of hierarchy, possibilities will surge forth unbidden. The establishment of life's ascendancy over survival is the historical movement that will undo history. Our true opponents have yet to be invented, and it is up to us to seek them out, to join battle with them on the far side—the childish side—of things.

Can humanity resume a dialogue with the cosmos, a dialogue comparable to the one that the earliest inhabitants of the earth must have engaged in, yet different, this time, in that it will occur on a higher plane, on a plane whence it is possible to look back at prehistory, on a plane devoid of the trembling awe of early humans faced by the mystery of the cosmos? In a word, can the cosmos be endowed with a human meaning—a highly desirable replacement for the divine meaning with which it has been encumbered since the dawn of time?

And what of that other infinity, the actual human being, complete with body, nervous system, muscular activity and errant dreams? Might not humanity one day become master of these too? Might not individual will, once liberated by collective will, put to shame the astounding if sinister wonders of control already achieved over human beings by police-state conditioning techniques? If people can be made into dogs, bricks, or Green Berets, who is to say that they cannot be made into human beings?

We have never put enough faith in our own infallibility. Perhaps out of pride, we have handed a monopoly of this pretension to a medley of hypostasized, wizened forms: Power, God, the Pope, the Führer, Other People. And yet, every time we refer to Society, God, or all-powerful Justice, we are referring—albeit feebly and indirectly—to our own power. At least we are one stage beyond prehistory—and on the threshold of a new form of human organization, a social organization in which all the energy of individual creativity will have free rein, so that the world will be shaped by the dreams of each, as harmonized by all.

Utopia? Far from it! Condescension could not be more ill-placed. I know of *no one* who does not cling with all their might to the hope of such a world. Many, of course, lose their grip on this hope—but they put as much desperate energy into falling as into hanging on. Everyone wants their own subjectivity to triumph; the unification of human beings ought therefore to be built on this common desire. Nobody can strengthen their subjectivity without the help of others, without the help of a group that concentrates subjectivity, that faithfully expresses the subjectivity of its members. So far, the Situationist International is the only revolutionary group resolved to defend radical subjectivity at all costs.

XXII The Space-Time of Lived Experience and the Rectification of the Past

The dialectic of decay and supersession is also that of dissociated and unitary space-time [1]. The new proletariat carries within itself the capacity for fulfilling the potential of childhood and childhood's space-time [2]. The history of separations tends slowly towards a resolution with the end of 'historicizing' history [3]. Cyclical versus linear time. Lived space-time is the space-time of transformation; the space-time of roles is that of adaptation. The function of the past and of its projection into the future is the interdiction of the present. Historical ideology is the screen which comes between the will to individual fulfilment and the will to make history, preventing any fraternization or melding between them [4]. The present is a space-time yet to be created and implies the rectification of the past [5].

1

As the experts organize the survival of the species, and assign the programming of history to their sophisticated plans, the will to change life by changing the world grows ever stronger among the mass of the people. The point has been reached where each particular human being finds himself face to face, just like humanity as a whole, with a general despair with no way out except either annihilation or supersession. Ours is a time in which historical and individual development tend to merge because both are headed in the same direction—towards the state of *things*, and the refusal of this state. The history of the species and the millions of individual histories seem to be coming together—either to perish or to begin EVERYTHING afresh. In this way the past returns to us, bearing the seeds of death along with the spark of life. And our childhood too is at the meeting-place—under the threat of Lot's curse.

This threat hanging over our childhood is, I dare to hope, going to provoke an upsurge of revolt against the ghastly aging process to which the forced feeding of ideology and gimmicks condemns the child. I like to point up the undeniable analogy, in terms of dreams and desires, between the will of the feudal lord and the subjective wishes of the child. If we fulfil the potential of childhood, that must surely imply that the fulfilment of the project of the old masters is likewise destined to be carried through by us, adults of the technocratic era, rich in what children lack, possessors of what was beyond the reach of even the great world-conquerors. To us it will fall to combine collective history and individual destiny in ways surpassing the wildest dreams of a Tamerlane or a Heliogabalus.

As I have noted, the establishment of life's ascendancy over survival is the historical movement that will undo history. The construction of everyday life and the fulfilment of history are now one and the same project. In what will the joint construction of a new life and of a new society consist? What will be the nature of the revolution of everyday life? Simply this: supersession will replace decline, as the consciousness of the reality of decline nourishes the consciousness of the necessity for supersession.

No matter how far back in history, all previous attempts at supersession are part and parcel of today's poetry of the reversal of perspective. They play a part in it directly, without mediation, leaping over or even breaking down the barriers of space and time. The end of all separations undoubtedly begins with the end of one particular separation, that between space and time. For all these reasons it is clear that the reconstitution of a primordial unity presupposes the critical analysis of childhood's space-time, of the space-time of unitary societies, and of the space-time of the fragmentary societies embodying the dialectic between decay and the long-awaited possibility of its supersession.

2

If care is not taken, survival sickness can swiftly turn a young person into a haggard old Faust, burdened down with regrets and yearning for a youth traversed without his even knowing it. Teenagers bear the first wrinkles of the consumer; little distinguishes them from sixty-year-olds. They consume faster and faster, and the sooner they surrender to inauthenticity, the sooner they are rewarded with a precocious entry into old age. If they are slow to regain control, the past will close up behind them: they will have no further prospect of revisiting what they have done, even for the purpose of redoing it. So much separates them from the children they were playing with only yesterday. They have entered the meretricious domain of the market, willingly trading away the poetry, freedom and subjective riches of childhood for an image in the society of the spectacle. And yet, if only they pull up short and fight their way out of this nightmare, what an opponent the authorities will face! An opponent capable, in defence of childhood, of turning the most fearsome weapons of technocracy against their doddering inventors. We have not forgotten the extraordinary prowess displayed by the young Simbas of Lumumba's revolution, their rudimentary weapons notwithstanding; how much more may be expected from a generation every whit as enraged, but armed much more effectively and loosed upon a battleground reaching into every corner of everyday life!

For, in a sense, every sphere of everyday life is experienced embryonically in childhood. Children pack such a host of events into a few days or even a few hours that their time does not trickle away like an adult's. Two months' holiday for them is an eternity; for an old man it is a fleeting moment. The child's days are exempt from grown-up time: they are time swollen by subjectivity, by passion, by dreams shot through with reality. Outside this universe the educators wait patiently, watch in hand, for the child to join in the round dance of adult time. Adults are the ones who 'have' the time. At first children experience the adult's imposition of grown-up time on them as an intrusion; but eventually they capitulate, and consent to grow old. Innocent of the ways of conditioning, they fall like young animals into the trap. Later on, possessed now of the arms of criticism and eager to turn them against the time that imprisons them, they will find that the years have carried them too far from the target. But childhood will remain with them, in their hearts, like an open wound.

So here we all are, haunted by a childhood that social organization seeks to destroy by scientific means. The psycho-sociologists are on the lookout, while the market researchers are already exclaiming, 'Look at all those sweet little dollars!' (as quoted by Vance Packard). In short, a new arithmetic.

Children are playing in the street. One of them suddenly leaves the group, comes up to me and tells me some of the most beautiful dreams I have ever heard. He teaches me something which had I but known it would have saved me, namely the thing that destroys the notion of age: the capacity for living a multitude of events—not just watching them flow by, but truly living and continually refashioning them. And now that I find myself at a point where all this is beyond my reach, yet where all has become clear to me, is it any wonder that a kind of wild urge for wholeness erupts in me from beneath so many false desires—a type of childishness now made fearsome by all the lessons learnt from history and the class struggle? How could the new proletariat fail to be the purest catalyst of childhood's fulfilment in the adult world?

We are the discoverers of a world new yet familiar, a world lacking only unity of time and space. A world still riddled with separations, still fragmented. The semibarbarity of our bodies, our needs, and our spontaneity—that is, our childishness, as refined by consciousness—vouchsafes us secret access to places never discovered over centuries of aristocratic rule, and never even dreamt of by the bourgeoisie. In this way we are able to enter the maze of unfinished civilizations and approach all the arrested attempts at supersession surreptitiously undertaken by history. May our rediscovered childhood desires rejoin the childhood of our desires. From the wild depths of a past that is still close to us, and in a sense still unfulfilled, let a new geography of the passions emerge.

3

As motion within the motionless, the time of unitary societies is cyclical. Beings and things follow their course, moving around the circumference of a circle whose centre is God. This God-pivot, unchanging yet at once nowhere and everywhere, is the measure of the duration of an eternal power. He is his own standard, and the standard of all that gravitates at a constant distance from him, unfolding and coming full circle but never coming to a complete halt and never in fact escaping its orbit. In Nerval's words, 'La treizième revient, c'est encor la première'.

As for the space of unitary systems, its organization is determined by time. Since there is no time but God's, no space seems to exist aside from that which God controls. This space extends from the centre to the circumference, from heaven to earth, from the One to the many. At first sight, time seems irrelevant here: it takes one neither closer to God nor further from him. By contrast, the way to God is spatial: the upward path of spiritual elevation and hierarchical promotion. Time belongs to God and God alone, but the space granted humans retains a specifically and irreducibly human quality. Human beings can ascend or descend, rise or fall in the social world, ensure their salvation or risk damnation. Space implies the presence of humans: it is the dimension of their relative freedom, whereas time imprisons them within its circle. And what is the meaning of the Last Judgement, if not the idea that God will one day gather time in to himself once more, the centre sucking in the circumference and concentrating the entirety of the space imparted to his creatures into this impalpable point? This desire to obliterate the human as *matter* (the human occupation of space) is clearly the project of a master incapable of completely possessing his slaves, and hence incapable of not being partly possessed by them.

Duration has space on a leash; it drags us towards death, gnawing away at the space of our life. In the course of history, however, the distinction between time and space is not always so apparent. Feudal societies are societies of separations, just as bourgeois societies are, for separation is the corollary of privative appropriation. But feudalism's advantage here lies in its startling ability to mystify.

The power of myth bridged separations and made a unitary life possible. That life was inauthentic, it is true, but at least the inauthenticity was One—and unanimously accepted by a coherent community (tribe, clan, or kingdom). God was the image or symbol of the supersession of space and time dissociated from each other. Everyone who 'lived' in God partook of this supersession. The majority did so in a mediated way. They submitted, in other words, within the space of their everyday lives, to the requirements of the organizers of a duly hierarchical space extending upwards from mere mortals to priests, to leaders, to God. As a reward for such submission they were offered eternal life, promised duration without space and guaranteed pure temporality in God.

There were those, however, who cared little for this bargain. Instead, they dreamt of an eternal present conferred by an absolute mastery of the world. One is continually struck by the parallel between the punctual space-time of children and the great mystics' yearning for unity. Thus Gregory of Palamas, in 1341, described 'illumination' as a sort of ethereal consciousness of unity: 'Light exists outside space and time. He who partakes of divine energy becomes himself in a sense Light; he becomes one with Light, and, like Light, he is fully aware of everything that remains obscure to those who have not received such grace.'

This confused hope, which was bound to remain hesitant if not inexpressible, has been vulgarized and clarified by the transient bourgeois era. The bourgeoisie has made it concrete by administering the *coup de grace* to the aristocracy and its spiritualism, and it has made it possible by allowing its own disintegration to become terminal. The history of separations comes slowly to an end with the end of separations them-selves. Little by little, the unitary feudal illusion is incorporated into the libertarian unity of a life yet to be constructed in a realm beyond mate-rially guaranteed survival.

4

Einstein's speculations about space and time are in their own way a reminder of the death of God. Once myth no longer papered over the rift between space and time, consciousness fell heir to the malaise that underpinned the heyday of Romanticism (the pull of the exotic, nostal-gic feelings about the passage of time, and so on).

What is time, to the bourgeois mind? No longer God's time, it has become the time of Power, of Power fragmented. A time—in-bits time whose unit of measurement is the instant—that instant which is but a feeble echo of cyclical time. No longer the circumference of a circle, but rather a finite yet endless straight line. No longer a mechanism setting each individual to God's time, but rather a sequence of states in which everyone chases after themselves, but in vain, as though the curse of Becoming somehow damned us to see nothing but our own backs, the human face remaining unknown, inaccessible, ever in the future. No longer a circular space encompassed by the eye of the Almighty at its centre, but rather a series of tiny points which, though seemingly inde-pendent, actually combine, according to a specific order of succession, into the line they form as each follows its predecessor.

In the mediaeval hourglass time *flowed*—even if it was always the same sand that passed back and forth between the two bulbs of the timer. As represented on the *circular* clock face, by contrast, time is dispensed unit by unit, and never returns. Such is the irony of forms: the new mentality took its form from a dead reality, and when the bourgeoisie gave a cyclical appearance to everything—from wrist-watches to its half-baked humanist yearnings—what it was really dressing up in this way was the death of time, the death of its own time.

There is nothing for it, however: ours is the day of the clockmaker. Economic imperatives turn people into walking chronometers, as signalled by the band about their wrists. Ours is the time of work, of progress, of output, the time of production, consumption, and planning. The specta-cle's time: time for a kiss, snapshot time. A time for everything and every-thing at its time (time is money). Commodity time. Survival time.

Space is a point along the line of time, a place in the machine that changes future into past. Time controls lived space, but it does so from without, by causing it to pass, by making it transient. The space of the individual life is not pure space, however, nor is the time that sweeps it along pure temporality. It is worth examining this a little more closely.

Each terminal point on the temporal line is specific and unique, yet no sooner is the next point added than its predecessor disappears into the line's uniformity, mere grist to the mill of a past to which nothing is new. It becomes quite indiscernible. Thus each point serves to extend the very line that makes it vanish.

This pattern of continual destruction and replacement is the way Power ensures its own *duration*; people who are spurred on to consume power destroy it, yet simultaneously they renew it by *enduring*. If Power destroys everything it destroys itself, and if it destroys nothing it is likewise destroyed. Power can only endure strung out between the two poles of this contradiction, a contradiction which the dictatorship of consumption worsens day by day. Power's durability depends simply on the continuing existence of people, that is to say, on their permanent *survival*. This is why the problem of dissociated space-time now has revolutionary implications.

No matter that lived space is a universe of dreams, desires and prodigious creativity: so far as its duration is concerned, it is merely one point following another, and its evolution obeys one logic only, that of its own destruction. It appears, waxes, then disappears into the anonymous line of the past, where its remains become raw material for flashes of memory and historical research.

The positive aspect of a point of directly experienced space is that it escapes in part from generalized conditioning; the drawback is that it has no existence in its own right. The space of everyday life manages to turn a little time to its own uses, capturing and appropriating it, but time-that-slips-away insinuates itself into lived space and intrudes the sense of time passing, the sense of destruction and death. Let me explain.

The punctual space of everyday life steals a portion of 'external' time, and in this way clears a small area of unitary space-time for itself. This is the space-time of the privileged moment, of creativity, of pleasure, of orgasm. The arena of this alchemy is minute, but it is experienced so intensely that it exercises an unrivalled fascination over most people. From Power's point of view, from the outside, such passionate moments are completely insignificant points, mere instants funnelled from the future into the past. The line of objective time knows nothing—and wishes to know nothing—of the present as immediate subjective presence. As for subjective life, crushed into mere points of space—joy, gratification, revery—it would rather know nothing of time-that-slips-away, linear time, the time of things. On the contrary, it seeks full knowledge of its present, for after all it is itself only a present.

So lived space filches a small portion of the time sweeping it away and makes a present out of it—or at least it seeks to do so, for the present is yet to be constructed. It seeks to create the unitary space-time of love, of poetry, of pleasure, of communication: direct experience without dead time. Meanwhile linear time—objective time, time-that-slips-away—in its turn invades the space captured by everyday life. It takes the form of negative time, dead time, and reflects the temporality of destruction. This is the time of *roles*, that time which, within life itself, fosters disembodiment, the repudiation of authentically experienced space and its repression and replacement by appearances, by the spectacular function. The space-time produced by this hybrid union is, quite simply, that of survival.

What is private life? It is the amalgamation within one instant, within one point headed for destruction along the line of survival, of a real space-time (the moment) and a false one (the role). Of course, the actual structure of private life does not conform strictly to this dichotomy, for interaction goes on continually. Thus the prohibitions that hem lived experience in on all sides, confining it to far too small a space, also exert pressure for that experience to be transformed into roles, to enter time-that-slips-away as a commodity, to become pure repetition and, in accordance with accelerated time, to create the illusory space of appearances. At the same time, however, the malaise produced by inauthenticity, by space experienced falsely, stimulates the search for a real time, for the time of subjectivity, for the present. So, in dialectical terms, private life is: *a real lived space + an illusory spectacular time + an illusory spectacular space + a real lived time.*

The more thoroughly illusory time combines with the illusory space that it creates, the closer we come to being things, to being pure exchange-value. The more thoroughly the space of authentic life combines with authentically lived time, the more human mastery asserts itself. Space-time lived in unitary fashion is the first guerrilla base, the spark of the qualitative in the night that still enshrouds the revolution of everyday life.

Objective time does not merely strive, then, to destroy punctual space by thrusting it into the past, it also eats at it from within by imposing on it the accelerated rhythm which creates the role's density (the illusory space of roles is produced by the rapid repetition of an attitude, rather as the repetition of a filmed image creates the illusion of life). The role invests subjective consciousness with time-that-slips-away, the time of aging, of death. This is Antonin Artaud's 'fold into which consciousness has been forced'. Dominated from without by linear time, from within by the temporality of the role, subjectivity has no option but to become a thing, a precious commodity. History speeds this process up, moreover. In fact roles are now the consumption of time in a society where the official time is that of consumption. And here too the single-mindedness of oppression will bring about an equally single-minded opposition. What is death in our time? The absence of subjectivity, the absence of a present.

The will to live always reacts in unitary fashion. Most people are already engaged in a genuine repurposing of time to the benefit of lived space. Provided their efforts to increase the intensity of lived experience, to expand authentic space-time, do not come to grief in confusion, or break up on the reefs of isolation, who can say that objective time, the time of death, might not be broken forever? Is not the revolutionary moment, after all, a moment of eternal youth?

//////

The project of enriching the space-time of direct experience requires an evaluation of what impoverishes it. Linear time has no hold over people save insofar as it prohibits them from *transforming* the world and thus forces them to *adapt* to it. Freely radiating creativity is Power's public enemy number one. And creativity's strength lies in the unitary. How does Power attempt to smash the unity of lived space-time? First and foremost, by transforming lived experience into a commodity and leaving it to the tender mercies of the law of supply and demand as applied to roles and stereotypes in the spectacular marketplace (see my discussion of roles in Chapter XV above). Two other tactics are also adopted by Power: (a) recourse to a particular kind of identification: the combined attraction of past and future, which destroys the present; and (b) the attempt to co-opt the will to build a unitary space-time of lived experience (in other words, to construct situations to be lived) by incorporating it into an ideology of history. I shall now consider these two tactics in more detail.

//////

(a) From Power's standpoint there is no such thing as lived moments (lived experience has no name), but merely a sequence of interchange-able instants constituting the line of the past. A whole system of conditioning has been developed to mass-market this view of things, and all kinds of hidden persuasions help us internalize it. The results are not far to seek. Where has the present gone? Can it be skulking in some dark corner of daily existence?

All we have are memory and anticipation. Meetings past and meetings future: two ghosts that haunt us. Each passing second shuttles me from the instant that was to the instant that will be. Each second spirits me away from myself; no *now* ever materializes. Empty commotion serves admirably to give everyone a fleeting quality, to pass the time (as we say so aptly), and even to make time run right through people. Schopenhauer's claim that 'Before Kant we were in time; since Kant time is in us' is a fine way of evoking the fact that consciousness is now flooded by the time of aging and advancing decrepitude. But it did not occur to Schopenhauer that what drove him as a philosopher to develop a mysticism of despair was precisely humanity's torment on the rack of a time reduced to an apparent split between future and past.

Imagine the distraction and despair of someone torn between two instants, forever zigzagging in pursuit of one or the other without ever reaching either—and without ever grasping hold of himself. If only passionate expectation were in play: under the spell of a past moment—a moment of love, say, and the woman you love is about to appear, you sense it, you already feel her touch . . . The kind of passionate expectation, in a word, that prefigures a 'situation to be constructed'. Alas, it must be acknowledged that most of the time the whirligig of memory and anticipation blocks both the expectation and the experience of the present by sweeping us into the millrace of dead time with its succession of hollow instants.

Seen through Power's glass, the only future is a past reiterated. A portion of familiar inauthenticity is projected by an act of what is known as prospective imagination into a time which it fills in advance with its utter vacuousness. Our only memories are memories of roles once played, our only future an endless remake. Human memory is supposed to answer to no requirement save Power's need to assert itself in time by perpetually reminding us of its presence. And this reminder takes the form: *nihil nove sub sole*—or, in the vulgar tongue, 'you always have to have leaders'.

The future sold as a 'different time' is a worthy complement to the different space sold as a place for us to unburden ourselves completely. Change eras, slough one's skin, turn the clock back or forward, change roles. The only thing that does not change is alienation. Whenever 'I is another', that other is condemned to hover between past and future. Roles *never* have a present. No wonder they can provide no well-being: if my present is a failure—*here* always being *elsewhere*—how could I possibly relate in a congenial way to either past or future?

//////

(b) Identification with past-and-future reaches its acme thanks to historical ideology, which turns the individual and collective will to master history upside down.

Time is a form of mental perception, clearly not a human creation but rather a dialectical relationship with external reality; a relationship therefore that contributes to alienation, and to humanity's struggle within and against alienation.

Animals, being entirely subject to the demands of adaptation, have no consciousness of time. Humans, however, refuse adaptation and attempt to change the world. Whenever they fail in this ambition to be a demiurge, they suffer the anguish of having to adapt, of knowing themselves reduced to animal-like passivity. Consciousness of the necessity for adaptation is also consciousness of time slipping away, which is why time is linked to human anxiety. As necessity for adaptation to circumstances overrides the desire and capacity for changing them, the stranglehold of the consciousness of time tightens. Survival sickness is surely nothing but the acute consciousness of evanescence in the time and space of the other—the consciousness, in other words, of alienation. Rejecting the consciousness of growing old, along with the objective preconditions of the growing-old of consciousness, implies a strengthening of the will to make history, an increase in that will's cogency and a greater consonance with everyone's subjective wishes.

An ideology of history has one purpose only: to prevent people from making history. What better way to distract people from their present than to draw them into that sphere where time slips away? This task falls to the historians. They organize the past, divide it up according to time's official line, and then assign events to *ad hoc* categories. These easy-to-use categories put past events into quarantine. Solid parentheses isolate and contain them, preventing them from coming to life, from rising from the dead and running once more through the streets of our everyday lives. The event is deep-frozen, so to speak. It becomes illegal to retrieve it, remake it, complete it, or attempt to supersede it. It is merely *there*—preserved forever in suspended animation, for the admiration of aesthetes. All it takes is a slight change of marker for this same past event to be transported into the future. The future amounts to the repetitions of historians, whose forecasts are a collage of memories—*their* memories. The much-vaunted notion of the goal of history has been so vulgarized by Stalinist thinkers that it has successfully stripped the future as well as the past of all humanity.

Prodded into identifying with another time and another personality, modern individuals have thus let themselves be robbed of their present in the name of historicism. Their taste for authentic life has been swallowed up by the spectacle's space-time: 'Comrades, you are entering upon the stage of History!' For those who reject the heroism of historical commitment, a complementary mystification is provided by the psychologists. History and psychology work in tandem, joining forces to produce the extreme poverty of co-optation. The choice is between history and a nice quiet life.

Historic or not, all roles are in decay. The crisis of history and the crisis of everyday life are no longer distinct. An explosive mixture. The task now is to repurpose history, to subordinate it to subjective ends, and to do so with the participation of all humanity. Marx, I might add, never sought anything less.

5

For most of the last century the chief tendencies in painting have presented themselves as playing games—even joking—with space. Nothing was better suited than artistic creativity to express the restless and impassioned search for a new, directly experienced space. And what better means than humour for conveying the feeling that art can no longer provide much of a solution? (I am thinking of the early Impressionists, the Pointillists, the Fauvists, the Cubists, the Dadaist collagists and the first abstract painters.)

A malaise first felt by artists has, with the degeneration of art, come to affect the awareness of an ever-growing number of people. The construction of an art of life is now a popular demand. There is a whole artistic past the fruits of whose research have been thrown thoughtlessly aside; the time has come to give its discoveries material form in a passionately experienced space-time.

Memories in this connexion are memories of mortal wounds. What is left uncompleted rots. The past is presented to us as irremediable, yet— supreme irony—the very people who characterize it as definitive spend all their time breaking it down, falsifying it and dolling it up according to the latest fashion. One thinks of poor Winston Smith, in Orwell's *1984*, obliged to rewrite old news items contradicted by the latest official version of the past.

There is only one valid way to forget, and that is to erase the past by fulfilling it. To avert decay by superseding it. No matter how far removed in time, the facts of the past have never spoken their last. A radical change in the present can always topple them from the museum shelf and bring them live within our grasp. There is no more poignant (nor can I conceive of a more exemplary) testimony to the way the past may be rectified than that offered by Victor Serge in *Conquered City*. At the close of a lecture on the Paris Commune given at the height of the Bolshevik Revolution, a soldier who resembles 'a clay figure from a shooting gallery' rises ponderously from a leather armchair at the back of the room.

> In low tones, but tones of authority, he was clearly heard to say, 'Tell us the story of Doctor Millière's execution.'
>
> Erect, a giant of a man, his head bowed so that all you could see of his face was his hairy jowls, sullen mouth and uneven, wrinkled brow—he put one in mind of certain masks of Beethoven—he listened to the story of Doctor Millière, in a dark blue frock coat and a top hat, dragged in the rain through the streets of Paris, forced to kneel on the steps of the Pantheon, crying 'Long live humanity!'—and the retort of the Versaillese sentry leaning on a railing a few steps away: 'Fuck your humanity, and fuck you!'
>
> In the dark night of the unlit street outside the meeting hall, the clay figure approached the lecturer. . . .

He clearly had a confidence to share, for his momentary hesitation was heavy with significance.

'I was also in the Perm government, last year when the kulaks rebelled. . . . I had just read Arnould's pamphlet, *Les morts de la Commune*—a fine pamphlet. So Millière was on my mind. And, Citizen, I avenged him myself! That was a wonderful day in my life—and there haven't been many. I avenged Millière perfectly. Just like that, on the steps of the church, I shot the biggest landlord of the place. I can't remember his name now, and I couldn't care less.'

After a brief pause he added: 'But this time it was I who shouted "Long live humanity!"'

Past revolts take on a new dimension in my present, the dimension of an immanent reality crying out to be brought into being without delay. The walks of the Luxembourg Gardens and the Square de la Tour Saint-Jacques still resound with gunfire and the cries of the Commune suppressed. There will be more firing-squads, though, and more piles of corpses will erase so much as the memory of the earlier ones. One day the revolutionaries of all time will be joined by the revolutionaries of all countries and together they will wash the Mur des Fédérés with the blood of the executioners.

Constructing the present means correcting the past, changing the signs that surround us, hewing our unfulfilled dreams and desires out of the veinstone in which they are trapped, and allowing individual passions to harmonize within a collective reality. Bridging the temporal gap between the insurgents of 1525 and the Mulelist rebels, Spartacus and Pancho Villa, or Lucretius and Lautréamont requires no more time than the duration of my will to live.

Waiting for radiant tomorrows kills our joy today. The future is worse than the vast ocean itself, for it contains nothing. Planning, prospects, long-range views—one might as well discuss a house's roof before the ground floor is constructed. It is true, though, that if one's present is solidly built, the rest will take care of itself.

Only the quick of the present, with its multiplicity, is of interest to me. Despite all the strictures, I want to bathe in today as in a great light; to convert alien time and the space of others into the immediacy of everyday experience. I want to make Sister Catherine's mystical formula into concrete reality: 'Everything that is in me is in me; everything that is in

me is outside me; everything that is in me is all around me; everything
that is in me is mine, and nowhere can I see anything that is not in me.'
For this is no more than subjectivity's rightful victory, which history has
now placed within our grasp—just so long as we tear down the Bastilles
of the future, restructure the past, and live each second as though an
eternal return ensured its exact recurrence forever in an endless cycle.

Only the present can be total. It is a point of incredible density. We
must learn how to slow time down, how to live the permanent passion
for unmediated experience. A tennis champion has recalled how, during
a very hard-fought match, when he had a difficult and critical return
shot to make, he suddenly saw everything in slow motion—so slow that
he had plenty of time to weigh up the situation, judge distances and
make a brilliant return. In the realm of true creation time dilates; in
that of inauthenticity, by contrast, it accelerates. Whoever masters the
poetics of the present may expect adventures comparable to that of the
little Chinese boy who fell in love with the Queen of the Seas. He went
searching for her in the depths of the ocean. When he returned to terra
firma he came upon a very old man pruning roses who said to him: 'It is
a strange thing, but my grandfather told me of a little boy lost at sea who
had just the same name as you.'

'All time resides in the moment', according to the esoteric tradition.
As for the claim of the *Pistis Sophia* that 'One day of light is a thousand
years in the history of the world', history's developing tray has revealed
its exact correspondence to Lenin's assertion that some days of revolution are worth centuries.

Resolving the contradictions of the present is always the main task,
never stopping half-way or getting 'distracted', but heading directly for
supersession. This task is collective, passionate, poetic and playful (eternity is the world of play, says Boehme). No matter how impoverished,
the present always contains the true wealth of possible creation. This is
the never-ending poem that can fill me with joy. But you all know—from
your own life—how great the forces are that wrest it from my grasp.

But how can I let myself be sucked into the whirlpool of dead time,
agree to grow old, to wear out slowly till nothing is left of my body and
my mind? Better to die as an act of defiance against duration. Citizen
Anquetil, in his *Précis de l'histoire universelle*, published in Paris in Year
VII of the Republic, tells the story of a Persian prince so offended by the
world's vanity that he withdrew to a castle along with forty of the most

beautiful and cultivated courtesans of the kingdom. There he died a month later from the effects of debauchery. What is death compared to such an infinity? If I must die, at least let me die as I have occasionally loved.

XXIII The Unitary Triad: Fulfilment, Communication, Participation

The repressive unity of Power under its three aspects—constraint, seduction and mediation—is simply the form, inverted and perverted by the techniques of dissociation, of a tripartite unitary project. In its chaotic, underground development, the new society expresses itself practically as a transparency in human relationships which promotes the real participation of all in the fulfilment of each. Three passions—for creation, love and play—are to life what the needs for nourishment and shelter are to survival [1]. The passion to create underpins the project of fulfilment [2]; the passion of love fuels the project of communication [4]; and the passion for play is the foundation of the project of participation [6]. Wherever these three projects are separated from each other, Power's repressive unity is reinforced. Radical subjectivity is the presence, discernible today in practically everyone, of an indivisible will to construct a passionate life [3]. The erotic is the spontaneous coherence which gives the enrichment of lived experience a practical unity [5].

1

The construction of everyday life implies the most thoroughgoing fusion of reason and passion. The mystery in which life has always been cloaked bespeaks an obscurantism intended to conceal the triviality of mere survival. The fact is that the will to live cannot be detached from the desire for a measure of organization. As things stand, the attraction for each of us of a rich and varied life is inevitably manifested as a striving which is subject in whole or in part to the social Power whose task it is to dash such aspirations. Just as the governance of human beings relies on three forms of oppression, namely constraint, alienating mediation and magical seduction, so the will to live draws its vitality and its coherence from the unity of three projects, namely self-fulfilment, communication and participation.

For a human history not reduced to the history of human survival—though not detached from it—the dialectic of this threefold project, in conjunction with that of the forces of production, can provide an adequate explanation for most behaviour. Every riot, every revolution embodies a passionate quest for exuberant life, for total clarity in human relationships, and for a collective way of transforming the world. Three basic passions seem in fact to underlie historical development, passions that are to life as the needs for nourishment and shelter are to survival. The desire to create, the desire to love and the desire to play interact with those needs for nourishment and shelter, while the will to live clashes continually with the need to survive. Of course, these factors are significant only in their historical context, but the history of their dissociation is precisely what I want to challenge here in the name of the unceasing struggle for totality.

As I have tried to show, the advent of the welfare state tends to incorporate the issue of survival into the problematic issue of life in general. In a historical situation where the economy of life is gradually subsuming the economy of survival, it is ever more plain to see that the dissociation of the three aforementioned projects, and of the passions underlying them, is an extension of the aberrant distinction between life and survival. Torn as it is between separation, which is the domain of Power, and unity, which is that of revolution, existence is obliged to find expression for the most part in ambiguous ways. I shall therefore discuss each project separately, but with their unity in mind.

//////

The project of self-fulfilment is born of the passion to create, at the moment when subjectivity wells up and aspires to reign universally. The project of communication is born of the passion of love, when individuals discover that the desire for amorous conquest in themselves is identical in others. The project of participation is born of the passion for play, when the group fosters the self-fulfilment of each individual.

The isolation of these three passions perverts them. Dissociated from one another, the three projects are falsified. The will to self-fulfilment is transformed into the will to power: in thrall to status and role-playing, it presides over a world of constraint and illusion. The will to communication turns into objective mendacity: founded now on relationships between objects, it provides the semiologists with the signs which it is their job to disguise as human. The will to participation serves to organize the loneliness of everyone in the crowd, setting up the tyranny of illusory community.

Once cut off from the others, each passion may be incorporated as an absolute into a metaphysical vision, thus rendering it inaccessible. Our philosophers have quite a sense of humour: first they break the circuits, then they say the power has failed. On this basis they can claim with impunity that self-fulfilment is a chimaera, transparent communication a pipe-dream, and the idea of social harmony mere whimsy. True enough, so long as separation is the order of the day, everyone confronts only the impossible. The Cartesian mania for cutting everything up into little pieces, and for proceeding only one step at a time, can produce only an incomplete and crippled reality. And crippled individuals are the only recruits available to the armies of Order.

2. The Project of Self-Fulfilment

Guaranteed material security leaves unused a large supply of energy formerly expended in the struggle for survival. The will to power seeks to harness this free-floating energy, otherwise available for the free development of individual life, and use it to buttress hierarchical slavery [a]. Conditioning by generalized oppression obliges the majority to withdraw strategically into their subjectivity, which they perceive as their only irreducible asset. It behoves the revolution of everyday life to give concrete form to the countless assaults launched daily by subjectivity against the objective world [b].

(a) The historical stage of privative appropriation has barred mankind from becoming a creator God itself, and humanity has had to be content, by way of compensation, with decreeing that as compensation for this rebuff humans must be content to create such a God in ideal form. At heart every human being wants to be God, but until now this desire has been turned against human beings themselves. I have shown how hierarchical social organization constructs the world by destroying human beings; how the perfection of its mechanisms and networks allows it to function like a giant computer whose programmers are themselves programmed; and how 'the coldest of all cold monsters' is epitomized by the cybernetic State now in preparation.

Under such conditions, the social struggles for enough to eat, creature comforts, stable employment and financial security—all formerly aggressive campaigns—are slowly but surely coming to resemble rearguard actions (their enduring importance notwithstanding). The need to survive has absorbed and continues to absorb a vast quantity of energy and creativity, so vast that it must soon overflow and descend on the so-called welfare state like a pack of ravening wolves. Fake conflicts and illusory action notwithstanding, this continually stimulated creative energy is no longer dissipating fast enough under the tyranny of consumption. What will become of this suddenly freed-up dynamism, this excess strength and vigour which neither constraint nor lies can now effectively exhaust? No longer co-opted by artistic and cultural consumption—by the ideological spectacle—such creativity can only turn spontaneously against the conditions and assurances of survival itself.

The rebellious have nothing to lose but survival. But they may lose survival in two ways: by losing life too, or by embarking on its construction. Since survival is a kind of slow death, there is a temptation, not devoid of passionate justification, to speed the process up and die more quickly—to go flat out in a fast car, as it were, and 'live' the negation of survival negatively. Alternatively, people may try to survive as anti-survivors, bringing all their energy to bear on the enrichment of everyday life and thus negating survival by drowning it in the joys of construction. Both alternatives clearly follow the single yet contradictory path of decay and supersession.

Self-fulfilment cannot be divorced from supersession. Desperate refusal, no matter how ferocious, cannot escape the authoritarian dilemma: survival or death. Acquiescent rebellion and wild creativity easily broken in by the order of things are expressions of the *will to power*.

//////

The will to power is the project of fulfilment travestied, cut off from communication and participation. It is the passion for creation—and for self-creation—entangled in the hierarchical system, condemned to drive the mill of repression and appearances. Status and humiliation, authority and submission—such is the quick march of the will to power. Heroes, in this light, are those who pay homage to roles and to brute force, those who, once exhausted, follow Voltaire's advice to cultivate their gardens.

Thereafter their mediocrity will continue to serve, in its lumbering way, as a model for ordinary mortals.

Betrayals of the will to live by heroes, leaders, stars, playboys, and experts are beyond count. Likewise the sacrifices they have made to force their image, their name and their aura of dignity on people—a few people, or a few million—whom they necessarily take for fools (otherwise they themselves would be fools!).

All the same, beneath its protective wrapping, the will to power does harbour traces of an authentic will to live. Think of the *virtù* of the *condottiere*, the exuberance of the giants of the Renaissance. But today the *condottieri* are no more. At best we have captains of industry, gangsters, arms dealers and art dealers—mercenaries all. For an adventurer, Tintin; for an explorer, Albert Schweitzer. Yet it is with such people that Zarathustra dreams of peopling the heights of Sils-Maria—in these runts that he claims to discern the lineaments of a future race! Truth to tell, Nietzsche was the last master, crucified by his own illusions. His death was a replay, with more piquancy and wit, of the drama of Golgotha. It shed light on the disappearance of the feudal lords just as Christ's shed light on the disappearance of God. As prone to disgust as he was, Nietzsche had no difficulty breathing in Christianity's ignoble stench by the lungful. By affecting not to understand that Christianity, for all its stated contempt for the will to power, was in reality its best shield, its most faithful henchman, stoutly opposed to the emergence of masters without slaves, Nietzsche gave his blessing to the permanence of a hierarchical world where the will to live dooms itself to be nothing more than the will to power. By signing his last letters 'Dionysus the Crucified', he revealed his own docility—the docility of anyone who has merely sought out a master for his compromised vitality. Nobody appeals to the witch-doctor of Bethlehem with impunity.

Nazism is Nietzschean logic called to order by history. The question was: what is the fate of the last masters in a society whence all true masters have vanished? And the answer: they become superslaves. Even the superman as conceived by Nietzsche, as weak as this figure may be, is obviously far superior to the flunkeys who ran the Third Reich. Fascism knows only one superman: the State.

The State as superman is the strength of the weak. This is why the demands of an isolated individual can always be satisfied by a role impeccably played in the official spectacle. The will to power is spectacular in nature. Isolated people detest others and hold them in contempt even if they themselves perfectly exemplify 'mass man'—the most contemptible being imaginable. Their aggressiveness reposes comfortably upon the crudest illusions of community and their combativeness serves only their own promotion in the rat race.

Managers, bosses, hard men, mobsters—they have all had to sweat and slave, take their knocks, and stand and fight. Their morality is no different from that of pioneers, boy scouts, soldiers and all other shock troops of conformity. 'No animal in the world would have done what I have had to do.' Since he cannot *be*, the mafia boss (say) is defined by a will to *appear*: he compensates for the emptiness of his existence by proclaiming his existence ever more loudly. Only lackeys take pride in their sacrifices. The rule of things is supreme here: if not the artificiality of the role, then the 'authenticity' of an animal. There are tasks fit for beasts but for no human being. The 'heroes' who march past behind brass bands—Red Army, SS, French paratroopers—are the torturers of Budapest, Warsaw and Algiers. Military discipline is sustained by the fury of the common soldier; as for the police, they are dogs who know when to bite and when to fawn.

The will to power is a reward for slavery. At the same time it is a hatred of slavery. The great notabilities of the past never identified themselves with a Cause. They preferred to conflate a Cause with their own desire for power. As great causes have crumbled and disappeared, great notabilities have likewise waned. But the game goes on. People embrace a Cause because they have been unable to embrace themselves and their own desires, yet in the Cause and in the sacrifice it demands what they seek, paradoxically, is their own will to live.

Sometimes a sense of freedom and play awakens among the irregulars of the ruling Order. I am thinking of a Salvatore Giuliano, before he was co-opted by the landowners, or a Billy the Kid, or various gangsters briefly close to the anarchist terrorists. Legionnaires and mercenaries have been known to defect to the Algerian or Congolese rebels, choosing the party of open insurrection and taking their taste for play to its logical conclusion: the breaking of all taboos and the quest for total freedom.

Youth gangs also come to mind. The very immaturity of their will to power has often kept their will to live almost uncontaminated. Obviously, young hoodlums are ever at risk of co-optation. First as consumers, because they want things they cannot afford; then, as they get older, as producers. But within the gang play remains so important that a genuine revolutionary consciousness is always possible. If the inherent violence of teenage gangs were not squandered in exhibitionistic and generally half-baked rumbles, and steered instead towards the real poetry to be found in rioting, then youthful game-playing could easily take on an insurrectionary colouring and set off a chain reaction—a qualitative shock-wave. Most people are aware of their desire to live authentically, to throw off constraints and roles. All that is needed is a spark—plus adequate tactics. Should juvenile delinquents ever attain a revolutionary consciousness, merely by grasping what they already are and by wanting to be more, they might conceivably become the epicentre of a reversal of perspective. Federating their groups would at once manifest such a consciousness for the first time and make its extension possible.

(b) Until now the centre has always been something other than man, and creativity has remained marginal, outside the gates of the city. Indeed the history of city planning clearly reflects the vicissitudes of the focus around which life has been organized over thousands of years. Ancient cities grew up around a stronghold or sacred spot, a temple or a church, a place where heaven and earth met. The dismal streets of workers' housing tend to surround factories and industrial plants, while administrative centres look out over soulless avenues. As for the new towns of today's planners, such as Sarcelles or Mourenx near Paris, there is simply no centre at all. Which makes things simpler: their point of reference is *always somewhere else*. In these labyrinths where the only thing you are really allowed to do is get lost, the ban on playing, on meeting others—in short, on *living*—takes the form of kilometres of plate-glass windows, an endless grid of roadways and towering, supposedly habitable blocks of concrete.

Oppression is no longer centralized, for it is everywhere. The positive aspect of this disintegration is that everyone begins to see, in their state of almost complete isolation, that they must first save themselves, make themselves the centre, and from their own subjectivity build a world where they can be at home anywhere.

A clear-sighted return to the self is also a return to the wellspring of other selves, the wellspring of the social. So long as individual creativity is not made the centre of social life, the only freedom of human beings will be the freedom to destroy and be destroyed. If you think for others, others will think for you. And those who think for you judge you; they reduce you to their own norms; and, whatever their intentions may be, they make you stupid—for stupidity comes not from a lack of intelligence, as stupid people imagine: it stems from self-renunciation, from self-abandonment. So if anyone asks you what you are doing, asks you to explain yourself, treat them as a judge—which is to say an enemy.

'I want heirs; I want children; I want disciples; I want a father; I don't want myself.' Such are the sentiments of people with minds addled by Christianity, whether of the Roman or the Peking variety. Unhappiness and neurosis are the certain outcome of these attitudes. My subjectivity is far too dear to me for me ever casually to solicit or reject help from others. The point is not to lose oneself in others, and even less in oneself. Anyone who realizes that in the end he relies on the collectivity must still first find himself; otherwise, all he will derive from others is his own negation.

Strengthening the subjective centre is such a special task that it is hard even to talk about it. In the heart of each human being there is a hidden room, a *camera obscura*, to which only the mind and dreams have access: a magic circle where the world and the self are reconciled, where every wish or whim is instantly satisfied. The passions flourish there, lovely, poisonous blossoms redolent with the mood of the times. I create a universe for myself and, like some temperamental and tyrannical god, reign there over beings who exist for me alone. In a few charming pages, James Thurber tells how Walter Mitty dreams that he is first a swashbuckling captain, then an eminent surgeon, then a cold-blooded killer, and finally a war hero. All this as he drives his old Buick and stops to buy some dog biscuits.

The significance of the subjective centre may be gauged by disparagement directed its way. People love to dismiss it as a haven of compensation, a meditational retreat, a dependency of poetry or a locus of introversion. Revery, they say, is inconsequential. But are not fantasy and the capricious visions of the mind starting-points and fomenters of the finest onslaughts on morality, authority, language and mystification? Are not subjectivity's riches the source of all creativity, the testing-ground of immediate experience and a bridgehead thrust into the Old World upon which coming onslaughts will depend?

For those able clearly to receive the messages and visions emanating from the subjective centre, the world is reshaped, values change, and things lose their aura and become simply tools. Thanks to the magic of the imagination, everything exists solely to be manipulated, caressed, broken apart, put back together or altered in any way I wish. Once the primacy of subjectivity is accepted the spell of things is broken. Started from other people, the search for the self is fruitless; we repeat the same futile gestures time after time. Started from oneself, on the other hand, actions are not repeated but rather revisited, corrected and fully realized.

Our innermost dreams secrete an energy that demands nothing better than to drive circumstances like turbines. The high technology of our time bars the way to Utopia; at the same time, however, it suppresses the purely magical aspect of the dream. All our wishes will come true once the modern world's technology is placed at their disposal.

Even now—and even without any help from technology—can subjectivity ever miss the mark? It is by no means impossible for me to give objective form to everything I have ever dreamt of being. Surely everyone, at least once in their life, has been a little like a Charles Lassailly or a Sergey Nechayev: like Lassailly, who passed himself off at first as the author of a book he had never written, but ended up as a true writer, as the author of *Roueries de Trialph* (1833); or like Nechayev, who began by cheating Bakunin out of money in aid of a nonexistent terrorist organization, but later on became the guiding light of a genuine nihilist group? The day must surely come when I shall actually be as I have wanted to seem to others: the image boosted in the spectacle by my wish-to-exist must eventually become authentic. For subjectivity can turn the roles and lies of the spectacle to its own ends: it can, as it were, reinvest appearances in reality.

Though strictly mental in nature, the subjective imagination always strives for practical fulfilment. There is no doubt that the force of attraction of the artistic spectacle—and especially in its narrative forms—plays on this striving for fulfilment, but only in order to capture it and use it to drive passive identification. Guy Debord rightly underlines this point in his agitational film *Critique of Separation:* 'In general, the things that happen in individual existences as at present organized, the things that really concern us and solicit our involvement, are those that deserve no more than to have us be distant spectators, bored and indifferent. Situations seen through the lens of some artistic transformation or other are often, to the contrary, the ones that attract us, that would justify our becoming actors, participants. This is a paradox that needs to be reversed—put back on its feet.' The forces of the artistic spectacle must be disbanded their matériel added to the arsenal of subjective dreams. Thus armed, those dreams will be far too dangerous to be treated as fantasies. The issue of the realization of art can be approached in no other way.

3. Radical Subjectivity

All subjectivities are different, but all obey the same will to fulfilment. Their variety needs to be subordinated to this common tendency so as to create a united front of subjectivity. Any attempt to build a new society must never forget two requirements: first, that the fulfilment of each individual subjectivity will be collective or it will not be; and, secondly, in the words of Saint-Just, that 'Each fights for what he loves: that is what is called the honest truth. Fighting for everyone else is merely the consequence.'

My subjectivity feeds on events. The most varied events: a riot, a broken heart, an encounter, a memory, a toothache. The shock-waves of reality-in-the-making reverberate through the caverns of the subjective. The vibrations reach me willy-nilly and, though not everything affects me with equal force, I am invariably confronted by the same paradox: no matter how easily my imagination takes possession of the facts, my wish truly to change them is almost invariably foiled. The subjective centre registers the transmutation of real into imaginary and simultaneously the return flow of the facts rejoining the uncontrollable course of things. A bridge must therefore be built between the work of the imagination and the objective world. Only radical theory can grant individuals inalienable rights over their surroundings and circumstances. Radical theory grasps human beings at the root—and that root is subjectivity, an irreducible zone that is the common property of all.

You cannot save yourself on your own or achieve fulfilment in isolation. How can any individual who has gained some measure of insight into himself and the world fail to recognize a will identical to his own in those around him—the same quest, the same starting-points?

All forms of hierarchical power are different, yet all perform identical oppressive functions. Similarly, all subjectivities are different, yet all embody an identical desire for complete self-fulfilment. This is the sense in which one may speak of a real 'radical subjectivity'.

Every unique and irreducible subjectivity is rooted in the same will to fulfil oneself by changing the world, to live every sensation, every experience, every possibility to the full. This will is present in everyone, its intensity varying according to the individual's level of consciousness and resolve. Its effectiveness naturally depends on the degree of collective unity it can attain without losing its own diversity. Consciousness of this necessary unity stems from what might be called an *identity reflex*—a tendency diametrically opposed to identification. Thanks to identification we lose our oneness in the plethora of roles; thanks to the identity reflex we enhance our multiplicity within the unity of federated subjectivities.

The identity reflex is the foundation of radical subjectivity, the questing vision of those who seek their self everywhere in others. 'While on a mission in the State of Chu,' says Confucius, 'I saw some piglets sucking on their dead mother. After a while they trembled and went away. They had sensed that she could no longer see them and that *she was not like them any more*. What they loved in their mother was not her body, but whatever it was that made that body alive.' Likewise, what I look for in other people is the richest part of myself hidden within them. Is the identity reflex bound to spread? Not necessarily. But present-day historical conditions certainly favour such a development.

There is no contesting the concern of human beings for nourishment, shelter, succour, and protection from adversity and disaster. Technological shortcomings—very quickly transformed into social ones— have postponed the satisfaction of these universal needs. Today, however, a planned economy allows us to foresee the final solution of the problems of survival. And with *survival* needs well on the way to being met— at least in the hyperindustrialized countries—it is apparent that there are also passions for *life* to be satisfied, that this is of vital importance to humanity at large, and indeed that failure to satisfy them will undermine, if not destroy all our gains in the realm of material survival. As the problems of survival are slowly but surely resolved, they clash more and more brutally with the problems of life, which, just as slowly and just as surely, continue to be sacrificed to survival imperatives. In a way, this split simplifies matters, for it shows clearly that socialist planning is at odds with the harmonization of our collective life.

//////

Radical subjectivity is the common front of identity rediscovered. Those who cannot recognize themselves in others are condemned forever to be strangers to themselves. I can do nothing for others if they can do nothing for themselves. This is the context in which we must reconsider such notions as 'knowledge' and 'recognition', and 'sympathetic' and 'sympathizer'.

Knowledge is of value only if it leads to the recognition of the common project—or in other words to the identity reflex. Fulfilment presupposes a certain style; it also calls for a good deal of knowledge of various kinds, but such knowledge is worthless in the absence of the style. As the first years of the Situationist International have shown, the main enemies of a coherent revolutionary group are those closest to the group in knowledge and furthest away from it in their lived experience and in the sense they give it. In the same way 'sympathizers' who identify with the group become an obstacle in its path: they understand everything except what is essential, what is radical. They beat the drum for their knowledge because they are incapable of beating the drum for their own selves.

By laying claim to myself I break other people's hold over me, while leaving them to recognize themselves in me. No one can develop freely without spreading freedom in the world.

'I want to be myself. I want to walk without impediment. I want to assert myself alone in my freedom. May everyone do likewise. Let no one agonize over the fate of the revolution: it will be safer in the hands of everyone than in the hands of parties.' Thus Ernest Coeurderoy—and I agree completely. Nothing entitles me to speak in the name of other people. I am delegated by myself alone. Yet at the same time I cannot shake off the idea that my life is not just a personal matter, and that by living the way I live, and struggling to live more intensely and more freely, I serve the interests of untold numbers of other people. Each of my friends embodies a social group no longer unaware of itself: each of us knows that in acting for oneself one acts for all. Only through such transparency can authentic participation be built up.

4. The Project of Communication

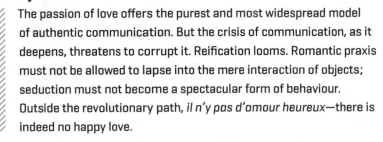

The passion of love offers the purest and most widespread model of authentic communication. But the crisis of communication, as it deepens, threatens to corrupt it. Reification looms. Romantic praxis must not be allowed to lapse into the mere interaction of objects; seduction must not become a spectacular form of behaviour. Outside the revolutionary path, *il n'y pas d'amour heureux*—there is indeed no happy love.

The three passions that underlie the threefold project of fulfilment, communication and participation have equal weight, but they are not equally repressed. Whereas play and creativity are blighted by prohibitions and by every sort of distortion, love, though not immune to oppression, remains the most widespread and most easily accessible experience—the most democratic, so to speak.

The passion of love is the model of perfect communication: the orgasm, the harmony of two partners at the moment of climax. The occasional lightning flash of the qualitative in the gloom of everyday survival. Considering its unmediated intensity, exaltation of the senses, emotional fluidity, and propensity for change and variety, love seems predestined to reimpassion the deserts of the Old World. Survival without passion cannot fail to engender a passion for a life that is both one and multiform. Love's gestures epitomize and distil both the desire for, and the reality of such a life. The universe true lovers build from their dreams and caresses is a transparent one: lovers want to be at home everywhere.

More successfully than the other passions, love has managed to conserve a measure of freedom. Creativity and play have always 'benefited' from an official image, an acknowledgement within the spectacle that alienates them, as it were, at source. Love, by contrast, has never been completely evicted from the clandestine existence that we call intimacy. It chanced to be protected by the concept of private life: banished from the day (reserved for work and consumption), it was thrust into the dark corners and dim lighting of the night. In this way it partly escaped the sweeping co-optation that ravaged daylight activities. As much cannot be said for the project of communication. The spark of passionate love is smothered by the ashes of false communication. Further aggravated by pressure to consume, falsification is now set fair to contaminate even the simple gestures of love.

//////

People who talk about communication when there is nothing but relations between things spread the lies and misconceptions that buttress reification. Harmony, understanding, agreement—what do such words mean when all I see around me are exploiters and exploited, bosses and underlings, actors and spectators, all of them so much grist for the mills of Power?

This is not to say that things express nothing. When someone invests an object with their own subjectivity, that object becomes human. But in a world ruled by privative appropriation, the object's only function is to justify its owner. If my subjectivity takes possession of its surroundings, if my vision lays claim to a landscape, this can only be in an ideal sense, without material or legal implications. In Power's perspective, people and things exist not for my enjoyment, but to serve a master; nothing really *is*, for everything is a function of an order based on property.

There can be no authentic communication in a world where most behaviour is governed by fetishes. The space between people and things is controlled by alienating mediations. And as Power becomes an abstract function its signs become so chaotic and numerous that they require interpretation by a host of scribes, semanticists and mythologists. Trained as they are to see only objects around them, proprietors require objective (and objectified) servants. The job of communications specialists is to organize lies for the benefit of these guardians of corpses. Only subjective truth, backed up by historical conditions, can resist them. Unmediated experience is the sole possible starting-point if the deepest inroads of the oppressive forces are to be smashed.

//////

The bourgeoisie's one pleasure has been the degradation of pleasure in all its forms. Not content with imprisoning the freedom to love in the squalid property relationship of the marriage contract (though releasing it as required for the purposes of adultery), not satisfied merely to vitiate passion with deception and jealousy, this class has found ways to separate lovers in the very throes of their love.

Despair in love arises not from the difficulty of finding a lover but rather from the fear that, once in each other's arms, lovers may fail ever to meet, each perceiving the other as an object. The hygienist notions of Swedish social democracy have already popularized a caricature of free love that treats love like a pack of cards.

The disgust provoked by a world stripped of authenticity provokes an insatiable desire for human contact. What extraordinary good fortune that love exists! At times I think that there is nothing so immediately real, so tangibly human, as the feel of a woman's body, the softness of her skin, the warmth of her sex. And indeed that nothing else exists— but that this one thing opens the door to a totality that even eternal life could not exhaust.

And then, even at the most intimate moments of passion, the inert mass of objects suddenly exerts its covert force. The passivity of a lover suddenly unravels the fabric being woven; the dialogue is interrupted before it has really begun. Love's dialectic freezes. Two recumbent tomb statues lie side by side. Nothing remains but a relationship between things.

Although love always arises *from* and *within* subjectivity—a girl is beautiful because I find her desirable—my desire cannot help objectifying what it hankers for. Desire always objectifies the loved person. But if I let my desire transform the loved person into an object, am I not doomed to collide with this object and (with habit doing its part) detach myself from it?

Perfect communication in love requires the reconciliation of two opposing tendencies: (a) the more I detach myself from the object of my desire and the more objective strength I accord my desire, the more I become a desire indifferent to its object; (b) the more I detach myself from my desire as an object, and the more objective strength I accord the object of my desire, the more my desire finds its *raison d'être* in the person loved.

In social terms, one way this interplay of attitudes might find expression is through the changing of partners combined with a more or less permanent attachment to a 'pivotal' partner. Such relations would be founded on a kind of dialogue amounting in fact to a single principle apprehended by all, a principle I have always longed to actualize: 'I know you don't love me, because you love only yourself. I am just the same as you. So love me.'

Love is impossible in the absence of radical subjectivity. The time is up for all Christian, self-sacrificial and politically militant forms of love. To love only oneself through other people, to be loved by others through the love they owe themselves—that is what the passion of love teaches, and what the conditions of authentic communication require.

//////

'Love' may also denote amorous conquest pursued by way of the inauthentic. To approach a woman via the spectacle is to doom oneself from the outset to a reified relationship. The playboy is the specialist here. The real choice is between spectacular seduction, based on braggadocio, and qualitative seduction, based on the attraction of someone not concerned to seduce.

Sade describes two possible approaches. On the one hand, the libertines of *The 120 Days of Sodom* can obtain gratification only by putting the objects of their seduction to death under horrifying torture (what more fitting homage to a *thing* than to make it suffer?); by contrast, the libertines of *Philosophy in the Bedroom,* warm and vivacious, do all they can to heighten their mutual gratification. The former exemplify the masters of old, quivering with hatred and revolt; the latter are already masters without slaves, discovering in each other nothing but echoes of their own delight.

The typical seducer of today is the sadist who refuses to forgive the desired person for being an object. Genuinely seductive people, to the contrary, possess the fullness of desire within themselves; they refuse to play roles and owe their seductiveness to this refusal. In Sade's work this would be Dolmancé, Eugénie, or Madame de Saint-Ange. This fullness can exist for the desired person, however, only if they recognize their own will to live in the other person who embodies it. Genuine seductiveness relies on truth alone. And not everyone deserves to be seduced. This is what Schweidnitz's *Béguines* and their thirteenth-century companions meant by saying that resistance to sexual advances was the sign of a crass spirit. The Brethren of the Free Spirit expressed the same idea: 'Any man who knows the God that lives in him carries his own heaven within himself. On the other hand, ignorance of one's own divinity constitutes a truly mortal sin. This is the meaning of the hell that one also carries with oneself in this life here below.'

Hell is the void left by separation, the anguish of lovers lying side by side but not together. Noncommunication is always reminiscent of the defeat of a revolutionary movement. The death wish takes up residence wherever the will to live runs aground.

//////

Love has to be freed from its myths, from its images, from its spectacular categories; its authenticity must be nourished, its spontaneity restored. There is no other way to combat its co-optation and reification by the spectacle. Love can withstand neither isolation nor fragmentation; untrammelled, it is bound to overflow into the will to transform the whole of human activity, into the necessity of building a society where lovers feel free everywhere.

The birth and dissolution of the moment of love are bound up with the dialectic of memory and desire. At the *inception* of this moment, desire and the memory of the earliest satisfied desires (implying no resistance to seduction) tend to reinforce one another. In the *moment* itself, memory and desire coincide: the moment of love is a space-time of authentic lived experience, a present where both the memory of the past and the tensed bow of desire aimed at the future coalesce. During the *break-up* stage, memory prolongs the passionate moment but desire gradually ebbs away. The present disintegrates, memory turns nostalgically towards past happiness, while desire senses the unhappiness to come. With *dissolution* separation is complete. The failure of the recent past cannot be erased from memory, and this eventually quells desire.

In dialogue, as in love, in the passion of love as in the project of communication, the problem is how to avoid the break-up stage. Remedies might include:

(a) Extending the moment of love by letting love flow into the channels open to it—by maintaining its links with the other passions and projects and transforming it from a mere moment into the true 'construction of a situation'.

(b) Encouraging collective experiments in individual self-fulfilment and multiplying the possibilities of sexual attraction by bringing together a great variety of possible partners.

(c) Permanently strengthening the pleasure principle, which sustains the passionate nature of the projects of self-fulfilment, communication and participation. Pleasure is the principle of unification; love is the passion for unity in a shared *moment*; friendship, the desire for unity in a shared *project*.

5. The Erotic, or the Dialectic of Pleasure

There is no pleasure that does not strive for coherence. The interruption of this quest, its nongratification, produces a disturbance analogous to what Wilhelm Reich called 'stasis'. Power's oppressive mechanisms keep human behaviour in a state of perpetual crisis. Pleasure, like the anxiety aroused by its absence, thus has an essentially social function. The erotic is the development of the passions in the process of their consolidation, an interplay between unity and multiplicity without which there can be no revolutionary coherence. ['Boredom is always counterrevolutionary' —*Internationale Situationniste* 3.]

Wilhelm Reich attributes most neurotic behaviour to disturbances of the orgasm, to what he called 'orgastic impotence'. He maintains that anxiety arises from the inability to experience a complete orgasm, from a sexual discharge that fails to release all the excitation aroused by the caressing, foreplay and so on that lead up to and make possible full sexual union. The energy thus accumulated and unspent floats free and is converted into anxiety. Anxiety from lack of gratification still further impedes future orgastic release.

But the problem of tensions and their relief is not an exclusively sexual matter. It characterizes all human relationships. And Reich, though he sensed that this was so, failed to emphasize strongly enough that the present social crisis is also a crisis of an orgastic nature. If it is true that 'the energy source of neurosis lies in the disparity between the accumulation and the discharge of sexual energy', it seems to me that our neurotic energy also derives from the disparity between the accumulation and the discharge of the energy mobilized by human relationships. Complete gratification is still possible in the moment of love, but no sooner do we seek to prolong this moment and give it a social character than we run into Reich's 'stasis'. The world of dissatisfaction and nonconsummation is a world of permanent crisis. What would a society without neurosis be like? An endless banquet. Pleasure is our only guide.

//////

'Everything is woman in what we love', wrote La Mettrie. 'The empire of love recognizes no boundaries other than those of pleasure.' But pleasure itself refuses to recognize boundaries. Pleasure which does not grow disappears. Repetition kills it, nor can it abide the fragmentary. The pleasure principle is inseparable from the totality.

The erotic is pleasure in search of coherence—the movement of passions on the way towards intercommunication, interdependence and integration; towards the re-creation in social life at large of the perfect pleasure experienced in the moment of love; and towards the establishment of the preconditions for interplay between the one and the many, or in other words for free and transparent participation in consummation.

Freud defines the goal of Eros as unification or the search for union. But when he maintains that fear of being separated and expelled from the social group stems from an underlying fear of castration, he has things the wrong way round: castration anxiety stems from the fear of expulsion, and not vice versa. It grows in proportion to the isolation of individuals in an illusory community.

Even as it seeks unification, Eros is essentially narcissistic—in love with itself. It wants a world to love as much as it loves itself. In *Life Against Death*, Norman O. Brown points up this contradiction. How, he asks, can a narcissistic orientation lead to union with objects in the world? 'The abstract antinomy of Self and Other in love can be overcome if we return to the concrete reality of pleasure and to the fundamental definition of sexuality as the pleasurable activity of the body, and think of loving as the relation of the ego to the sources of pleasure.' But it needs to be made clear that the sources of pleasure reside less in the body than in the possibility of expansion into the outside world. The concrete reality of pleasure is based on the freedom to unite with all those who help one unite with oneself. The fulfilment of pleasure depends on the pleasure of fulfilment, the pleasure of communication on the communication of pleasure, and participation in pleasure on the pleasure of participation. It is in this sense that the narcissism turned towards the outside world of which Brown speaks can only lead to the complete overthrow of social structures.

The more intense pleasure becomes, the more it demands the whole world. That is why I heartily second André Breton's truly revolutionary exhortation: 'Lovers, you should make one another come more and more!'

Western civilization is a civilization of work and, as Diogenes observed, 'Love is the occupation of the idle.' With the gradual disappearance of forced labour, love is bound to retrieve all the ground it has lost. This naturally poses something of a threat to every kind of authority. Precisely because the erotic is unitary, it embodies the freedom of multiplicity. No propaganda serves freedom better than people serenely enjoying the pleasures of the senses. Which is why pleasure is for the most part driven underground, why love is locked in the bedroom, why creativity is exiled to the backstairs of culture, and why alcohol and drugs cower under the long arm of the law.

The morality of survival condemns the diversity of pleasures just as it does all unitary multiplicity in favour of repetition. Whereas pleasure-anxiety is satisfied by the repetitive, true pleasure is predicated on diversity in unity. The simplest paradigm of the erotic is no doubt the pivotal couple: partners striving to make their experience as transparent and free as possible—an infectious complicity with the charm of an incestuous relationship. A wealth of shared experience inevitably fosters a brother-and-sister-like bond. Great loves have always had something incestuous about them, which suggests that love between brothers and sisters was special from the very first, and that it should be encouraged; only one small (and desirable) step is required to put an end once and for all to one of the oldest and most absurd of taboos. I am tempted to coin the term 'sororization' for an arrangement where one has a wife-cum-sister all of whose friends are also one's wives and sisters.

In the erotic realm there is no perversion save for the negation of pleasure—its distortion into pleasure-anxiety. What does the spring matter so long as the water runs? As the Chinese say: motionless in one another, pleasure carries us away.

Finally, there is no better way than the search for pleasure to keep the spirit of play alive. It guarantees real participation, protecting it against self-sacrifice, coercion and lies. The intensity of pleasure is the measure of subjectivity's hold on the world. Caprice is the play of nascent desire; desire is the play of nascent passion. And the play of passion itself finds its most coherent expression in the poetry of revolution.

Does this mean that the search for pleasure is incompatible with pain? Not at all—but pain has to be reinvented. Pleasure-anxiety is neither pleasure nor unpleasure, but the kind of scratching that merely makes an itch worse. So what is authentic pain? A setback in the play of desire or passion: a pain that is positive, thus all the more passionately focused on the creation of new kinds of pleasure.

6. The Project of Participation

The organization of survival can abide only false, spectacular forms of play. But with the crisis of the spectacle, the spirit of play, hounded almost out of existence, tends to reemerge on all sides. It is now taking the form of social upheaval and already foreshadows, over and above this negative aspect, the future society based on true participation. The praxis of play implies the refusal of leaders, of sacrifice and of roles; it also implies freedom to pursue self-fulfilment and transparency in social relationships [a]. Tactics is the contentious phase of play. Individual creativity needs organization to focus and strengthen it. Tactics cannot be detached from hedonistic considerations. Every action, no matter how circumscribed, must be aimed at the total destruction of the enemy. Adequate forms of guerrilla warfare must be extended to industrial societies (b). Repurposing (*détournement*) is the only revolutionary use of the spiritual and material values promoted by consumer society—and the ultimate weapon of supersession (c).

(a) The needs of the economy and play do not mix. Financial transactions are deadly serious. There is no trifling with money. The element of play still present within the feudal economy was gradually squeezed out by the rationality of monetary exchange. A playful approach to exchange meant barter conducted, if not without any common measure, then at least without any rigid pricing. But as soon as capitalism foisted its commercial relationships on the world, all traces of fancy were banished; and today the dictatorship of the commodity shows clearly that this system intends to enforce these relationships everywhere, and at every level of life.

In the high Middle Ages pastoral social relationships tempered the purely economic necessities of the feudal system with a measure of freedom; a playful spirit often prevailed even over the *corvée*, the dispensing of justice, or the settling of accounts. By throwing almost the whole of everyday life onto the battlefield of production and consumption, capitalism represses the urge to play while at the same time trying to co-opt it as a source of profit. Over the last few decades, consequently, we have seen the attraction of the unknown turned into mass tourism, adventure turned into scientific missions, the game of war turned into operational strategy, and the taste for change fobbed off with mere changes in taste.

Generally speaking, present-day social organization banishes all real play. Play has become something for children only. And even children, be it said, are ever more insistently offered gadget-type toys that reward passivity. As for adults, they are allowed only fake and co-opted forms of play: competitions, TV game shows, elections, casino gambling and so on. Naturally, such impoverished substitutes can never squelch the spontaneous richness of the passion for play—least of all today, when history is providing play with optimum conditions for expansion.

The order of the sacred tolerated profane and iconoclastic playfulness, as witness the irreverent decoration and obscene carvings to be found on capitals and elsewhere in cathedrals. So far from muting them, the Church openly embraced cynical mockery, caustic fantasy and nihilistic scorn. Under its mantle, demoniacal playfulness found shelter under its wing. Bourgeois power, on the other hand, had to quarantine play, isolate it in a special ward, as though afraid that it might infect other human activities. This privileged and rather disdained area of the nonprofitable was the bailiwick of art. And so things remained until the imperium of the economy reached even this sphere and set about converting it to commodity production. Ever since, the passion for play has been hunted down, yet it continues resurgent on all sides.

When a new breach first opened in the layers of prohibition covering the spirit of play, it occurred at the weakest point, the area where playfulness had held out the longest, namely the artistic sphere. This eruption was Dada. 'The Dadaist shows,' recalls Hugo Ball, 'struck a chord in their audience, awakening a long-repressed primitive-irrational play instinct.' Once embarked on the fatal path of pranks and scandals, art was bound to bring down with it the whole edifice which the spirit of seriousness had erected to the greater glory of the bourgeoisie. As a result play in our time has donned the robes of insurrection. Unfettered playfulness and the revolution of everyday life are now indistinguishable.

Ejected from hierarchical social organization, the passion for play has returned to destroy that organization, and in so doing construct a new type of society founded on real participation. Without presuming to foretell the precise characteristics of that society, where play will be completely unrestricted, we may safely say that it will embody the rejection of all leaders and all hierarchies, the rejection of self-sacrifice, the rejection of roles, the freedom to pursue genuine self-fulfilment, and transparency in social relationships.

//////

Play is inconceivable without rules—and without playing with the rules. Watch children at play. They know the rules of the game, they can remember them perfectly well, but they are always cheating, always dreaming up new ways of getting round them. But cheating, for children, does not have the connotations it does for adults. Cheating is part of the game, they play at cheating, complicit even in their disputes. What they are really doing is spurring themselves on to create new games. And sometimes it works: a new game emerges and unfolds. In this way they revitalize the passion for play without arresting its flow.

The moment an authority solidifies, becomes irrevocable and assumes a magical aura, play comes to a halt. But playfulness, however light-hearted, always involves a certain spirit of organization and the discipline this implies. Even if leaders of the game are called for, their decision-making power must never be wielded to the detriment of each player's autonomy. Rather, that power is the point of convergence of all individual wills, the collective echo of each particular demand. The project of participation requires a coherent organization that makes it possible for the decisions of each to be the decisions of all. Obviously small intimate groups—microsocieties—offer the best conditions for such experiments. Within them, the game can be the sovereign arbiter of the intricacies of communal life, harmonizing individual whims, desires and passions. This is especially true since the game envisaged here is an insurrectionary one necessitated by the group's resolve to live outside the world's official rules.

The passion for play is incompatible with self-sacrifice. You may lose, pay the forfeit, submit to the rules, have a rough time; but this is the logic of the game, not the logic of a Cause, not the logic of sacrifice. Once the idea of sacrifice appears the game becomes sacrosanct and its rules become rites. In true play, the rules encompass ways of getting round the rules, of playing with them. In the realm of the sacred, by contrast, rituals are not to be toyed with, they can only be broken, transgressed (and let us not forget that profaning the altar is still a form of homage to the Church). Only play deconsecrates—opening the door to boundless freedom. Play is the basis of the principle of *détournement*, the freedom to repurpose, to change the meaning of everything that serves Power: the freedom, say, to turn Chartres Cathedral into a funfair, a labyrinth, a shooting-range, or a dream landscape.

In a group founded on the passion for play, boring or arduous tasks might for instance be assigned as penalties—as the price paid, as it were, for losing a point or a game. Or, more simply, they could be used to fill dead time, as a kind of recreation from passionate activity, a stimulus making the more intense moments to come still more exciting. The construction of situations will inevitably embody the dialectics of presence and absence, richness and poverty, pleasure and pain, with the intensity of each pole heightening that of its opposite.

Meanwhile, technology deployed in an atmosphere of sacrifice and coercion invariably loses much of its impact. Encumbered in this way with a repressive function, its instrumental value is compromised, while oppressed creativity diminishes the efficiency of the machinery of oppression. The only guarantee of unalienated, truly productive work is the magnetic attraction of play.

In genuine play, roles are inconceivable if they are not played *with*. Roles in the spectacle demand complete conviction; a playful role, by contrast, implies a certain detachment, an attitude that allows one to see oneself as playing yet free, rather like a seasoned actor given to joking *sotto* voce between dramatic tirades. Spectacular organization cannot abide this sort of behaviour. The Marx Brothers showed just what a role can be when taken over by playfulness, and they achieved this despite more or less effective co-optation by the cinema. Just think what would happen if playing with roles had real life as its epicentre!

Anyone who enters the realm of play with a rigid, serious role will either fail or ruin the game. Consider the *agent provocateur*. Provocateurs are specialists in collective play, of which they have mastered the technique but not the dialectic. They might even be effective promoters of a revolutionary group's *offensive* goals (they always urge attack, after all), were they not fated, unlucky souls, to defend only their own role and mission, and thus quite incapable of representing the group's *defensive* interests. This contradiction always gives agents provocateurs away, sealing their sad fate. And the epitome of the provocateur is the game leader who has mutated into a leader pure and simple.

The passion for play is the only adequate basis for a community whose interests are indistinguishable from those of its individual members. Unlike provocateurs, traitors appear spontaneously in revolutionary groups. They do so whenever the passion for play wanes, thus warping the project of participation. The traitor is someone who cannot find authentic fulfilment through the sort of participation offered and decides to 'play' against this participation: not in order to correct but to destroy it. Treachery is the senile disorder of revolutionary groups. And the abandonment of the principle of play is the prime treachery, the one that justifies all the others.

Since it mobilizes the consciousness of radical subjectivity, the project of participation enhances the transparency of human relationships. The game of insurrection cannot be detached from the project of communication.

//////

(b) *Tactics.* Tactics is the polemical stage of play. It provides the necessary continuity between poetry *in statu nascendi* (play) and the organization of spontaneity (poetry). Essentially technical in nature, it prevents spontaneity from being dissipated and lost in the confusion. We know how cruelly absent tactics have been from most popular uprisings. We also know just how offhand historians can be about spontaneous revolutions. No serious study, no methodical analysis, nothing remotely comparable to Clausewitz's book on war. One might say that revolutionaries have ignored Makhno's battles as devoutly as bourgeois generals have studied Napoleon's.

Though a more thoroughgoing analysis cannot be offered here, a few remarks are in order.

An army well organized hierarchically can win a war, but not a revolution; an undisciplined mob can win neither. The problem is how to organize without creating a hierarchy; in other words, how to make sure that the 'leader of the game' does not become a tyrant. The spirit of play is the best safeguard against authoritarian sclerosis. Creativity armed is an unstoppable force. We have seen how the troops of Villa or Makhno could destroy the most battle-hardened forces. On the other hand, if playfulness calcifies, the battle is lost. The revolution fails so that its leader can be infallible. Why was Villa defeated at Celaya? Because he neglected to renew his strategy and tactics. Technically speaking, Villa was led astray by memories of Ciudad Juárez, where, by breaking through the walls of house after house, his men had taken the enemy from the rear and crushed them, and consequently he now disdained all the military advances of the First World War, with its machine-guns, mortars, trenches and so on. Politically, meanwhile, a certain narrowness of view led him to keep the industrial proletariat at arm's length. Tellingly, Obregón's army, which defeated Villa's Dorados, included both working-class militias and German military advisers.

The strength of revolutionary armies lies in their creativity. Often the first days of an insurrection bring stunning victories because the rules the enemy plays by are broken, because a new game is invented and because everyone participates fully in its development. But should this creativity flag, should it lapse into repetitiveness, should a revolutionary army come to resemble a regular army, the enthusiasm and even hysteria that gradually manifest themselves are naturally helpless to compensate for the decline in combativeness, while nostalgia for past victories breeds terrible defeats. The mystique of Cause and Leader replaces the conscious unity of the will to live and the will to win. In 1525, having held the combined forces of two princes at bay for two years, some forty thousand peasants, for whom tactics had been replaced by religious fanaticism, were hacked to pieces at Frankenhausen; the feudal army lost but three men. In 1964, in Stanleyville, hundreds of Mulelists, convinced that they were invincible, let themselves be massacred by surging onto a bridge defended by two enemy machine-guns. These were the same men who had earlier captured trucks and arms from the National Congolese Army by pitting the road with elephant traps.

Hierarchical organization and its opposite, the lack of discipline and coherence, do have one thing in common: they are both ineffective. In classical warfare, the inefficiency of one side triumphs over the inefficiency of its adversary by virtue of technical superiority. In revolutionary war, the poetic force of the insurgents deprives the enemy of its arms, and of the time to use them, thus stripping them of their only possible advantage. No sooner, however, do the guerrillero's tactics become predictable than the enemy learns to play by his rules, and an antiguerrilla campaign will then have every prospect of destroying or at least blocking the people's already slackened creativity.

//////

How can the discipline required by combat be ensured among troops who refuse blind obedience to a leader? How can cohesion be maintained? Generally, revolutionary armies either succumb to the devil of submission to a Cause or plunge into the deep blue sea of a heedless search for pleasure.

The call to self-sacrifice and renunciation in the name of freedom is the foundation-stone of future servitude. On the other hand, premature rejoicing and half-baked pleasure-seeking invariably herald the repression and *semaines sanglantes* of reaction. No, the game has to have coherence and discipline, but these must flow from the pleasure principle itself. The risk of pain is part and parcel of the quest for the greatest possible pleasure, whence the energy with which this quest is pursued; there is no other explanation, for instance, for the verve with which the roistering soldiery of pre-Revolutionary France would attack a town over and over again, no matter how many times they were repelled. What drove them onward was their passionate anticipation of the celebration to come—in this case, a celebration of pillage and debauchery. Pleasure is heightened for being long in the making. The most effective tactic is one able to integrate hedonism. The will to live, brutal and unfettered, is the fighter's most deadly secret weapon—and one liable to be turned against any who threaten it: with his own skin in the balance, a soldier has every reason to shoot his superiors. For the same reason, a revolutionary army has everything to gain by making its every member into a skilled tactician and, above all, into their own master, into someone who strives systematically to create their own pleasure.

In the struggles to come, the desire to live intensely will replace the old motive of pillage. Tactics will become a science of pleasure, for the search for pleasure is itself pleasurable. Such tactics, moreover, can be learned every day. The form of play known as armed combat differs in no essential way from the free play sought by everyone, more or less consciously, at every instant of their everyday lives. Anyone who is ready to learn, from their simple everyday experience, what tends to kill them and what tends to fortify them as a free individual, is well on the way to qualifying as a tactician.

There is no such thing, however, as a tactician in isolation. The will to destroy the old society demands a federation of tacticians of everyday life. To equip such a federation, to supply its technical needs, is one of the immediate goals of the Situationist International. Strategy, meaning the collective construction of the ramp to revolution, is founded on the tactics of individual everyday life.

//////

The ambiguous notion of humanity sometimes generates a degree of indecision in spontaneous revolutions. Too frequently the desire to make the individual the central concern opens the door to a paralysing humanism. How often revolutionary movements have spared their future executioners! How often they have accepted a truce that gives the enemy forces time to regroup! The ideology of humanism is a weapon in the hands of reaction, and it ends up justifying the worst inhumanity: think of Belgian paratroopers in Stanleyville.

No compromise is possible with the enemies of freedom—and humanism does not apply to mankind's oppressors. The destruction of counterrevolutionaries is the only humanitarian act that averts the cruelties of bureaucratized humanism.

A final problem of spontaneous insurrection derives from the paradoxical fact that it must destroy Power *totally* by means of *partial* actions. The struggle for economic emancipation alone has made survival possible for everyone, but it has also subjected everyone to survival's limitations. There can be no doubt, of course, that the masses have always fought for a much broader objective, for an overall transformation of their condition, a change in life as a whole. At the same time, the will to change the whole world in one fell swoop partakes of magical thinking, which is why it can so easily mutate into plain old reformism. The tactics of apocalypse and the tactics of gradual reform are bound to come together sooner or later in a marriage of reconciled antagonisms. Have not all pseudo-revolutionaries ended up by identifying tactics with compromise?

The ramp to revolution avoids partial victories and frontal assaults alike. Guerrilla war is a total war. This is the path on which the Situationist International is set: calculated harassment on every front—cultural, political, economic, and social. The battlefield is everyday life, which guarantees the unity of the struggle.

//////

(c) *Détournement*. In its broadest sense, repurposing means *putting everything back into play*. It is the act whereby the unifying force of play retrieves beings and things hitherto frozen solid in a hierarchy of fragments.

One evening, for example, as night fell, some friends and I wandered into the Palais de Justice in Brussels, a familiar elephantine edifice whose mass dominates the poor districts below while standing guard over the affluent Avenue Louise (which we shall one day turn into a fabulous adventure playground). As we drifted through a maze of corridors, staircases and suite after suite of rooms, we pondered how the place might be rearranged. For a while we occupied enemy territory; the magic of our imaginings transformed that sinister pile into a fantastic fairground, a sunny pleasure dome, where the most exhilarating adventures would allow themselves to be directly experienced.

In a word, *détournement* is the most elementary form of creativity. In daydreams subjectivity repurposes the world. Sometimes such repurposing resembles Monsieur Jourdain speaking prose; sometimes it is more like James Joyce writing *Ulysses*. Which is to say that it may be spontaneous or it may require a good deal of reflection.

It was in 1955 that Debord, struck by Lautréamont's systematic use of this device, first drew attention to its rich possibilities. In 1959, Asger Jorn described *détournement* as 'a game made possible by the fact that things can be *devalued*. All components of past culture must be reinvested or else disappear'. Returning to the subject later that year, in *Internationale Situationniste* 3, Debord elaborated as follows: 'The two fundamental principles of *détournement* are the loss of importance of each originally independent element (which may even lose its first sense completely), and the organization of a new signifying whole which confers a fresh meaning on each element.' Historical conditions have since bolstered these remarks, and it is now clear that:

(i) As the swamp of cultural disintegration broadens, spontaneous repurposing proliferates. The age of consumable values is remarkably well suited to the creation of 'new signifying wholes'.

(ii) Nor is culture now an especially privileged sphere in this regard. Repurposing can be an integral part of all forms of resistance in everyday life.

(iii) Under the dictatorship of the fragmentary, repurposing is the only subversive technique that serves the totality. No other revolutionary act is more coherent, more demotic or better adapted to insurrectional practice. Thanks to a sort of natural process—the desire to play—it fosters extreme radicalization.

                              //////

Amid the decay affecting the entirety of spiritual and material behaviour—and made inevitable by the imperatives of consumer society—the 'devaluing' phase of *détournement* has in a sense been taken over and guaranteed by historical conditions themselves. With negativity embedded in factual reality, repurposing comes increasingly to resemble a tactic of supersession—an essentially positive act.

Although the abundance of consumer goods is hailed on all sides as a major step forward, the way the social system deals with these goods, as we have seen, corrupts any good use of them. The primacy of the commodity-as-gimmick as a source of profit for capitalist and bureaucratic regimes alike means that commodities must be deprived of utility. The ideology of consumerism thus acts like a defect in manufacture, sabotaging the commodity it packages and turning what could be the material basis of happiness into a new form of slavery. In this context, repurposing popularizes other ways of using goods—of inventing superior uses for them whereby things marketed with a view to manipulating subjectivity can instead be manipulated by subjectivity to its own benefit. The crisis of the spectacle will reassign forces now serving lies to the camp of directly experienced truth. The main tactical and strategic issue is how to turn the weapons that commercial pressures oblige the enemy to distribute against that enemy itself. A user's guide to repurposing should be available to all consumers who want to stop consuming.

The weapon of repurposing, first used in the sphere of art, has now been deployed in every sphere. The technique emerged amid the cultural turmoil of the years between 1910 and 1925, but its use has gradually spread to every area touched by social disintegration. The fact remains that the artistic realm continues to offer repurposing a viable area for experiment; the fact remains, too, that much must still be learnt from the past. Thus Surrealism's premature attempt—in a perfectly suitable context—to reinvest Dadaist antivalues which had not yet been reduced to zero shows that trying to build on inadequately devalued elements can only result in co-optation by the prevailing mechanisms of social organization. The 'combinatorial' approach to art by today's cyberneticians goes so far as to prize any accumulation of disparate elements whatsoever, even if the particular elements *have not been devalued at all*. Consider Pop Art or the work of Jean-Luc Godard: the same apologetics of the junkyard.

Artistic expression also makes it possible, albeit tentatively and cautiously, to explore new forms of agitation and propaganda. In 1963, for instance, Michèle Bernstein produced a series of relief-plaster works with embedded lead soldiers, cars, tanks, etc. With such titles as *Victory of the Bonnot Gang*, *Victory of the Paris Commune*, *Victory of the Budapest Workers' Councils of 1956*, these works were meant to spur efforts to rectify and improve certain historical events artificially frozen in the past—to revisit the history of the workers' movement and at the same time to fulfil art. No matter how limited it may be, no matter how speculative, agitational art of this kind opens the door to everyone's creative spontaneity, if only by proving that in the especially distorted realm of art repurposing is the only language, the only action, that contains its own self-criticism.

Creativity has no limits; repurposing knows no bounds.

XXIV The Interworld and the New Innocence

> The interworld is the waste-land of subjectivity, a place where the corroding remnants of Power clash with the will to live [1]. The new innocence liberates the monsters of the inner world, projecting the murky violence of the interworld back against the old order of things which is its cause [2].

1

There is a Wild West of subjectivity plagued by the ills of Power: a zone rife with undying hatreds, vengeful gods, the tyranny of envy and the snarling of frustrated will. Its corruption is marginal, yet it threatens on every side. It is an 'interworld'.

The interworld is the waste-land of subjectivity. It contains cruelty in its starkest forms—the cruelty of the cop and the cruelty of the rebel, the cruelty of oppression and the cruelty of the poetry of revolt. Resisting spectacular co-optation yet never heeding the call of insurrection, the dreamer's superior space-time assumes monstrous forms here in accordance with the norms of individual will but always within Power's perspective. The growing impoverishment of everyday life has eventually made it into a public realm hospitable to every kind of experiment, an exposed battlefield where creative spontaneity confronts the forces that corrupt it. Intrepid explorer of the mind that he was, Artaud was able to describe this uncertain combat with great clarity in 'Supplement to the Journey to the Land of the Tarahumaras' (1944):

> The unconscious belongs to me only in dreams, and even there I cannot tell if what I see lingering is a form marked for birth or filth that I have rejected. The subconscious is what emerges from the premises of my internal will, but I am very unsure as to who reigns there, though I suspect that it is not I, but rather a horde of countervailing wills which, for reasons unknown to me, think in me, but have never had any other thought than that of usurping

my own place in my body and in my self. But in my preconscious, where their temptations harry me, I can see them, all those countervailing wills, bearing down on me, but I am armed now with full awareness, so what do I care, because I feel myself *there*.

A few lines earlier, Artaud had recounted how he 'came to feel that I must travel upstream, and delve into my preconscious until I could see myself evolving and *desiring*. Peyote got me there.'

All the same, the itinerary of the hermit of Rodez sounds a warning. Artaud's break with the Surrealist movement is significant. He reproached the group for allying itself with Bolshevism; for putting itself at the service of a revolution (one drenched, be it said, in the blood of the Kronstadt sailors) instead of putting the revolution at the service of Surrealism. Artaud was consummately right in attacking Surrealism's failure to base its revolutionary coherence on its most admirable feature, namely a commitment to the primacy of subjectivity. No sooner had he broken off with Surrealism, however, than Artaud sank into solipsistic ravings and magical thinking. Any notion of fulfilling subjective will by transforming the world went by the board. Instead of externalizing the inner world, he set out to make it sacrosanct, to discover, in the rigid world of analogies, some eternal founding myth; but the only route to that kind of revelation is the road of impotence. Those who hesitate to cast out the flames that devour them from within can only burn, can only be themselves consumed, in accordance with the laws of consumption, in ideology's shirt of Nessus. Ideology—be it the cult of drugs, of art, of psychoanalysis, of theosophy or of revolution—is the one thing that never changes history in the slightest.

//////

The imaginary is the exact science of possible solutions, not a parallel universe granted to the mind in compensation for real failures in the outside world. It is a force intended to bridge the gap between internal and external worlds. A praxis condemned to inaction.

With its phantoms, its obsessions, its outbursts of hate, its sadism, the interworld is like a cage of wild animals driven mad by their imprisonment. Anyone may descend thither by way of dreams, drugs, alcohol or the disordering of the senses. Its violence asks only to be freed. A good atmosphere in which to steep oneself, if only to attain the consciousness

...nat dances and kills—the consciousness that Norman O. Brown calls 'Dionysian'.

2

The red dawn of riot cannot dispel the monstrous creatures of the night. It clothes them in light and fire and disperses them over town and countryside. The new innocence is the actualization of malevolent dreams. Subjectivity cannot be built without destroying the obstacles in its path; it draws the violence needed for this from the interworld. The new innocence means lucidly embarking on an annihilation.

The most peaceable people are inhabited by dreams of blood. How hard it is to be solicitous towards those whom one cannot kill on the spot; to disarm by kindness those one cannot conveniently disarm by force. For those who have very nearly ruled over me I feel a great hatred. How can this hate be eliminated without eliminating its causes? The barbarity of riots, the arson, the people's savagery—all the excesses that terrify bourgeois historians—are exactly the right vaccine against the cold-blooded atrocity of the forces of law, order and hierarchical oppression.

With the new innocence, the interworld suddenly bursts its bounds and sweeps oppressive structures away. The play of sheer violence is subsumed by the pure violence of the game of revolution.

The shock of freedom works miracles. Nothing can withstand it—not sickness of mind, not remorse, not guilt, not the sense of powerlessness, not the brutalization produced by the world of Power. When a water pipe broke in Pavlov's laboratory, not one of the dogs that survived the flood showed the slightest trace of their long conditioning. Could the high tide of social upheaval have less effect on people than a broken water pipe on dogs? Reich recommends provoking explosions of anger in neurotics with emotional blocks and muscular armouring. That kind of neurosis is, I think, particularly widespread today; it is, simply, what I call survival sickness. And the most coherent explosion of anger will very likely bear a suspicious resemblance to general insurrection.

Three thousand years of darkness cannot withstand ten days of revolutionary violence. And the reconstruction of society will surely mean the simultaneous reconstruction of everyone's unconscious.

//////

The revolution of everyday life will obliterate the notions of justice, of punishment, of torture—notions determined by exchange and by the reign of the fragmentary. We want to be not dispensers of justice but masters without slaves, rediscovering, beyond the destruction of slavery, a new innocence, a life of grace. The point is not to judge the enemy but to destroy him. Whenever he liberated a village, Durruti gathered the local peasants together and asked them to point out the Fascists. These he summarily executed. The coming revolution will do likewise. With equanimity. We know that there will be no one to judge us thereafter: judges will be no more, for we shall have gobbled up every last one of them.

The new innocence means the destruction of an order of things that has ever impeded the art of living, and that today threatens what little remains of authentic life. I need no justification for defending my own freedom. Not a moment passes without Power's placing me in a posture of legitimate self-defence. The spontaneous jurisprudence of the new innocence is well expressed in this exchange between the anarchist Duval and the policeman sent to arrest him:

'Duval, I arrest you in the name of the Law!'

'And I suppress you in the name of freedom!'

Things don't bleed. Those heavy with the dead weight of things will die the death of things. Victor Serge recounts in *Conquered City* how, during the sack of Razumovskoe, some soldiers were rebuked for smashing porcelain for the fun of it. Their reply was: 'We would smash all the porcelain in the world to change life. . . . You love things too much and men too little. You love men too much, men like things, and Man too little.' Everything that does not have to be destroyed should be saved: that, in a nutshell, is our future penal code.

XXV You Won't Fuck with Us Much Longer!

A Sequel to *Vous foutez-vous de nous? Addresse des braves sans-culottes à la Convention nationale* [Are You Fucking with Us? Address of the Valiant Sans-Culottes to the National Convention [Sans-Culottes Printshop, Rue Mouffetard, Paris, 9 December 1792]]

Watts, Prague, Stockholm, Stanleyville, Turin, Mieres, Santo Domingo, Amsterdam: wherever passionate acts and a passionate consciousness of refusal shut down the factories of collective illusion, the revolution of everyday life is underway. Resistance intensifies as poverty becomes more general. The precipitating cause of so many particular issues that have long sparked confrontation—hunger, constraint, anomie, illness, anxiety, isolation, deceit—has now been exposed in its fundamental logic, its empty and all-enveloping form, its horrifyingly oppressive abstractness. It is the *whole world* of hierarchical power, of the State, of sacrifice, of exchange, of the quantitative—the commodity as will and representation of the world—that is now coming under attack from the driving forces of an entirely new society, a society still to be invented yet already with us. Revolutionary praxis casts its revealing light upon every last corner of the globe, changing negative into positive, lighting up the hidden face of the earth with the fires of insurrection and mapping out the planet's imminent conquest.

Only genuine revolutionary praxis can invest plans for armed rebellion with the precision they must have if they are not to remain hopelessly tentative and relative. But this same praxis becomes eminently corruptible once it breaks with its own logic. Revolutionary rationality is concrete rather than abstract, superseding the empty and universal form of the commodity. It is the only way to a nonalienating objectification—to the fulfilment of art and philosophy in the direct experience of the individual. Its thrust and extension are determined by a nonfortuitous encounter between two poles under tension: it is the spark that links subjectivity—whose will to be everything arises from the very totalitarianism of oppressive conditions—with the objective decay which, thanks to history, now affects a generalized commodity system.

Existential conflicts do not differ qualitatively from those which affect mankind as a whole. People cannot hope to control the laws governing their collective history if they do not at the same time master their individual histories. To embrace revolution while abandoning oneself—as all *militants* do—is to work arse-backwards. Down with voluntarism—but down likewise with the mystique of revolution's historical inevitability! We must devise an approach route to revolution—a plan at once rational and passionate which dialectically unites immediate subjective demands and the objective conditions of the age. Within the dialectic of partial and total, the *launching ramp of the revolution* is the project of configure everyday life, in and through the struggle against the commodity form, in such a way as to ensure that each phase of the revolutionary process is a faithful reflection of the ultimate goal. No maximum programme, no minimum programme—and no transitional programme; rather, an overall strategy framed by reference to the essential traits of the system to be destroyed, traits against which our first assaults must be directed.

When the time for insurrection comes (and hence, as a practical matter, *right away*), revolutionary groups must be capable of a *global* formulation of the problems created by a diversity of circumstances, just as the proletariat will solve problems globally in the process of its self-dissolution. Here are some of issues that must be addressed: how to achieve the concrete supersession of work, of the division of labour and of the gulf between work and leisure (the reconstruction of human relations by means of a passionate and conscious praxis affecting every sphere of social life, etc.); how to achieve the concrete supersession of exchange (the dethronement of the value of money, including the subversive use of counterfeiting, the establishment of relationships incompatible with the old economic system, the elimination of parasitic social strata, etc.); how to contrive the concrete supersession of the State and of every kind of alienating collectivity (the construction of situations, of self-managing assemblies, of *positive* laws designed to encourage every freedom and eradicate backward sectors, etc.); and how to organize the movement and extend it outwards from key areas so as to overthrow prevailing conditions everywhere (self-defence, relations with unliberated areas, promotion of the use and manufacture of arms, etc.).

Between the old society in tatters and the new society yet to be built, the Situationist International exemplifies a group in search of revolutionary coherence. Its significance, like that of any group that gives voice to the poetic impulse, is that it will supply a model for future social organization. It is essential, therefore, that external oppressive structures (hierarchy, bureaucratization) not be allowed to reproduce themselves within the group. This can be ensured only by making participation conditional upon the maintenance of real equality among members—not as a metaphysical right, but as the norm to be respected. It is precisely in order to avoid both authoritarianism and passivity (leaders and militants) that a revolutionary group should unhesitatingly sanction any drop in theoretical level, any practical backsliding, any compromise. There is no good reason for putting up with people whom the dominant system puts up with only too well. Expulsions and breaks are the only way to defend an imperilled coherence.

By the same token, the project of massing poetry's disparate forces presupposes the ability to recognize or catalyse autonomous revolutionary groups, to radicalize and federate them without ever assuming leadership. A group such as the Situationist International has an axial function: to serve everywhere as an axis rotated in the first instance by the power of popular resistance but augmenting and disseminating this initial motor force. The Situationists' only yardstick for identifying their allies is revolutionary coherence.

The long revolution prompts us to build a parallel society opposed to the dominant system and poised to replace it. Or, more precisely, towards the establishment of federations of microsocieties—authentic guerrilla *focos* fighting for *generalized self-management*. True radicalism permits every variation and guarantees every freedom. The Situationists do not come with some plan in hand for a new kind of society; they do not say 'Here is the ideal form of social organization. All hail!' They merely show, by fighting for themselves and maintaining the highest possible consciousness of that struggle, why people really fight and why becoming conscious of the fight is paramount.

1963–1965

Postscript (1972)
A Toast to Revolutionary Workers

Radical criticism has merely analysed the Old World and its negation. It must now either fulfil itself in the practice of the revolutionary masses or betray itself by opposing that practice.

So long as the project of the whole human being is still the spectre haunting the absence of unmediated self-fulfilment, so long as the proletariat has not *in reality* reappropriated theory from those who have derived it from the proletariat's own movement, so long will each radical step forward be followed by ideology's two steps back.

By urging proletarians to lay hold of a theory derived from direct everyday experience (and from the lack of it), the *Traité de savoir-vivre à l'usage des jeunes générations* cast its lot unequivocally with the cause of supersession. But by the same token it laid itself open to all the falsification bound to accompany any delay in its insurrectional application. No sooner is radical theory separated from the self-movement of revolutionary consciousness, as when that consciousness is suddenly slowed by history, than it becomes other than itself while remaining itself, and cannot completely evade capture by a parallel but contrary movement— by a relapse into detached thought, into the grip of the spectacle. The fact that it embodies its own self-criticism merely exposes it not only to ideological parasites, running the gamut in this instance from subjectivists to nihilists, via communitarians and apolitical hedonists, but also to our old friends the puffed-up bullfrogs of critical criticism.

Radical working-class action will in due course place the spheres of production and consumption (which it alone is able, *in the first instance*, to repurpose) at the service of individual passions and needs; what delay here shows is that the portion of the proletariat with no direct control over economic processes, capable at best, in an ascendant phase, of framing and disseminating a theory which it cannot itself fulfil or correct, is liable; in a period of defeat, to transform this theory into a regression of the intellect, for consciousness with no true utility can only justify its existence as a second-hand item.

The subjective expression of the Situationist project was at its best
as it prepared the ground for May 1968 and nurtured consciousness of
the new forms of exploitation; thereafter, it fell to its lowest ebb in the
intellectualizing discourse which many accepted out of frustration at not
being able to destroy what can *only* be destroyed (and indeed by sabotage
and repurposing rather than by occupations) by workers with hands on
the levers of production and consumption.

All the same, inasmuch as the Situationist project represented the
most advanced practical thought of the aforementioned proletarian
sector with no power over the market process, and inasmuch, too, as this
project never for a moment relinquished as its unique, self-appointed
task the destruction of the social organization of survival in favour of
generalized self-management, its real internal movement must sooner
or later resurface in a working-class context, leaving the spectacle and its
hot-air specialists to 'discover' the Situationist movement and adorn it
with their *apparatus criticus*.

Radical theory belongs to whoever enhances it. To defend it against
books or other cultural commodities wherein it reposes too often and
too long *on display* is not to glorify an antiwork, antisacrifice, antihi-
erarchy worker in contrast to a proletarian restricted to an unarmed
consciousness of the same refusals; rather, it is to call upon those who
find themselves at the most basic level of the unitary struggle against
the society of survival to use the forms of expression most effectively
available to them, and to perform revolutionary acts that forge their
own language by creating conditions from which there is no possible
turning back. Sabotage of the forced-labour system, destruction of the
processes of commodity production and reproduction, repurposing of
stores and plant to the benefit of the revolutionary forces and of all
those siding with them out of passionate attraction—here are means
capable of putting an end, not only to the bureaucratic reserve army
constituted by both intellectualizing workers and workerist intellectuals, but also to the brain-hand dichotomy itself—and indeed eventually
to the whole world of separations. Down with the division of labour and
the universal factory! Long live the unity of nonwork and generalized
self-management!

The main theses of the *Traité de savoir-vivre* must now find corrob-
oration of a concrete sort in the actions of its antireaders: not in the
form of student agitation but in that of total revolution. The task of

theory is to carry violence where violence already holds sway. Workers of Asturias, Limburg, Poznan, Lyons, Detroit, Csepel, Leningrad, Canton, Buenos Aires, Johannesburg, Liverpool, Kiruna, Coimbra—it is up to you to enable the entire proletariat to extend the pleasure of making revolution for one and for all to the everyday joys of making love, breaking taboos and revelling in the joys of passion!

Without the criticism of arms, the arms of criticism are suicide weapons. Many proletarians successfully avoid the despair of terrorism and the poverty of militantism only to become voyeurs of the working class, spectators of their own shelved potential. Cuckolded and defeated as revolutionaries sans revolution, they settle for the role of revolutionaries-by-proxy, awaiting the moment when the falling rate of petty-bureaucratic power hands them a chance to act as mediators and play the leader under the banner of their objective inability to smash the spectacle. This is why it is so vital that the organization of insurgent workers—the only revolutionary organization needed henceforth—must be the creation of the insurgent workers themselves, and thus the model for the proletariat at large in its fight for generalized self-management. Its advent will mark the final passing of repressive organizations (States, parties, unions, hierarchical groups of all kinds) along with their critical corollary, the fetishism of organization that thrives in the ranks of the nonproductive proletariat. The unmediated practice of such an organization will eradicate the contradiction between voluntarism and realism that indicated the limitations of the Situationist International: confronted by the perpetual reemergence within itself of the relationships characteristic of the dominant world, the group found that its own methods of dealing with this, namely expulsions and breaks, were inadequate, and never managed to harmonize intersubjective agreements and differences. (I left the Situationist International and its growing burden of empty self-importance in November 1970.) Lastly, this development will prove that that the portion of the proletariat with no practical prospect of repurposing the means of production is in need not of organizations but rather of individuals acting for themselves. Such individuals may on occasion join forces as action groups for the purposes of sabotage (attacks on the repressive networks, occupation of radio stations, etc.); they may be expected to intervene wherever and whenever opportunities for tactical and strategic effectiveness present themselves. Their sole aim will be to pursue unrestrained gratification and, *inseparably*, to kindle the fire of working-class guerrilla warfare—that negative and positive fire which, though it arises from the very depths of the proletariat, is nevertheless the only possible basis for that class's self-abolition as part of the abolition of class society as a whole.

The workers may still lack the coherence needed to realize their full effectiveness, but they can be sure that they will succeed in achieving that potential, and in a definitive way. The recent history of wildcat actions and riots is the writing on the wall that announces the resurgence of workers' councils and the return of Communes. The sudden reappearance of these forms—sure to be met by a repressive counterattack whose violence will put the repression of intellectual movements in the shade—will come as a surprise only to those unable to discern, beneath the diversity of the spectacle in its immobility, the unitary progression of the old mole, the proletariat's ongoing clandestine struggle for the appropriation of history and the global overthrow of all the prevailing conditions of everyday life. The necessity of *history-for-itself* is likewise discernible in all its cunning in the *negative* coherence which is the most that an unarmed proletariat can achieve: a sort of defensive unanimity that serves as a ubiquitous objective warning to whatever threatens the radicalism of the working class from within. Such threats include intellectualizing tendencies, which cause consciousness to regress to the level of book learning and culture; unchecked mediators with their bureaucratic 'critique'; status-seekers, more attached to new roles than to the dissolution of all roles in the playful emulation that characterizes basic guerrilla action; and all those forces which press for the abandonment of practical subversion, of the revolutionary conquest of territory, of the unitary, international march towards the end of separations, the end of self-sacrifice, the end of forced labour, the end of hierarchy, and the end of the commodity in its every last manifestation.

The danger reification poses to each individual's creativity no longer lies in some theoretical *What Is to Be Done?* It resides rather in practical revolutionary action. Those who fail to discover in revolution the crucial passion which opens the door to all the others can attain only a pale imitation of pleasure. In this sense, the *Traité de savoir-vivre* sought to find the shortest route from individual subjectivity to its fulfilment in history-made-by-all. From the standpoint of the long revolution, it was just one point, albeit a starting-point, on the communalist road to generalized self-management. It was no more than a sketch, but a sketch of the death sentence which the society of survival pronounces upon itself and which will one day be executed without appeal by the international of factories, fields and streets.

We have a world of pleasures to win, and nothing to lose but boredom.

October 1972

Appendix 1 Author's Preface to the First French Mass-Market Edition [1992]¹

The Everyday Eternity of Life

The *Traité de savoir-vivre à l'usage des jeunes générations* announced the emergence of a radically new era from the bosom of a waning world.

With the quickening of the current that has for a short while now been carrying beings and things along, the *Traité* has grown, so to speak, ever more clairvoyant.

The stratified past still clung to by those who grow old with time is ever more easy to distinguish from the alluvia, timeless in their fertility, left by others who awake to themselves day by day (or at least strive to do so).

For me, these are two moments of a single fluctuating existence in which the present is continually shedding old forms.

A book that seeks to interpret its time can do no more than bear witness to a history imprecise in its becoming; a book that wreaks change on its time cannot fail to sow the seeds of change in the field of transformations yet to come. If the *Traité* has something of both, it owes this to its radical bias, to the preponderance in it of that 'self' which is in the world without being of the world, that self whose emancipation is a *sine qua non* for anyone who has discovered that learning to live is not the same thing as learning to survive.

In the early 1960s I conjectured that the examination of my own subjectivity, far from constituting an isolated activity, would resonate with other, like endeavours; and that if this examination was in tune with the times, it would in some way modulate those times in harmony with our desires.

To attribute the same ennui that textured my own everyday existence to a few others, and to enlist them in the dismal task of denouncing its causes, was not a little presumptuous on my part. Yet what an alluring challenge it was to wager on my presentiment that a passion for life was

---

1 Paris: Gallimard, Folio/Actuel, 1992.

on the increase, a passion the impossibility of defining which contrasted so sharply with the rigour of the criticism directed at the conditions ranged against it.[2]

In 1968 the hitherto underground work of vivisecting survival—a veritable *opus nigrum*—brutally shattered the barrier of prevailing sensibilities. Thirty years on, consciousness is slowly opening itself up to a reversal of perspective in the light of which the world ceases to be apprehended as prey to a negative fate and begins instead to be ordered on the basis of a new positivity, on the basis of the acknowledgement and expansion of the life forces within it.

Violence has changed its meaning. Not that the rebel has grown weary of fighting exploitation, boredom, poverty and death: the rebel has simply resolved no longer to fight them with the weapons of exploitation, boredom, poverty and death. For the first victims of such a struggle are those who engage in it full of contempt for their own lives. Suicidal behaviour is an inevitable part of the logic of a system that battens on the gradual dilapidation of nature and human nature alike.

If the ancient cry 'Death to the Exploiters' no longer echoes through the streets, it is because it has given way to another cry, one harking back to childhood and issuing from a passion which, though more serene, is no less tenacious. That cry is 'Life First!'

The rejection of commodities implicit in the shattered shop windows of 1968 marked such a clear and public breach in a millennia-old economic boundary-line drawn around individual destiny that archaic reflexes of fear and impotence immediately obscured the insurrectionary movement's truly radical character. Here at long last was a chance to make the will to live in each of us the basis for a society which for the first time in history would attain an authentic humanity.

Many people, however, treated this moment as an opportunity to

---

2 The *Traité* was written between 1963 and 1965, and the manuscript sent to thirteen publishers, all of whom rejected it. The last refusal was from Gallimard, on whose reading committee the book was supported only by Raymond Queneau and Louis-René Des Forêts. As it happened, on the day the returned manuscript and Gallimard's rejection letter reached me, *Le Figaro littéraire* published an article decrying the influence of the Situationists on the Provos of Amsterdam. That same evening Queneau sent me a telegram requesting that the manuscript be resubmitted. As a result I cut short a closing discussion of workers' councils as a social model (the book's Postscript, added in 1972, shows signs of an attempt to redress this). The *Traité* eventually appeared on 30 November 1967, six months before those 'events' which—precisely because their most innovative aspects are even now only just becoming apparent—are still not referred to as the Revolution of May 1968.

set up shop as merchandisers of opposition, ignoring any need to change behaviour wedded to the mechanics of commodity rule. Among the *Traité's* readers were some who seized upon my account of a certain *mal de vivre* (from which I wanted above all to free myself) as an excuse for offering no resistance whatsoever to the state of survival to which they were in thrall (and which the comforts of the welfare state, with its abundant and bitter consolations, had until then concealed from them).

It was not long before these people had run up new character armour for themselves at the verbal forge of militant terrorism. Later still (without ever abandoning their incendiary rhetoric) they became career bureaucrats and covered themselves with glory as cogs in the *apparat* of State and marketplace.

//////

In the 1960s a mutation of the economy took hold whose effects are increasingly evident today. With the benefit of hindsight I can now see much more easily how I was able to take advantage, in effect, of a kind of interregnum—during which the old authority was losing its grip but the new had still not thoroughly consolidated its power—to rescue a subjectivity that was widely discredited and to propose, as the basis of a projected society, *an enjoyment of self that proclaimed itself one with enjoyment of the world.*

To begin with, there were three or four of us who partook of, and shared among us, the passion for 'constructing situations'. The way each of us cultivated this passion at that time depended on their goals for their own existence, but it has lost nothing of its urgency, as witness both the inexorable advance of the life forces and the investments that an ecological neocapitalism is obliged to make in them.

The last thirty years have visited more upheavals upon the world than the several preceding millennia. That the *Traité* should have contributed in the slightest to the acceleration thus suddenly imposed upon events is in the end far less a source of satisfaction to me than the sight of the paths now being opened up, within some individuals and some societies, that will lead from the primacy now at long last accorded to life to the likely creation of an authentically human race.

May 1968 was a genuine decanting, from the kind of revolution which revolutionaries make against themselves, of that permanent revolution which is destined to usher in the sovereignty of life.

There has never been a revolutionary movement not governed from start to finish by the expanding empire of the commodity. The economy, with its iron collar of archaic forms, has always smashed revolution by means of freedoms, modelled on the freedom of trade, which because of the inherent constraints of the law of profit swiftly become the building-blocks of new tyrannies.

In the end the economy picks up whatever it put in at the outset—plus appreciation. This is the whole meaning of the notion of *récupération* (co-optation). Revolutions have never done anything but turn against themselves and negate themselves at the speed of their own rotation. The revolution of 1968 was no exception to this rule. The commodity system, finding generalized consumption more profitable than production, itself speeds up the shift from authoritarianism to the seductions of the market, from saving to spending, from puritanism to hedonism, from an exploitation that makes the earth and mankind sterile to a lucrative reconstruction of the environment, from capital as more precious than the individual to the individual as the most precious capital.

The impetus of the 'free' market has reunified the capitalist system by precipitating the collapse of bureaucratic, so-called communist state capitalism. The Western model has made *tabula rasa* of the old forms of oppression and instated a democracy of the supermarket, a self-service autonomy, a hedonism whose pleasures must be paid for. Its racketeering has exploded all the great ideological balloons of earlier times, so laboriously inflated from generation to generation by the winds of political seasons.

A religious flea-market has been set up among the sex-shops and the novelty emporia. The system has realized in the nick of time that a living human being is a more paying proposition than a dead human being—or one ravaged by pollutants. Little wonder that another vast market has grown up to cash in on the tender feelings and troubles of the human heart.

The critique of the spectacle has itself been travestied as critical spectacle: with the saturation of the market for denatured, tasteless, useless products, consumers unable to proceed any further down the road of stupidity and passivity are hoisted into a competing market where profitability depends on claims of quality and 'naturalness'. Suddenly we are obliged willy-nilly to demonstrate discernment—to retrieve the shreds of intelligence that old-style consumerism forbade us to use.

Power, State, religion, ideology, army, morality, the Left, the Right—
that so many abominations should have been sent one after another to
the wrecker's yard by the imperialism of the market, for which there is no
black and no white, might seem at first glance good reason to rejoice; but
no sooner does the slightest suspicion enter one's mind than it becomes
obvious that all these forces have simply redeployed, and are now waging
the same war under different colours. Green, lest we forget, is also the
colour of the dollar bill. The new and improved consumerism may be
democratic, it may be ironic, but it always presents its account, and the
account must always be settled. A life governed by sanctioned greed is by
no means freed thereby from the old tyranny of having to forfeit one's
life merely to pay for it.

If there is one area where the achievement of consciousness comes
into its own as a truly essential act, it is the realm of everyday life, where
every passing instant reveals once again that the dice are loaded and that
as per usual we are being taken for a ride.

From the agrarian structures that gave birth to the first city-states to
the world-wide triumph of the free market, the history of the commodity
system has continually swung back and forth between a closed economy
and an open one, between withdrawal into protectionism and embrace of
the free circulation of goods. Each advance of the commodity has engen-
dered on the one hand formal freedoms, and on the other a consciousness enjoying the incalculably great advantage over those freedoms of
potential incarnation within the individual, of potential conflation with
the very movement of desire.

The ideology of freedom that rode the wave of all past revolutions,
from the communalist insurrections of the eleventh and twelfth centuries to 1789, 1848, 1871, 1917, and 1936, never lost any time reducing and
rechannelling all libidinal exuberance into bloody violence.

Only one revolution (apropos of which it will someday be acknowledged that, in sharp contrast to all its predecessors, it truly wrote finis to
several millennia of inhumanity) did not end in a whirlwind of repressive violence. Indeed it simply did not end at all.

In 1968 the economy closed the circle: from its apogee it plunged
into nothingness. This was the moment when it abandoned the authoritarian puritanism of the production imperative for the (more profitable)
market in individual gratification. The suffusion of attitudes and *mores*
by permissiveness echoed the official world's recognition of pleasure—so

long, of course, as the pleasure in question was a profitable one, tagged with an exchange value and wrested from the gratuitousness of real life to serve a new mercantile order.

And then the game was over. Cold calculation had drawn too close to the heat of passion. The danger was that the will to live, aroused and denied simultaneously, would eventually reveal the artificiality of the market's definition of freedom. Where was the silver-tongued lie that would serve business's ecological new look by promoting the timidest imaginable defence of life forces while still preventing individuals from reconstructing both their desires and their environment as part of an indivisible process?

A fate that has overwhelmed fomenters of revolution from time immemorial decreed that the 1968ers should go where the economy beckoned: to modernity for the economy—and to disaster for them. If this fate was defied in 1968, it was thanks to a subjective consciousness of where real life lay. The rejection of work, sacrifice, guilt, separation, exchange, survival, so readily susceptible to intellectual co-optation, drew nourishment on this occasion from a lucidity that went far beyond *contestation* (or perhaps rather stopped far short of it) by choosing to hone desire and join the struggle of an embryonic everyday life at loggerheads with everything that seeks to exhaust and destroy it.

A consciousness severed from life forces is blind. The dark glasses of the negative can obscure the fact that what seems like forward motion is just the opposite. The social analyses of our fashionable thinkers are notable in this regard for the singular tenacity with which they cling to quite ridiculous claims. They toss such ideas as revolution, self-management and workers' councils into the dustbin at the very moment when state power is suffering the onslaught of groups whose collective decision-making admits of no intrusion by political representatives, shuns all organizers or leaders and combats all hierarchy.

I do not underestimate the shortcomings of practices of this kind, which have for the most part been confined to reactions of a defensive kind. But they are unquestionably a manifestation, bearing no *appellation d'origine contrôlée*, of a type of behaviour that breaks utterly with the old mass movements. Groups of individuals formed in this way could not be further removed from hordes of people manipulable at will.

Everyday life itself is even more replete with shortcomings—one has but to consider how little light is shed on it by those who wander through at the whim of its pleasures and pains.

But after all, the Judaeo-Christian era itself had to end before we found out that the well-worn word 'life' concealed a reality long overlain by the mere *survival* to which all life has been reduced by the commodity system, which mankind produces and which reproduces mankind in its own image.

There is no one who is not embarked upon a process of personal alchemy, yet so inattentive, so short-sighted are those who call their own passivity and resignation 'fate' that the magistery cannot get beyond the *opus nigrum*, cannot emerge from the atmosphere of putrefaction and death which is the ordinary product of desires forced into self-negation.

I consider the feeling (inevitably a desperate one) of having fallen prey to a universal conspiracy of hostile circumstances to be contrary to any will to autonomy. The negative is nothing but an excuse for resigning oneself never to be oneself, never to grasp the riches of one's own life.

My goal, instead, has been a lucidity grounded in my desires; by continually illuminating the struggle of the life forces against death, such a lucidity must surely counter the commodity's logic of disintegration. As a sort of research report, a single book has neither the best nor yet the most insignificant role to play in the passionate day-to-day struggle to winnow out from one's life whatever blocks or depletes it. *The Revolution of Everyday Life*, *The Book of Pleasures*, and *Adresse aux vivants* (Address to the Living) may be seen as three phases of a continuum connecting several concordances between a changing world and footholds secured from time to time in a persistent attempt at once to create myself and to re-create society.

The diminishing return from the exploitation and destruction of nature was the motor of the late-twentieth-century development of an ecological neocapitalism and of new modes of production. The profitability of life forces is no longer founded on their exhaustion but instead on their reconstruction. Consciousness of the life to be created progresses because the direction taken by reality itself contributes to it. Never have desires, returned now to their childhood, enjoyed such power within each individual to destroy everything that inverts, negates and reifies human beings and turns them into objects of exchange.

Something is taking place today that no one has ever dared imagine: the process of individual alchemy is on the point of transmuting an inhuman history into nothing short of humanity's self-realization.

September 1991

Appendix 2 Concerning the Translation

Raoul Vaneigem's 'treatise on *savoir-vivre*' will soon be fifty years old. The work has never gone out of print and has long been freely downloadable in several languages from the Internet. It would be impossible to quantify its circulation over the decades, but there is no doubt that it has been a 'life-changing book' for a host of readers and that it fully deserves its reputation as a 'classic of subversion'.

As for the *Traité*'s life in English translation, the version which I settled for in 1983, published jointly by Rebel Press in London and Left Bank Books in Seattle, was the culmination of the efforts of several translators in the 1970s (see my preface to that edition below). In the effervescence of the 1960s and '70s portions of the book were very widely circulated as pamphlets in the English-speaking world. In those days (and I believe I can speak for all of us), we wanted to maximize the practical impact of Raoul Vaneigem's words, to produce a *texte de combat,* and to this end we subordinated the customary criteria of literary translation to considerations of accessibility and topicality. We thought (correctly, I think) that the text belonged to us—to 'our party' in the sense in which Marx and Engels used this expression—and that we could (and should) do more or less what we liked with it—or rather what best served our collective aims.

Much time has passed, and when I returned to the translation I discovered to my surprise—and somewhat to my distress!—that a proper revision would entail not perhaps a reversal, but at least a shift of perspective. What I now offer, therefore, is a version much more faithful to the original, making no attempt to find 'English' equivalents for cultural references, and striving, so far from 'updating' anything, to preserve a feeling for those times. Which said, it is my hope that this newfound fidelity to the French and respect for the venerability of Vaneigem's work will in no way detract from its enduring relevance and power to provoke, not to mention its stunning prescience. How far I have succeeded in this I naturally leave it to the reader to judge.

D. N.-S., September 2011

Translator's Note to the Rebel Press Edition [1983]

This translation of Raoul Vaneigem's *Traité de savoir-vivre à l'usage des jeunes générations* was done a few years ago at the suggestion of Free Life Editions, New York. Although Free Life ceased all publication before the book could be brought out, I would like to thank them for sponsoring the project and for assisting me in a variety of ways while work was in progress.

I am also indebted to earlier translators of all or parts of the *Traité*, among them John Fullerton and Paul Sieveking, who in 1972 published the only full-length version that I know of (London: Practical Paradise Publications). I have stolen shamelessly from all such precursors, and I am especially obliged to CW [Chris Whitbread], CG [Chris Gray] and BE [Bruce Elwell].

Thanks are due too, for various forms of essential aid, to PL and YR in Paris; to RE and TJC in the United States; and to Rebel Press in London.

I must also express my gratitude to Raoul Vaneigem, who authorized the translation and answered all my queries without betraying the slightest sign of fatigue.

The Revolution of Everyday Life is not a title I care for; I would have preferred *The Rudiments of Savoir-Vivre: A Guide for Young Persons Recently Established in the World*, or more simply *The Facts of Life for Younger Readers*. The publishers are doubtless right, however, in preferring not to depart from the title by which the work has by now become known to the English-speaking public.

I have obstinately resisted the well-intentioned urgings of many people that I should overstep the role of translator and become an editor as well, by adding footnotes, glosses, biographical sketches of 'obscure personages', etc., etc. Nobody, I am afraid, has persuaded me of the need for any such spoonfeeding of the reader.

I wish it were not necessary to state (though I am quite sure it is) that my part in the publication of this book does not imply my adherence to any or all of its theses, much less my affiliation with any real or conjectured, 'Vaneigemist' or 'Debordist', post-, pro-, crypto-, neo- (or, for that matter, anti-) Situationist tendency or clique. The ardent student of the Situationist International, who is not such a *rara avis* as common sense might lead one to expect, may readily ascertain that I was expelled from that organization in 1967. That parting of the ways seemed to me then—and still seems to me—thoroughly justified on both sides.

It is nonetheless my earnest hope that this new edition of Vaneigem's book will serve both to enlighten another 'younger generation' and, by increasing the work's warts-and-all accessibility to English-language readers, militate against those absurd hagiographical impulses which mystify the Situationist International's doughty contributions instead of rescuing them from the clutches of enemies and pillagers with a shared interest in consigning them to oblivion.

I should like to dedicate this translation to Cathy Pozzo di Borgo.

D.N.-S, October 1982

Index

The Author

Raoul Vaneigem was born in 1934 in Lessines, Belgium, a small town whose traditional claim to fame was the production of paving stones but which in the twentieth century also produced the Surrealist painter René Magritte and the Surrealist poet Louis Scutenaire. Vaneigem grew up in the wake of World War II in a working-class, socialist and anticlerical milieu. He studied Romance philology at the Free University of Brussels and embarked on a teaching career that he later abandoned in favor of writing.

In late 1960 Vaneigem was introduced to Guy Debord by Henri Lefebvre, and soon afterwards he joined the Situationist International, which Debord and his comrades-in-arms had founded in 1957. He was a leading light in the group throughout the 1960s.

Vaneigem is a prolific writer and a relentless critic of late capitalism. Among his works translated into English are *The Totality for Kids* (London: Christopher Gray/Situationist International, 1966 ['Banalités de Base', 1962–63]); *Contributions to the Revolutionary Struggle* (London: Bratach Dubh, 1981 [*De la grève sauvage à l'autogestion généralisée*, 1974]); *A Cavalier History of Surrealism* (San Francisco: AK Press, 1999 [1977]); *The Book of Pleasures* (London: Pending Press, 1983 [1979]); *The Movement of the Free Spirit* (New York: Zone Books, 1994 [1986]); and *A Declaration of the Rights of Human Beings* (London: Pluto, 2003 [2001]).

PM Press plans soon to publish two more titles: *The Knight, the Lady, the Devil, and Death* (2003) and *The Inhumanity of Religion* (2000).

The Translator

Born in Manchester, England, Donald Nicholson-Smith is a New Yorker by adoption. A sometime Situationist (1965–1967), he has translated Guy Debord's *The Society of the Spectacle* and Henri Lefebvre's *The Production of Space*, as well as works by Apollinaire, Jean-Patrick Manchette, Jean Piaget, Thierry Jonquet, Paco Ignacio Taibo II, and many others.

ABOUT PM PRESS

PM Press was founded at the end of 2007 by a small collection of folks with decades of publishing, media, and organizing experience. PM Press co-conspirators have published and distributed hundreds of books, pamphlets, CDs, and DVDs. Members of PM have founded enduring book fairs, spearheaded victorious tenant organizing campaigns, and worked closely with bookstores, academic conferences, and even rock bands to deliver political and challenging ideas to all walks of life. We're old enough to know what we're doing and young enough to know what's at stake.

We seek to create radical and stimulating fiction and non-fiction books, pamphlets, T-shirts, visual and audio materials to entertain, educate and inspire you. We aim to distribute these through every available channel with every available technology — whether that means you are seeing anarchist classics at our bookfair stalls; reading our latest vegan cookbook at the café; downloading geeky fiction e-books; or digging new music and timely videos from our website.

PM Press is always on the lookout for talented and skilled volunteers, artists, activists and writers to work with. If you have a great idea for a project or can contribute in some way, please get in touch.

PM Press
PO Box 23912
Oakland, CA 94623
www.pmpress.org

FRIENDS OF PM PRESS

These are indisputably momentous times—the financial system is melting down globally and the Empire is stumbling. Now more than ever there is a vital need for radical ideas.

In the four years since its founding—and on a mere shoestring—PM Press has risen to the formidable challenge of publishing and distributing knowledge and entertainment for the struggles ahead. With over 175 releases to date, we have published an impressive and stimulating array of literature, art, music, politics, and culture. Using every available medium, we've succeeded in connecting those hungry for ideas and information to those putting them into practice.

Friends of PM allows you to directly help impact, amplify, and revitalize the discourse and actions of radical writers, filmmakers, and artists. It provides us with a stable foundation from which we can build upon our early successes and provides a much-needed subsidy for the materials that can't necessarily pay their own way. You can help make that happen—and receive every new title automatically delivered to your door once a month—by joining as a Friend of PM Press. And, we'll throw in a free T-shirt when you sign up.

Here are your options:

- **$25 a month** Get all books and pamphlets plus 50% discount on all webstore purchases

- **$40 a month** Get all PM Press releases (including CDs and DVDs) plus 50% discount on all webstore purchases

- **$100 a month** Superstar—Everything plus PM merchandise, free downloads, and 50% discount on all webstore purchases

For those who can't afford $25 or more a month, we're introducing **Sustainer Rates** at $15, $10 and $5. Sustainers get a free PM Press T-shirt and a 50% discount on all purchases from our website.

Your Visa or Mastercard will be billed once a month, until you tell us to stop. Or until our efforts succeed in bringing the revolution around. Or the financial meltdown of Capital makes plastic redundant. Whichever comes first.

Portugal: The Impossible Revolution?

Phil Mailer
with an afterword by Maurice Brinton

ISBN: 978-1-60486-336-9
$24.95   288 pages

After the military coup in Portugal on April 25, 1974, the overthrow of almost fifty years of Fascist rule, and the end of three colonial wars, there followed eighteen months of intense, democratic social transformation which challenged every aspect of Portuguese society. What started as a military coup turned into a profound attempt at social change from the bottom up and became headlines on a daily basis in the world media. This was due to the intensity of the struggle as well as the fact that in 1974-75 the moribund, right-wing Francoist regime was still in power in neighboring Spain and there was huge uncertainty as to how these struggles might affect Spain and Europe at large.

This is the story of what happened in Portugal between April 25, 1974, and November 25, 1975, as seen and felt by a deeply committed participant. It depicts the hopes, the tremendous enthusiasm, the boundless energy, the total commitment, the released power, even the revolutionary innocence of thousands of ordinary people taking a hand in the remolding of their lives. And it does so against the background of an economic and social reality which placed limits on what could be done.

"An evocative, bitterly partisan diary of the Portuguese revolution, written from a radical-utopian perspective. The enemy is any type of organization or presumption of leadership. The book affords a good view of the mood of the time, of the multiplicity of leftist factions, and of the social problems that bedeviled the revolution."
— Fritz Stern, *Foreign Affairs*

"Mailer portrays history with the enthusiasm of a cheerleader, the 'home team' in this case being libertarian communism. Official documents, position papers and the pronouncements of the protagonists of this drama are mostly relegated to the appendices. The text itself recounts the activities of a host of worker, tenant, soldier and student committees as well as the author's personal experiences."
— Ian Wallace, *Library Journal*

"A thorough delight as it moves from first person accounts of street demonstrations through intricate analyses of political movements. Mailer has handled masterfully the enormous cast of politicians, officers of the military peasant and workers councils, and a myriad of splinter parties, movements and caucuses."
— *Choice*

with PM Press

Against Architecture

Franco La Cecla
Translated by Mairin O'Mahony

ISBN: 978-1-60486-406-9
$14.95   144 pages

First published in 2008, (as *Contro l'architettura*),
Against Architecture has been translated into French
and Greek, with editions forthcoming in Polish
and Portuguese. The book is a passionate and
erudite charge against the celebrities of the current
architectural world, the "archistars." According to Franco La Cecla, architecture
has lost its way and its true function, as the archistars use the cityscape to build
their brand, putting their stamp on the built environment with no regard for the
public good.

More than a diatribe against the trade for which he trained, Franco La Cecla
issues a call to rethink urban space, to take our cities back from what he calls
Casino Capitalism, which has left a string of failed urban projects, from the
Sagrera of Barcelona to the expansion of Columbia University in New York City.
As he comments throughout on the works of past and present masters of urban
and landscape writing, including Robert Byron, Mike Davis, and Rebecca Solnit,
Franco La Cecla has given us a book that will take an important place in our
public discourse.

*"To tell the truth, Franco La Cecla is not wrong. There is too much building, sometimes
only to put a signature, a stamp on a spot, without any worry about the people who
are going to live there. In other situations it is easy to be used by the institutions
that support speculation. It is the reason why I refused many projects, because, I am
lucky—and I can choose."*
— Renzo Piano in *La Repubblica*

*"La Cecla's book is a delight, in the way that he dismantles the glory of the 'archistar'
in their proud myopic grandeur that totally ignores people and their rights to a better
urban life."*
— Sebastian Courtois, *La Reforme*

Revolution at Point Zero: Housework, Reproduction, and Feminist Struggle

Silvia Federici

ISBN: 978-1-60486-333-8
$15.95   208 pages

Written between 1975 and the present, the essays collected in this volume represent thirty years of research and theorizing on questions of social reproduction and the transformations which the globalization process has produced. Originally inspired by Federici's organizational work in the Wages For Housework movement, topics discussed include the international restructuring of reproductive work and its effects on the sexual division of labor, the globalization of care work and sex work, the crisis of elder care, and the development of affective labor. Though theoretical in style, the book is written in an explanatory manner that makes it both accessible to a broad public and ideal for classroom use.

"Finally we have a volume that collects the many essays that over a period of four decades Silvia Federici has written on the question of social reproduction and women's struggles on this terrain. While providing a powerful history of the changes in the organization of reproductive labor, Revolution at Point Zero documents the development of Federici's thought on some of the most important questions of our time: globalization, gender relations, the construction of new commons."
— Mariarosa Dalla Costa

Catastrophism: The Apocalyptic Politics of Collapse and Rebirth

Sasha Lilley, David McNally, Eddie Yuen, and James Davis with a foreword by Doug Henwood

ISBN: 978-1-60486-589-9
$16.00   192 pages

Our times are riven by catastrophe. The world is reeling from the deepest economic crisis since the Great Depression, with the threat of further meltdowns ever-looming. Global warming and myriad dire ecological disasters worsen—with little if any action to halt them—their effects rippling across the planet in the shape of almost Biblical floods, fires, droughts, and hurricanes. Governments warn that no alternative exists than to take the bitter medicine they prescribe—or risk devastating financial or social collapse. The right, whether religious or secular, views the present as catastrophic and wants to turn the clock back. The left fears for the worst, but hopes some good will emerge from the rubble. Visions of the apocalypse and predictions of impending doom abound. Across the political spectrum, a culture of fear reigns.

Catastrophism explores the politics of apocalypse—on the Left and Right, in the environmental movement, and from capital and the state—and examines why the lens of catastrophe can distort our understanding of the dynamics at the heart of these numerous disasters—and fatally impede our ability to transform the world. Lilley, McNally, Yuen, and Davis probe the reasons why catastrophic thinking is so prevalent, and challenge the belief that it is only out of the ashes that a better society may be born. The authors argue that those who care about social justice and the environment should eschew the Pandora's box of fear—even as it relates to indisputably apocalyptic climate change. Far from calling people to arms, they suggest, catastrophic fear often results in passivity and paralysis—and, at worst, reactionary politics

"This groundbreaking book examines a deep current—on both the left and right—of apocalyptical thought and action. The authors explore the origins, uses, and consequences of the idea that collapse might usher in a better world. Catastrophism *is a crucial guide to understanding our tumultuous times, while steering us away from the pitfalls of the past."*
— Barbara Epstein, author of *Political Protest and Cultural Revolution: Nonviolent Direct Action in the 1970s and 1980s*

William Morris: Romantic to Revolutionary

E.P. Thompson
with a foreword by Peter Linebaugh

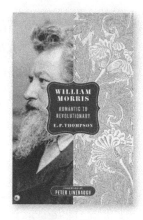

ISBN: 978-1-60486-243-0
$32.95   880 pages

William Morris—the great 19th century craftsman, architect, designer, poet and writer—remains a monumental figure whose influence resonates powerfully today. As an intellectual (and author of the seminal utopian News From Nowhere), his concern with artistic and human values led him to cross what he called the 'river of fire' and become a committed socialist—committed not to some theoretical formula but to the day by day struggle of working women and men in Britain and to the evolution of his ideas about art, about work and about how life should be lived.

Many of his ideas accorded none too well with the reforming tendencies dominant in the Labour movement, nor with those of 'orthodox' Marxism, which has looked elsewhere for inspiration. Both sides have been inclined to venerate Morris rather than to pay attention to what he said.

Originally written less than a decade before his groundbreaking *The Making of the English Working Class*, E.P. Thompson brought to this biography his now trademark historical mastery, passion, wit, and essential sympathy. It remains unsurpassed as the definitive work on this remarkable figure, by the major British historian of the 20th century.

"Two impressive figures, William Morris as subject and E. P. Thompson as author, are conjoined in this immense biographical-historical-critical study, and both of them have gained in stature since the first edition of the book was published… The book that was ignored in 1955 has meanwhile become something of an underground classic—almost impossible to locate in second-hand bookstores, pored over in libraries, required reading for anyone interested in Morris and, increasingly, for anyone interested in one of the most important of contemporary British historians… Thompson has the distinguishing characteristic of a great historian: he has transformed the nature of the past, it will never look the same again; and whoever works in the area of his concerns in the future must come to terms with what Thompson has written. So too with his study of William Morris."
— Peter Stansky, *The New York Times Book Review*

"An absorbing biographical study… A glittering quarry of marvelous quotes from Morris and others, many taken from heretofore inaccessible or unpublished sources."
— Walter Arnold, *Saturday Review*

All Power to the Councils!: A Documentary History of the German Revolution of 1918–1919

Edited and translated by Gabriel Kuhn

ISBN: 978-1-60486-111-2
$26.95   344 pages

The defeat in World War I and the subsequent end of the Kaiserreich threw Germany into turmoil. While the Social Democrats grabbed power, radicals across the country rallied to establish a socialist society under the slogan "All Power to the Councils!" The Spartacus League staged an uprising in Berlin, council republics were proclaimed in Bremen and Bavaria, and workers' revolts shook numerous German towns. The rebellions were crushed by the Social Democratic government with the help of right-wing militias like the notorious Free Corps. This paved the way to a dysfunctional Weimar Republic that witnessed the rise of the National Socialist movement.

The documentary history presented here collects manifestos, speeches, articles, and letters from the German Revolution, introduced and annotated by the editor. Many documents, like the anarchist Erich Mühsam's comprehensive account of the Bavarian Council Republic, are made available in English for the first time. The volume also includes appendixes portraying the Red Ruhr Army that repelled the reactionary Kapp Putsch in 1920, and the communist bandits that roamed Eastern Germany until 1921. All Power to the Councils! provides a dynamic and vivid picture of a time with long-lasting effects for world history. A time that was both encouraging and tragic.

"The councils of the early 20th century, as they are presented in this volume, were autonomous organs of the working class beyond the traditional parties and unions. They had stepped out of the hidden world of small political groups and represented a mass movement fighting for an all-encompassing council system."
— Teo Panther, editor of Alle Macht den Räten: Novemberrevolution 1918

"The German Revolution of 1918–1919 and the following years mark an exceptional period in German history. This collection brings the radical aspirations of the time alive and contains many important lessons for contemporary scholars and activists alike."
— Markus Bauer, Free Workers' Union, FAU-IAA

"The struggles of the German working class in the early 20th century are perhaps some of the most bitter and misunderstood in European history, and it is time they were paid more attention."
— Richard Parry, author of The Bonnot Gang

A Living Spirit of Revolt:
The Infrapolitics of Anarchism

Žiga Vodovnik with an introduction
by Howard Zinn

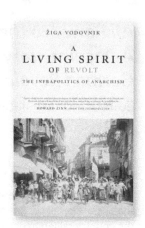

ISBN: 978-1-60486-523-3
$15.95   232 pages

*"The great contribution of Žiga Vodovnik is that his
writing rescues anarchism from its dogma, its rigidity, its
isolation from the majority of the human race. He reveals
the natural anarchism of our everyday lives, and in doing*
so, enlarges the possibilities for a truly human society, in which our imaginations, our
compassion, can have full play."
—Howard Zinn, author of *A People's History of the United States*, from the
Introduction

At the end of the nineteenth century, the network of anarchist collectives
represented the first-ever global antisystemic movement and the very center of
revolutionary tumult. In this groundbreaking and magisterial work, Žiga Vodovnik
establishes that anarchism today is not only the most revolutionary current
but, for the first time in history, the only one left. According to the author, many
contemporary theoretical reflections on anarchism marginalize or neglect to
mention the relevance of the anarchy of everyday life. Given this myopic (mis)
conception of its essence, we are still searching for anarchism in places where
the chances of actually finding it are the smallest.

*"Like Marx's old mole, the instinct for freedom keeps burrowing, and periodically
breaks through to the light of day in novel and exciting forms. That is happening
again right now in many parts of the world, often inspired by, and revitalizing, the
anarchist tradition that is examined in Žiga Vodovnik's book. A Living Spirit of
Revolt is a deeply informed and thoughtful work, which offers us very timely and
instructive lessons."*
— Noam Chomsky, MIT

*"Žiga Vodovnik has made a fresh and original contribution to our understanding of
anarchism, by unearthing its importance for the New England Transcendentalists and
their impact on radical politics in America. A Living Spirit of Revolt is interesting,
relevant and is sure to be widely read and enjoyed."*
— Uri Gordon, author of *Anarchy Alive: Anti-Authoritarian Politics from Practice to
Theory*

CPSIA information can be obtained
at www.ICGtesting.com
Printed in the USA
BVHW050000020623
665169BV00002B/2